THE HANDICAPPER'S
STAKES FESTIVAL

THE
HANDICAPPER'S
STAKES FESTIVAL

CLASS EVALUATION, SIMULCASTING, CROSS-TRACK BETTING, AND THE NATION'S NEW STAKES MENAGERIE

James Quinn

WILLIAM MORROW AND COMPANY, INC.

NEW YORK

It is the policy of William Morrow and Company, Inc., and its imprints and affiliates, recognizing the importance of preserving what has been written, to print the books we publish on acid-free paper, and we exert our best efforts to that end.

Library of Congress Cataloging-in-Publication Data

Quinn, James, 1943–
    The handicapper's stakes festival : class evaluation,
  simulcasting, cross-track betting, and the nation's new stakes
  menagerie / by James Quinn.
      p.   cm.
    ISBN 0-688-12790-8
    1. Horse racing—Betting.   2. Horse racing—Betting—United
  States.   I. Title.
  SF331.Q5475   1995
  798.401—dc20   94-23885
                                                             CIP

Printed in the United States of America

First Edition

1 2 3 4 5 6 7 8 9 10

BOOK DESIGN BY RICHARD ORIOLO

CONTENTS

My biggest score of the past season (1992) occurred at Keeneland Race Course, in Lexington.

The bet was placed at Santa Anita Park, in Los Angeles.

Until handicapping the Keeneland race the night before, I had never even heard of my benefactor, but I fell in love with the filly on first sight.

She was entered in the Ashland Stakes, a Grade 1 event for 3YO fillies, to be simulcast the next afternoon at Santa Anita. Separate betting pools!

Southern California horsemen had shipped a trio of the circuit's leading fillies to Keeneland, the crucial detail. I thought none of the southern California shippers would win. I knew each of them would be overbet at Santa Anita.

My unfamiliar filly, undefeated, no less, was shipping to Keeneland as well, from stakes efforts at Churchill Downs and

Ellis Park. I knew, too, she would be underbet at Santa Anita.

Coincidence played a part. Early in the week I had received an unexpected consulting fee of $2,700. I decided immediately, impulsively, uncharacteristically, but unequivocally, to risk $2,000 of it on the Keeneland simulcast. It's as if the king-sized wager constituted the rite of passage to a brave new world. The world of unfamiliar horses, simulcasting, and cross-track betting.

My filly, Prospector's Delight, looked to me a cinch in her past performances. Not only was she a multiple graded-stakes winner of impeccable consistency and soaring figures that shaped up as the lone front-runner on pace analysis, but also the trio of southern California fillies were overrated.

As is inevitably true of an overwhelming intuition at the racetrack, this one had blazed to life from a deeply rational force.

That Saturday, at Santa Anita, Prospector's Delight was not the irresistible overlay I had imagined. She was 4–1, third choice behind two of the southern California shippers. At Keeneland she was 2–1.

With enthusiasm, I bet.

Prospector's Delight sailed unmolested to the front out of the gate. Nothing pressed her down the backstretch. Passing the three-eighths pole, the southern California filly Magical Maiden advanced on the outside.

Prospector's Delight drew away by a couple of lengths around the far turn. She blasted clear in the upper stretch. She won handily, unbothered early, unthreatened late. After taking more late betting than I had noticed, Prospector's Delight paid $9.60 at Santa Anita.

I had underestimated the savvy of southern California bettors perhaps, but not the possibility of a windfall attributable to unfamiliar horses, simulcasting, and cross-track betting.

Months later, in the fall, at Oak Tree, in another stakes, a Bobby Frankel–trained grass runner named Incessant suffered a troubled but well-disguised trip as the heavy favorite. I put Incessant on the Horses To Watch list.

I never managed the bet.

On the Friday afternoon preceding the Breeders' Cup championship races at Gulfstream Park, Incessant won a stakes on the Gulfstream grass. Frankel had sent the horse to Florida to participate in the stakes program specially arranged for the racing days before and after the Breeder's Cup. Gulfstream Park had billed the three-day weekend as a stakes festival, which it was.

Underbet at Gulfstream Park, Incessant paid $14.60 to win. In a similar spot at Santa Anita, the horse would have paid less than half that amount.

The Breeders' Cup support stakes were not simulcast events in southern California. No wagering occurred at Santa Anita. But Incessant represented a Horse To Watch going postward at an inflated price, and a wager might have been placed in Las Vegas, at another simulcast site taking Gulfstream Park, or at Gulfstream Park itself.

The missed opportunity aroused in me a powerful, almost primitive reaction. The experience has affected my approach to playing the better races ever since. Incessant was not the first stakes winner in recent seasons I had lost to another time, another place.

I vowed Incessant would be the last.

THE HANDICAPPER'S STAKES FESTIVAL

THE
UNFAMILIAR
EDGE

Racetracks large, medium, and small of late have been staging "stakes festivals" of colorful varieties, commonly a compacted program of added-money events intended to support the track's signature race, or merely to spice the local program with extra stars. Stakes festivals might encompass a day, a weekend, three days, or even a week.

The so-called festivals of stakes races have been multiplying rapidly, track executives everywhere having been impressed by the accompanying increases in attendance and handle. No doubt the trend will continue, and persevere.

The implications for handicappers are intriguing, and promising. With an abundance of stakes races crowded into a short schedule, many of the horses will be unfamiliar to local bettors. Several may be shippers from a faraway distance. Certain contenders, therefore, will be underbet, and others overbet. The wagering inefficiencies will be numerous from season to season, and so will the corresponding wagering opportunities. As a result, handicappers can anticipate unprecedented chances for windfalls in the stakes divisions.

At the same time, similar betting inefficiencies have been characteristic of numerous nationwide simulcast events, where cross-track betting occurs. To a remarkable degree, local handicappers have proved to be misguided as frequently as not about the relative abilities of stakes horses that look new and unfamiliar.

The phenomenon has occurred in major stakes as well as in routine weekend features. When Thirty Slews won the Breeder's Cup Sprint at Gulfstream Park in 1992, he paid $37.80 in Florida, only $12.80 at Santa Anita, home base, but an astonishing $80.00 in New York. Thirty Slews was an underlay at Santa Anita, an overlay at Gulfstream Park, and a ridiculous overlay at Belmont Park.

Outrageous examples of the same phenomenon continue to find their way into conversations among horseplayers everywhere, but few of them have bothered to grab the advantage. The cornerstone proposition of this book holds that whenever stakes festivals, simulcasting, and cross-track betting converge, excellent handicappers will have an edge. Partially hidden to local eyes, the best and fastest horses may figure absolutely. The odds may be amazingly high in relation to real chances. Handicappers who know what to look for may find their best opportunities of the week, month, or season.

The key to unlocking stakes races with admirable consistency is class evaluation. Not speed figures, pace analysis, form cycles, trainers, or pedigree, and certainly not workouts, although all of the above, and more, may influence and complement the essential analysis, either strengthening or weakening the fundamental case.

As horse racing has changed throughout the 1980s and continuing in the 1990s, declining in competitive quality, so have the standards of class evaluation. Nowhere have the alterations been more dramatic than in the stakes.

A decade ago I argued that Grade 1 races should be won by Grade 1 horses. Thousands of handicappers saluted the aphorism, implemented it effectively, and have abided by it steadfastly. But it's no longer true, and therefore the standard no longer serviceable. Traditional standards of class evaluation in Grade 1 stakes will be unreliable.

The same observation applies to other graded and open-stakes. Handicappers need revised standards of class evaluation, and selection guidelines suitable to the times. The good news is the class evaluation of stakes horses survives as a topic surprisingly uncomplicated. It can be reexamined succinctly in the next section.

NEW DEFINITIONS Handicappers had every right to be shaken the day at Santa Anita in 1993 when an allowance route was won by a $12,500 claiming horse that had been losing at the lower level. What's happening, anyway?

Restricted allowance conditions had been broken occasionally at Santa Anita by $25,000 claiming horses and a $16,000 horse had stolen one of the races, but the $12,500 upset registered like an insult, a slap.

Later in 1993, a southern California handicapper of *Daily Racing Form* broke into print with his observation that the non-winners allowance races for 3UP had been won persistently by older horses. He relayed the data for the season. The advice was to discount 3YOs in allowance races open to older horses.

Throughout a two-decade career, I had understood the non-winners allowance series as favorable conditions for the lightly raced, impressively improving 3YOs that might be any kind and today will be taking a relatively small step towards better non-claiming company. Do handicappers of spring and summer prefer four- and five-year-olds that have never won an allowance race, or two? I hope not. But nowadays too many handicappers do.

The melancholy truth is that the quality of competition at major U.S. tracks has declined so severely for so many seasons that almost anything goes. Class barriers have been shattered. Hardly a week passes at the majors anymore when one or two of the weekday cards are not plainly awful.

I recall a distasteful incident on a Friday afternoon in the Santa Anita Turf Club two seasons ago. Only a handful of the luncheon tables on the turf terrace were occupied. The first race had ended. A businessman in a three-piece suit arrived hurriedly and animatedly. As the gentleman was seated, a guy at a table located above called down to say he was alive in the double.

"I hadn't intended to come," said the latecomer, "but it's a warm day and I just wanted to get out of the office."

The businessman ordered lunch and dived headlong into the past performances. Approximately a half hour drifted by. The businessman looked up agitatedly from the Form and in a firm tone called to the guy above, "This card sucks. I can't believe how bad these races are. Is this Santa Anita? I should have stayed at work."

Nobody who has been paying attention will rebut the observation that a persistent deflation factor in the competitive quality of races has been pounding down conventional class barriers. In claiming and allowance races, class drops and class rises have been more numerous, and more precipitous, than ever. In the stakes divisions, ordinary horses that formerly did not get close are winding up in the nation's winners circles, the happily surprised owners and trainers eagerly telling turf writers where the next added-money spot might be. Nobody mentions that the horses do not really belong.

A proliferation of stakes juxtaposed to a decline in the competitive quality has rendered too many stakes outcomes analagous to Andy Warhol's projection of fifteen minutes of fame for everybody. As a result, too many handicappers have concluded the class factor no longer counts. It's speed and pace and trips and biases and trainers and jockeys, but it isn't class.

The mounting frustration with slow horses and bad races cannot be dismissed. Still, handicappers should resist all temptation to abandon class as a fundamental factor of handicapping. The class factor is never unimportant in thoroughbred racing, even at low levels of competition, and it remains prominent much more frequently than not in this book's territory, the stakes.

It's sad that slower, cheaper horses have been winning too many stakes titles. In part, the anomaly can be accepted as temporary. As the inordinate number of racing dates and stakes races are pared back and the Arabs, Japanese, and other foreigners discontinue to purchase roughly 40 percent of America's select yearling crops, the competitive quality of stakes will improve.

Regardless, the majority of stakes races, graded-stakes especially, will be won by the best horses, the contenders that combine the attributes of speed, endurance, and determination to the optimal degrees. The longer the race and the stronger the opposition, the greater the importance of recognizing which horses are actually best.

In step with the times, a general strategy for assessing relative class can be reformulated. From the Grade 1 features to the restricted types, when evaluating horses in stakes races, handicappers can favor contenders that have (a) won twice already at today's class level, or (b) won once against or finished close to stakes winners clearly superior to today's opposition.

The insistence that stakes horses have won twice at today's class level or higher represents the key modification. The stricter standard protects handicappers from the grossest errors of class evaluation.

A decade ago it remained positively true that Grade 1 races were won by Grade 1 horses. A single title was definitive. These impressive horses typically towered over lower-level stakes horses, even multiple Grade 2 winners. In turn, Grade 2 stakes were won by Grade 2 horses. And these winners typically towered over the Grade 3 winners and stakes winners below Grade 3.

Of the class ladders in the stakes divisions, handicappers found a convenient and orderly hierarchy.

The changing times notwithstanding, the new definitions, and recommended modifications, should be elementary, familiar, and readily adapted. Here are six:

1. A Grade 1 stakes horse has won *two* or more Grade 1 stakes.
2. A Grade 2 stakes horse has won *two* or more Grade 2 stakes.
3. Under Grade 1 conditions, where no horse in the field has won two Grade 1 stakes, accept as comparable winners of one Grade 1 stakes and one Grade 2 stakes.
4. Under Grade 1 and Grade 2 conditions, where no horse in the field has won a single Grade 1 stakes, accept as contenders (a) horses having two or more Grades, Listed, or Open stakes wins in the last six starts and (b) any impressively improving 3YO or 4YO having speed figures within two lengths of the older stakes par.

   The Beyer Speed Figures of *Daily Racing Form* will be 106 to 110; figures of fillies and mares will be 98 to 102.
5. In Grade 3, Listed, and Open stakes, prefer horses that have won two or more Grade 3, Listed, or Open stakes having purses of $100,000 or higher.
6. In any restricted stakes, prefer horses well suited to the class demands of the exact eligibility conditions, i.e.:

   • if for nonwinners of a stakes race, prefer the lightly raced, improving younger horses of fine pedigree and good connections that have been moving rampantly through allowance conditions with above-par speed figures and pace figures in combination . . .
   • if for nonwinners of a specified amount of first money

since a specified date, prefer horses that have been inactive or active infrequently since the specified date and prior to the specified date won either (a) better races having higher purses or (b) an allowance race convincingly.

In a context of declining quality and malaise, the above definitions and guidelines work remarkably well. They provide handicappers with flexibility, without careening into carelessness.

At every level of stakes competition, the new definitions and guidelines indicate that multiple wins will be a far safer barometer of genuineness than a single win. The revised standards serve another equally beneficial purpose. They prevent handicappers from committing either of two persistent blunders when analyzing the stakes.

The first is believing that because a horse has won a Grade 1 or Grade 2 stakes it holds a decisive class edge, when it does not.

The second is thinking horses will be outgunned at today's class level, when they are not.

A fascinating, and complicated, topic regards the general reliance on speed figures to evaluate the contenders in stakes races. Usually, the figures will be helpful, and sometimes they will be decisive. The analyses of this book will refer to speed and pace figures repeatedly. Certain limits, however, should be strictly observed.

First, in graded stakes at the classic distance (a mile and one-quarter), speed figures recorded at middle distances do not apply. It's a crucial divide.

Bertrando qualifies as a quintessential case. The leading handicap horse of 1993, Bertrando never got a mile and one-quarter comfortably. His lone impressive speed figure at ten furlongs was earned at Del Mar on a speed-biased track surface having an abbreviated stretch. At middle distances, alternately, Bertrando coasted to victory with soaring speed figures. He posted a Beyer 125 at nine furlongs in the slop at Belmont Park.

Handicappers that relied upon Bertrando's figures at nine furlongs when evaluating the horse at ten furlongs were readily misled. Coming off sensational nine-furlong performances each time, Bertrando blew the ten-furlong Strub Stakes at 1–5 to the unranked Siberian Summer and he surrendered the Breeder's Cup Classic rather helplessly to the longest shot on the board.

Second, speed figures recorded in stakes at mid-level and minor tracks do not transfer to the majors as reliably as speed handicappers would prefer. Those figures too often reflect only outlays of speed, but not as often and not nearly as well, the qualities of endurance or determination. Those intangibles will be in demand considerably less at many racetracks.

Three-year-olds that have earned a Beyer Speed Figure of 104 during spring at Turfway Park, for example, will be unlikely to repeat the number when they arrive at Belmont Park or Hollywood Park. Class analysts should demand that shippers showing lofty speed figures at mid-level and minor tracks also have demonstrated (a) consistency, (b) versatility, and (c) the ability to press a rapid pace and still finish fast.

Lacking any of that evidence, the 3YO stakes winners moving ahead in class likely will be defeated on the intial try at major tracks or in major stakes. The maneuver represents one of the steepest class hikes in the game, and regularly fails.

Later, after seasoning and maturation have played significant roles, 3YO stakes winners from the lower-level ovals may repeat or surpass previously high speed figures. Perceptive figure analysts sometimes can anticipate the later successes. They rely upon patterns of speed figures, which connects to another caution.

Third, in the vast majority of stakes races at sprint and middle distances, patterns of speed figures should supersede any figure standing independently. A high figure sticking out like a giraffe's neck is automatically suspect.

When evaluating 3YOs, handicappers should routinely consult the highest figure earned against the most advanced conditions of eligibility. Where form is intact, and circumstances positive, that's the figure horses should be expected to duplicate, or to exceed.

Fourth, with 3YOs especially, not only is the ability to run to par at today's class level fundamental, so is the ability to record a pace figure within two lengths of par. The satisfactory pace figure should be mandatory for front-runners, pressers, and stalkers moving ahead in class.

Even when speed figures prove inconclusive in analyzing the stakes, almost always they serve to identify the leading contenders. As later sections will show, speed figures cannot tell handicappers which colt will prevail in the Kentucky Derby, or which division leaders will survive on Breeders' Cup Championship Day, to cite the most controversial situations. At each defining moment, however, speed figures do identify the horses qualified to rise to the occasion. Horses that are not fast enough simply cannot be expected to win.

The limits set, the caution signs posted, handicappers must understand it's the stakes races where speed handicapping and class evaluation form their most natural and powerful nexus. Because speed and class denote horses' intrinsic abilities as no other factors of handicapping can, where top figures have been earned against the best opposition, the horses will be difficult to deny.

What's the best bet at the racetrack? Prices aside, one of the best is the fastest horse that has already beaten the most advanced competition.

This book affirms the complementary relationship between speed and class at the highest levels of competition. It invokes the use of speed figures when analyzing stakes races, but in a broader, more meaningful context that relates speed to class. The emphasis that is placed there, belongs there.

Furthermore, where the speed and class interplay remains inconclusive, as happens frequently enough, several other factors should be considered. Specifying the priorities and emphases to be accorded those factors constitutes a noble purpose of this book. The objective is to help handicappers play the stakes races consistently well. The actual handicapping of numerous stakes at numerous tracks should satisfy that purpose, and I can warn casual handicappers up front they will not unravel many stakes races by resorting to judgments based upon jockeys, weight, and post position.

Following the national stakes calendar from January to December, and implementing a specific strategy and focus, this book offers an approach to beating the stakes that simulcast handicappers can mimic from season to season. I make this promise with confidence. Simulcast bettors who adhere closely to this book's guidelines and routine will accumulate greater profits in the stakes races than ever.

Among handicappers for whom stakes races have persistently defied their best efforts, the book's contents offer the potential for nothing less than a change to positive results.

And because stakes races today are invariably wrapped around exotic wagers such as the trifecta, Pick 3, and Pick 6, handicappers who learn how to extract bigger profits from the stakes soon enough will find creative ways to translate the newfound profits into windfalls, and maybe an occasional gigantic score.

We begin at Santa Anita Park during winter. The point of departure makes perfect sense, not only to southern California handicappers, but also to simulcast handicappers throughout the country. At present, more than 400 simulcast sites carry the winter signal from Santa Anita, either full card or partial card, and in either circumstance including the stakes. Southern California racing is fast becoming a national circuit.

Simulcast bettors should rejoice in the trend. By tuning in to the Santa Anita stakes program from January to April, they will prepare themselves to make a fantastic array of intelligent wagers for the remainder of the year.

A subplot of the book tracks the nation's most talented 3YOs, not merely to the Kentucky Derby, but beyond, and this trek too begins in winter. Attending smartly to the 3YO stakes at Santa Anita, Gulfstream Park, Oaklawn Park, Belmont Park, and Keeneland may not reveal the winner of the Kentucky Derby and other spring classics, but I guarantee handicappers the process will produce the eventual winners of numerous other 3YO stakes. And many of them will pay generous mutuels.

As spring follows winter and shifts into summer, the book's emphasis shifts subtly but just as inexorably from the 3YO stakes to stakes horses 4UP. Simulcast handicappers can stay on alert for shippers from Santa Anita's ninety-day winter season to other spots. Season after season, juicy opportunities will arise. Underrated runners-up and also-rans at Santa Anita may be splendid bets at other tracks. Overrated winners at Santa Anita are practically guaranteed to go postward as underlays elsewhere. At either extreme, alert, well-prepared handicappers will want to seize the moment.

As summer dovetails into fall, we'll pay attention to the preliminary stakes, then take the best horses to the Breeder's Cup championship races. For handicappers who have become experts on the nation's stakes divisions, the preliminaries to the championship races will serve as happy hunting grounds. I want to assure class handicappers they can look forward to clobbering the Breeders' Cup preparatory stakes for substantial money season after season.

The climax will be the Breeders' Cup championship races themselves, carded in 1993 at Santa Anita Park. As challenging as the championship races can be, the experience of nine Breeders' Cups has contributed a strategy for navigating through the seven-race program successfully. Each of the seven million-dollar races will be examined in detail.

At each juncture of the journey, handicappers will take special delight in the stakes festivals. From Oaklawn Park's Racing Festival of the South in April to Hollywood Park's International

Turf Festival in December, handicappers will want to discover the underbet, unfamiliar horses that represent this book's unfamiliar edge.

As do stakes races in general, the innovative stakes festivals go hand in hand especially well with class evaluation, simulcasting, and cross-track betting. Because the odds on so many of the best horses will be higher than they should be, irresistible really, I have dubbed the innovations, aptly, I think, as The Handicapper's Stakes Festival. The multifaceted stakes programs of today go hand in hand best of all with superior skill in handicapping.

Finally, for skeptical handicappers who insist the stakes races are too tough, or don't pay enough, I intend to keep score. In the end, the action complete, the book presents the accounts of a $20 bettor and $200 bettor, respectively. Most handicappers should appreciate the stakes races more than ever, and many skeptics might be persuaded to change their minds.

Of the large but unfashionable group of horse players who like to portray themselves as class handicappers, and have attacked the stakes races with enviable success all along, I want to send out notice that the stakes festivals, simulcasting, and cross-track betting represent the advances of a lifetime. Your time, your chance for the kill is now. Specialists on the class factor will have no defensible excuse if they fail to transform their annual profits from moderate to huge.

And not to be overlooked, playing the stakes game is good, clean, challenging fun. Everybody does it. Ideas and methods aside, handicappers like to debate the probable outcomes of the major stakes. Most enjoy watching the leading stakes stars in ferocious combat.

Why not resolve to convert the habit into as profitable a venture as handicappers can?

WINTER

With cold covering the Northeast, snow blowing through the Midwest, and rain falling on the West Coast, New York horses head to Florida, Chicago horses invade Oaklawn Park, and southern California horses prepare to ship to stakes opportunities wherever hungry horsemen spot them.

Ah, the charms of U.S. winter racing!

Images of Aqueduct's infamous inner course, jockeys in ski masks, and dirt surfaces frozen hard aside, nothing so characterizes winter racing among the thoroughbreds as the shipping of stakes horses to stakes races somewhere else. It's a practical imperative, and especially congenial to this book's purpose and to thousands of winterized handicappers country wide.

For something else has changed with the weather. The horses of winter may be forced to ship out, but simulcast handicappers are not.

JANUARY

At Santa Anita's winter season, track announcer Trevor Denman daily reminds the trackside crowd The Great Race Place's signal is being beamed to more than 400 simulcast sites. Staying warm, in relative comfort, while being fed, simulcast handicappers coast-to-coast can now play the races at Santa Anita, and they are strongly encouraged to do just that as frequently as schedules permit.

Whether handicappers of the Midwest, East, and South have done so previously or not, they are strongly urged to do as follows:

1. Closely monitor the outcomes of stakes races in all divisions at Santa Anita.
2. Track the nonclaiming 3YOs at Santa Anita as they develop and mature, and follow them when they ship to other tracks for derbies and other stakes.

The first pursuit acknowledges that Santa Anita offers the best racing of winter. Every season, stakes winners and close runners-up at Santa Anita will be sent to important stakes races virtually everywhere throughout the spring, summer, and fall.

The second pursuit supports the universal objective of winter racing in the stakes division. The road to the Kentucky Derby winds long, bumpy, grinding, and hard. Fewer than twenty of the classic hopefuls will eventually compete in the Kentucky Derby, but dozens will compete in the numerous preliminary stakes to Louisville. Dozens more will enter the unheralded derbies scattered across the land, whether it's the Bay Meadows Derby, the Tampa Bay Derby, the Illinois Derby, the Ohio Derby, the Pennsylvania Derby, or another derby somewhere else.

The stakes program at Santa Anita provides telltale clues to important stakes activity for the rest of the year. The track presents a unique series of graded stakes limited to 4YOs. The San

Fernando (Gr. 2) and Strub Stakes (Gr. 1) for colts and the El Encino (Gr. 3) and La Canada Stakes (Gr. 1) for fillies usually deliver winners and runners-up that later will be serious contenders in the open and graded stakes open to older runners everywhere.

Can the leading 4YOs from Santa Anita whip their older counterparts there, and elsewhere? Simulcast handicappers should determine to find out as much as they can about the Santa Anita 4YOs.

An intriguing, underestimated aspect of winter racing regards the leading stakes stars of last season. Which have declined? It's a provocative question. Year after year, many will have tailed off, but an unsuspecting public continues to favor the horses. If stakes horses have declined, most of them figure to lose, unless lowered in class from established heights. The scenario repeats itself annually, in particular under Grade 1 conditions. If former stakes stars that have weakened have not been dropped in class, they nonetheless will be overbet. The possibilities for handicappers in the know are obvious. Santa Anita is a marvelous testing ground for a number of last year's stakes stars.

As 1993 began, the outstanding Cal-bred Best Pal had returned to training following a seven-month layoff. A good but unexceptional 3YO of 1991, Best Pal had matured sensationally at four and in 1992 proved himself indisputably (except to insiders who voted instead for Pleasant Tap) the standout handicap horse in America. Impressive winner of four consecutive Grade 1 stakes, including the million-dollar Santa Anita Handicap, in each event Best Pal had recorded speed figures restricted to championship caliber only. At four, until insured in spring, Best Pal was as good as it gets.

How will Best Pal perform at five, a season that could find him at his chronological peak? If Best Pal has been rejuvenated, only true-blue stakes stars can stay with him. If Best Pal has declined, however, his speed and pace figures will tell the tale soon enough. Betting opportunities on other ranking horses might follow.

As a new season opens, these issues and others can be framed in ways that makes following the stakes races an exercise in pattern recognition.

But there is another more fundamental, and more valuable, purpose for handicappers, notably handicappers that confess to pratfalls in analyzing stakes races. The stakes program at Santa Anita presents a handicapping challenge unsurpassed in quality, diversity, and difficulty. Handicappers that can make it there, so to speak, can make it anywhere. Simulcast viewers will be exposed to a variety and complexity of stakes competition many of them have never sampled before.

During its 85–90 day winter-spring session, Santa Anita runs 55–60 stakes featuring many of the most talented racehorses on the continent. The 1993 schedule included 12 Grade 1s, 14 Grade 2s, 11 Grade 3s, 5 Listed stakes, 2 Open but unlisted stakes, and 11 Restricted stakes. Forty-one of the 55 stakes were hundred granders, or richer. Twenty-one stakes occurred on the grass, although typically many of those were shifted to the main track due to rains, a circumstance that presents its own peculiar handicapping charms.

To illustrate the fantastic possibilities, consider what happened at the outset. It's January 3, two days into the new stakes calendar. Imagine simulcast bettors playing Santa Anita's races at Suffolk Downs, in Boston. Those handicappers are unfamiliar with California horses and the eighth-race stakes offering looks like this:

7 FURLONGS. (1.20) 53rd Running of THE CALIFORNIA BREEDERS' CHAMPION STAKES. $100,000 added. 3–year–old (Foals of 1990). Bred in California. By subscription of $100 each to accompany the nomination, $250 to pass the entry box and $750 additional to start, with $100,000 added, of which $20,000 to second, $15,000 to third, $7,500 to fourth and $2,500 to fifth. Weight, 122 lbs. Winners of two races of $40,000 2 lbs. extra.; of three such races, 4 lbs. extra, Non–winners of $50,000 allowed 3 lbs.; of $25,000, 5 lbs.; of a race other than maiden or claiming, 8 lbs. Starters to be named through the entry by closing time of entries. A trophy will be presented to the owner and breeder of the winner. (Maiden and claiming races not considered.) Closed Wednesday, December 23, 1992 with 16 nominations.

Contemplating the eligibility conditions, not an unimportant departure, what do handicappers appreciate already?

This is a restricted stakes; to Cal-breds. It invites three-day-old 3YOs. It's a long sprint. The purse is generous, $100,000-added.

Relative class may be unclear, and may be unimportant, unless a Cal-bred that has won (or finished close) a listed or graded sprint stakes in swift time happens to be eligible and entered. Speed figures recorded at two might remain below the 3YO stakes par, maybe by several lengths. Several of the state-bred youngsters may be exiting best-efforts in maiden races and non-winners once allowances.

With that frame of reference, scan the past performances. Identify the staunchest contenders.

Lucky's First One
PINCAY L JR (23 4 3 3 .17)
Own.—Johnston & Johnston & Stonebraker
B. c. 3(Jan), by Something Lucky—Prone Position, by Long Position
Tr.—Warren Donald (4 1 0 0 .25)
Lifetime 4 1 2 0 $27,250
1992 4 1 2 0 $27,250
114

Offshore Pirate
VALENZUELA P A (14 3 2 2 .21)
Own.—Herrick Denan & William J
Dk. b. or br. c. 3(May), by Pirate's Bounty—Glass Tumbler, by Pass the Glass
Br.—Wygod Mr-Mrs Martin J (Cal)
Tr.—Vienna Darrell (3 1 1 0 .33)
Lifetime 3 2 1 0 $30,600
1992 3 2 1 0 $30,600
117

Moscow Changes
McCARRON C J (15 2 1 5 .13)
Own.—Harris Farms Inc
B. g. 3(Jan), by Moscow Ballet—Thailard's Pearl, by Thailard—GB
Br.—Harris Farms Inc (Cal)
Tr.—Zucker Howard L (2 0 1 0 .00)
Lifetime 5 2 2 1 $110,043
1992 5 2 2 1 $110,043
122

Boating Pleasure
STEVENS G L (26 9 2 2 .35)
Own.—Stephen Rickard J
Ch. c. 3(Feb), by Flying Paster—Committee Boat, by Secretariat
Br.—Mabee Mr-Mrs John C (Cal)
Tr.—Bellase Wallace (1 0 0 1 .00)
Lifetime 9 3 0 1 $87,075
1992 9 3 0 1 $87,075
122

El Atroz
PEDROZA M A (26 5 3 4 .19)
Own.—Cuadra TYT Inc
B. g. 3(Mar), by Timeless Native—Black Star-II, by Welmar
Br.—Cuadra TYT Inc (Cal)
Tr.—Sadler John W (5 0 0 0 .00)
Lifetime 6 2 0 2 $37,300
1992 6 2 0 2 $37,300
117

Enlightened Energy
FLORES D R (21 2 3 3 .10)
Own.—Wygod Mr-Mrs Martin J
Br. c. 3(Feb), by Pirate's Bounty—Radiant Glow, by Northern Dancer
Br.—Wygod Mr-Mrs Martin J (Cal)
Tr.—Hendricks Dan L (1 0 0 0 .00)
Lifetime 5 2 1 0 $43,400
1992 5 2 1 0 $43,400
117

Kingdom Found
NAKATANI C S (23 3 4 4 .13)
Own.—Dilbeck Ray
B. c. 3(Apr), by The Bart—Amiga La G, by Delaware Chief
Br.—Dilbeck Ray (Cal)
Tr.—Jones Gary (4 2 0 1 .50)
Lifetime 2 1 0 1 $19,300
1992 2 1 0 1 $19,300
114

Glowing Crown
SOLIS A (17 2 3 2 .12)
Own.—Franks John
Dk. b. or br. c. 3(Feb), by Hale—Hairless Heiress, by Baldski
Br.—Jawl Brothers & Tathem Thomas P (Cal)
Tr.—Van Berg Jack C (10 2 1 3 .20)
Lifetime 4 1 1 0 $23,300
1992 4 1 1 0 $23,300
114

No horse has won or finished close in an open, listed, or graded stakes. The Beyer Speed par for this race at Santa Anita hovers near 96. No horse has met that standard. Only one has approached par, Glowing Crown's 95, recorded against state-bred maidens.

But six of the newborn 3YOs are graduating from maidens (2) or allowances (4) to the state-bred stakes. That circumstance should be provocative. What does it suggest?

It suggests, or should, that the decisive factor might be early pace, as it frequently will be among 3YOs in sprints (and numerous routes) below Grade 2. Keep in mind that where pace figures have been low and lightly-raced colts will be moving ahead in class, the faster pace regularly contributes to a slower final time. Genuinely good 3YOs will survive the rapid pace, but ordinary horses do not.

Consider first the Beyer Speed Figures, in descending order, and the class level at which they were recorded:

Glowing Crown	95	state-bred maidens, Hol
El Atroz	89	NW1 Alw, BM
Kingdom Found	88	state-bred maidens, Hol
Boating Pleasure	82	state-bred route stk, Hol
	88	claiming sprint, SA
Offshore Pirate	83	state-bred Alw, Hol
Enlightened Energy	78	NW1 Alw, Hol
Lucky's First One	77	NW1 Alw, Hol
Moscow Changes	77	restricted sprint stk, SA

The contenders on speed include Glowing Crown, El Atroz, Kingdom Found, Boating Pleasure, and Offshore Pirate, with Glowing Crown fastest by three lengths and the others within three lengths of each other. Because the gelding had won a restricted stakes, I dug deeper on Moscow Changes, but each of its attempts featured either a low pace figure or low speed figure. Out.

I discarded Boating Pleasure too. Not only has its speed figures declined since the high-water mark of October 8, but also the youngster was blown to bits last out in the Hollywood Futurity (Gr. 1). As a rule, I seldom will favor 3YOs that have been crushed by superior horses in a recent try, even when dropping. The shellacking extracts a toll and normally young 3YOs will need a race or a respite to recover.

In the popular press coverage prior to the race, Kingdom Found was touted as a positively good thing, presumably because (a) it had crushed maidens when bet to 3/5 and (b) was handled by leading trainer Gary Jones.

With that in mind, examine the Quirin-style speed & pace figures of the main contenders:

Glowing Crown	97	105
El Atroz	103	103
Kingdom Found	(94)	103
Offshore Pirate	102	103

Here lies the crux of the analysis, which will be the case often in 3YO stakes of winter. Immediately, without reservation, and notwithstanding its final figure, manner of victory, trainer, or anything else, Kingdom Found can be discarded.

Kingdom Found trounced state-bred maidens exhibiting a pace figure roughly five lengths slower than today's probable pace. Talented 3YOs can sometimes improve their pace figures by five lengths and prevail against better, but the large majority do not. Kingdom Found shapes up as an underlay having a pace weakness. Playing the percentages and probabilities, Kingdom Found must be abandoned as the 2–1 favorite, an extremely vital distinction.

Glowing Crown reveals a soft pace figure too, but only two to three lengths slower than today's probable pace. That's a tougher call. Nonclaiming 3YOs often can run a couple of lengths faster to the pace call and repeat prior best efforts. But handicappers should not ignore the well-documented symmetry between speed and pace figures. When pace figures improve, speed figures normally decline, the common pattern among unexceptional horses.

Dismissing Kingdom Found, I preferred Glowing Crown, El Atroz, and Offshore Pirate as the main contention in a closely competitive match. The odds approaching post clarified the decision-making as nothing else had:

Kingdom Found	2–1
Glowing Crown	7–2
El Atroz	40–1
Offshore Pirate	7–2

The shipper from Bay Meadows lit up the tote at 40–1, a magnificent overlay that extended from Santa Anita to simulcast bettors near and far.

Why El Atroz was dismissed eludes me still. The trainer was John Sadler, a top man. The jockey was Martin Pedroza, merely the hottest rider early in the Santa Anita season.

Sure enough, nonclaiming 3YOs rising in class and shipping from minor tracks to major tracks generally will be outgunned in the stakes, but their chances improve (a) during the first four months of the year (b) in restricted stakes and (c) in shorter races, notably if their speed and pace figures have been competitive. All conditions were satisfied by El Atroz.

I backed El Atroz to win and hooked him top and bottom in exactas with Glowing Crown, Offshore Pirate, and even Kingdom Found, who I refused to let beat me out of a bulging mutuel.

The result chart is a joy to behold:

EIGHTH RACE

Santa Anita

JANUARY 3, 1993

7 FURLONGS. (1.20) 53rd Running of THE CALIFORNIA BREEDERS' CHAMPION STAKES. $100,000 added. 3-year-old (Foals of 1990). Bred in California. By subscription of $100 each to accompany the nomination, $250 to pass the entry box and $750 additional to start, with $100,000 added, of which $20,000 to second, $15,000 to third, $7,500 to fourth and $2,500 to fifth. Weight, 122 lbs. Winners of two races of $40,000 2 lbs. extra.; of three such races, 4 lbs. extra, Non-winners of $50,000 allowed 3 lbs.; of $25,000, 5 lbs.; of a race other than maiden or claiming, 8 lbs. Starters to be named through the entry by closing time of entries. A trophy will be presented to the owner and breeder of the winner. (Maiden and claiming races not considered.) Closed Wednesday, December 23, 1992 with 16 nominations.
Value of race $108,850; value to winner $64,850; second $20,000; third $15,000; fourth $7,500; fifth $2,500. Mutuel pool $422,462.
Exacta pool $441,564.

Last Raced	Horse	M/Eqt.A.Wt	PP St	¼	½	Str	Fin	Jockey	Odds $1
13Dec92 8BM10	El Atroz	LB 3 117	5 7	6hd	51	31½	1½	Pedroza M A	43.20
28Nov92 4Hol1	Offshore Pirate	LBb 3 117	2 4	2nd	2nd	1½	21½	Valenzuela P A	3.60
24Dec92 4Hol1	Glowing Crown	LBb 3 114	8 6	71	6hd	52	32¾	Solis A	3.70
4Dec92 3Hol1	Kingdom Found	LBb 3 114	7 2	51	41	2hd	41	Nakatani C S	2.40
7Nov92 5SA3	Moscow Changes	LB 3 122	3 3	1hd	3½	4hd	52½	McCarron C J	5.60
20Dec92 8Hol6	Boating Pleasure	LB 3 122	4 1	4hd	7½½	7½	61¾	Stevens G L	4.00
19Dec92 3Hol1	Enlightened Energy	L 3 117	6 8	8	8	8	7hd	Flores D R	18.00
19Dec92 3Hol2	Lucky's First One	B 3 117	1 5	3½	1hd	6½	8	Pincay L Jr	23.80

OFF AT 4:18. Start good. Won driving. Time, :22², :45 , 1:10 , 1:23² Track fast.

$2 Mutuel Prices:

5-EL ATROZ	88.40 26.60	9.40
2-OFFSHORE PIRATE	5.60	4.00
8-GLOWING CROWN		4.40

$2 EXACTA 5-2 PAID $487.40.

B. g, (Mar), by Timeless Native—Black Star-It, by Welmar. Trainer Sadler John W. Bred by Candra TYT Inc (Cal).

EL ATROZ, outrun early but not far back, loomed menacingly a quarter of a mile out, angled to the outside turning into the stretch to get a clear path, came into the stretch four wide, responded in the drive, came in a bit approaching the sixteenth marker while under left handed pressure, was under right handed pressure late and proved best. OFFSHORE PIRATE dueled for the lead the entire way and grudgingly had to settle for the place when not quite able to outfinish EL ATROZ. GLOWING CROWN, outrun early but not far back, raced wide down the backstretch, entered the stretch four wide and came home well enough to gain the show. KINGDOM FOUND attended the early pace, raced wide down the backstretch, battled for the lead around the far turn, continued battling for command early in the drive before weakening and was checked approaching the sixteenth marker when EL ATROZ came in a bit. The stewards conducted an inquiry into the stretch run involving the top four finishers and made no change in the order of finish when ruling that any interference had no affect on the original order of finish. MOSCOW CHANGES vied for the early lead and weakened in the drive. BOATING PLEASURE, away alertly, also vied for the early lead, raced wide down the backstretch. LUCKY'S FIRST ONE vied for the early lead and faltered.

POSTSCRIPT This may register as an unbelievable introduction to the stakes season, but the outcome was no fluke. Kingdom Found got a huge clarion call from announcer Trevor Denman while rallying on the far turn, but he will not be the last 3YO to disappoint at low odds while stepping up in class with a low pace figure. Throw them out, without mercy. Exceptions are deep closers, whose pace figures reflect running styles, not abilities.

Relative class proved unimportant here. But if the lineup had boasted a Cal-bred that already had won an open, listed, or graded stakes in faster time than today's opposition, that horse would qualify as the one to beat. El Atroz might have been beaten, but at 43–1 he would have demanded a bet regardless.

Before leaving this Cal-bred sprint stakes, here's a hot tip for simulcast handicappers. State-bred races of southern California are routinely comparable to open races at the same levels. Figure handicappers normally make no adjustments to claiming pars. Nonclaiming state-bred races will be slower than the open kind more frequently, but by one or two lengths only. In subsequent races, do not mark Cal-breds down unfairly, even when exiting the state-bred stakes.

The day after the race, I consulted handicapping colleague Scott Finley in Boston on an unrelated matter. Finley had watched the Santa Anita simulcast the day before at Suffolk Downs. As I recounted the $88.40 caper, believe it or not, Finley announced he had played the same horse. Ah, yes, simulcasting!

Last, but not least, a $20 wager on El Atroz returned $884. A $200 investment cleared $8,840. A $2 exacta box coupling two of the three main contenders got $487.40. A $10 exacta box cleared another $2,077.

This is the kind of kickoff that convinces handicappers as nothing else can that they are playing the fastest game in town. And while tallying up the dollars, I might as well come clean about the bonus I snatched.

While sipping wine in the turf club shortly before the eighth race with a new friend and major client of my brother, the CPA, I casually noted that El Atroz at 40–1 was a fabulous overlay.

I did not see the gentleman again until the ninth race had ended the day, but I met him at the bar for a brief celebration. The grin he held spoke volumes. An aggressive bettor, the gentleman had scored. As we shook hands, he extended me a glass of burgundy, and quickly, to my surprise, stuck a handful of folded bills in my jacket pocket. I did not unwrap the bills until arriving at my residence an hour later. They totaled $800, the richest finder's fee I've collected in two decades of play.

The next week's slate of stakes proved uneventful on the Santa Anita tote, but not unimportant in the scheme of things. January is the month to focus tightly on the 4YOs. The stakes series for 4YO colts should reveal whether southern California will be a dominant force later in the older handicap division.

First, the 4YO filly Pacific Squall returned from an August layoff in the Grade 2 El Encino Stakes. Prior to the lay-up, I felt Pacific Squall was sailing to the brim of the 3YO filly division and might challenge boldly in the 1992 Breeders' Cup Distaff. Needing the race, and seeking bigger prizes long haul, few Grade 1 division leaders 4UP are intended to land their best blows following a lengthy layoff.

Pacific Squall won nonethelesss, and in an impressively game manner. The race became meaningful in two ways: (1) This filly now qualifies as among the best of her generation, not to mention as a legitimate challenger to Paseana in the older filly and mare division and (2) Pacific Squall has an especially good chance to disappoint in her next start, and a major 4YO objective, the La Canada Stakes, only three weeks away.

On the second point, review the result chart of the El Encino:

EIGHTH RACE

Santa Anita

JANUARY 10, 1993

1 1/16 MILES. (1.39) 29th Running of THE EL ENCINO STAKES (Grade II). $100,000 added. Fillies. 4-year-olds. By subscription of $100 each to accompany the nomination, $1,000 additional to start with $100,000 added, of which $20,000 to second, $15,000 to third, $7,500 to fourth and $2,500 to fifth. Weight: 122 lbs. Non-winners of $100,000 twice at one mile or over in 1992-93, allowed 3 lbs.; of such a race in 1992-93 or $60,000 any distance since October 5, 5 lbs.; of $50,000 at one mile or over or $30,000 any distance at any time, 7 lbs. Starters to be named through the entry box by the closing time of entries. A trophy will be presented to the owner of the winner. (Claiming races not considered.) Closed Wednesday, December 30, 1992 with 19 nominations.

Value of race $108,900; value to winner $63,900; second $20,000; third $15,000; fourth $7,500; fifth $2,500. Mutuel pool $350,220. Exacta pool $335,403.

Last Raced	Horse	M/Eqt.A.Wt	PP St	1/4	1/2	3/4	Str	Fin	Jockey	Odds $1
15Aug92 8Sar3	Pacific Squall	B 4 119	3 4	2½	2½	1½	1¹½	1²½	McCarron C J	1.80
8Dec92 6Lrl1	Avian Assembly	B 4 118	6 7	6²½	6²½	4²½	2¹½	2⁶	Valenzuela P A	3.50
27Dec92 8SA5	Magical Maiden	LB 4 119	7 5	3¹½	3¹	2ʰᵈ	3¹½	3ʰᵈ	Stevens G L	1.30
8Nov92 6BM7	Autumn Mood	4 115	4 6	7	7	6⁴	6¹⁵	4ⁿᵒ	Atkinson P	42.20
13Dec92 7Hol3	Secretly	LB 4 115	5 3	5²	5½	5³½	5½	5⁹	Lopez A D	a-7.90
27Dec92 8SA3	Terre Haute	B 4 117	2 1	1¹	1¹	3¹	4ʰᵈ	6²⁶	Flores D R	a-7.90
28Nov92 8BM4	Certam De May	LBb 4 117	1 2	4ʰᵈ	4¹	7	7	7	Nakatani C S	17.20

a-Coupled: Secretly and Terre Haute.

OFF AT 4:22. Start good. Won driving. Time, :23², :47², 1:12¹, 1:38⁴, 1:45³ Track sloppy.

$2 Mutuel Prices:

4-PACIFIC SQUALL		5.60	3.60	2.40
7-AVIAN ASSEMBLY			4.20	2.80
8-MAGICAL MAIDEN				2.20

$2 EXACTA 4-7 PAID $28.20.

Dk. b. or br. f, by Storm Bird—Rambolie, by Ruffinal. Trainer Gonzalez J Paco. Bred by Folson & Jones & McCombs (Ky).

PACIFIC SQUALL sat just off the early pace while being rated, wrested the lead with three furlongs remaining, was under left handed pressure early in the drive when in front and to the inside of AVIAN ASSEMBLY, drifted out a bit approaching the sixteenth marker with the rider immediately switching to right handed pressure and gradually increased her advantage in deep stretch while all out. AVIAN ASSEMBLY lacked early speed, rallied to loom menacingly at the quarter pole, came through between rivals turning into the stretch, threatened PACIFIC SQUALL early in the drive, shied away from that opponent when that opponent drifted out a bit approaching the sixteenth marker, could not match PACIFIC SQUALL's response in deep stretch but proved clearly best of the rest. A claim of foul against PACIFIC SQUALL by the rider of AVIAN ASSEMBLY for alleged interference through the stretch was not allowed by the stewards when they ruled that the incident was minor and had no bearing on the original order of finish. MAGICAL MAIDEN sat within close range of the early pace, pressed the issue on the far turn but weakened

POSTSCRIPT An "all-out" effort following a long layoff anticipates the notorious "bounce" phenomenon among horses reappearing within six weeks. The pattern is not applicable as forcibly to leading stakes horses but constitutes a circumstance that persistently repeats itself and must be respected, certainly among horses that will be heavily bet.

Moments after she had returned to glory in the El Encino Stakes, I was looking forward to betting against Pacific Squall in the La Canada Stakes.

Drawing that fast conclusion relates to a clever trick of the trade when playing the stakes game. A helpful habit handicappers should cultivate is projecting the results of today's performance to the subsequent objective. Aided by visual skills, speed and pace figures, trip and bias notes, and the results charts, the projections sometimes can be plainly and interestingly stark. With turf writers extolling the virtues of Pacific Squall's comeback, and public selectors certain to overrate her next time, it's advantageous for handicappers to realize that on that next occasion Pacific Squall will be an underlay—and figures just as well to lose.

Comes now another inside tip for simulcast handicappers. Of the winter stakes limited to 4YOs, experience has convinced me Santa Anita's San Fernando Stakes across nine furlongs usually will be the most important. Now Grade 2, the race determines whether a southern California 4YO is primed to rush to the top of the older handicap division nationwide.

Because the race occurs at a middle distance, not ten furlongs, where many developing 4YOs will slip, a truly dominant 4YO can unleash the kind of exceptionally powerful performance. If the San Fernando outcome proves unexceptional, so presumably will be the southern California 4YOs.

In 1993, the San Fernando Stakes would be as far removed from the ordinary as ever. In a devastating run that could not have been anticipated before the gates opened, the field was overwhelmed by the front-runner Bertrando. Handicappers should pause to appreciate the situation for what it represented by revisiting Bertrando's record prior to the San Fernando Stakes:

A Grade 1 winner and obviously talented, Bertrando nonetheless had accomplished nothing sensational. Although he had laughed at the opposition as a juvenile in the Grade 1 Norfolk Stakes, he then surrendered the Santa Anita Derby to A.P. Indy (later Horse of the Year) in unexceptional time and manner. In two graded stakes at three, Bertrando's speed pace figures looked like this:

San Felipe	110	106	Par 106
Santa Anita Derby	112	107	Par 108

The figures can be considered characteristic of numerous speedy 3YOs, the capacity to surpass par at the pace call by two to three lengths while equaling par at the finish. This translates to a successful career in the stakes, but not to classic titles, and not to championships.

Away since April of 1992, Bertrando returned at seven furlongs in the Grade 2 Malibu, a race he lost while posting his first Beyer Speed Figure above 100. His Quirin-style figures in the Malibu improved to 103–112, the final figure exceeding the sprint par for older stakes horses (111), but the pace figure was soft. Bertrando should be a factor in big races, but he would probably "bounce" in the San Fernando. Frankly, I anticipated that.

Winning in a runaway, Bertrando's figures for the San Fernando crashed through conventional barriers: Pace 122, Speed 116. That's a performance five lengths faster than par at the pace call and three lengths faster than par at the finish. When dispensed by a front-runner, that performance equates to sheer brilliance.

Consider a comparison between Bertrando's San Fernando and that of the previous season's winner, a gelding who on that day had demonstrated he had qualified as the best older racehorse in the nation:

| Bertrando | 122 | 116 | Speed & Pace | 238 |
| Best Pal | 121 | 120 | Speed & Pace | 241 |

Best Pal, not a front-runner, exploded into a faster-than-par pace and sustained the powerful surge to the finish. Bertrando had proved he could set an extraordinary pace and sustain it all the way, at least for nine furlongs. The best thoroughbreds can press a brilliant pace and deliver a powerful finish.

In addition, Bertrando had been pushed early in the San Fernando by an outstanding colt, The Wicked North. Bertrando flicked his challenger aside nearing the quarter-pole and hustled home in hand, jockey Chris McCarron gazing back a couple of times.

Another complication. It was raining on San Fernando day, the track surface muddy. Wet surfaces favor front-runners. Yet the track surface was not wet-fast, certainly not producing the flaming fractions that often result from a tightly sealed dirt course. Bertrando's actual times were 110.7 seconds for six furlongs and 151⅕ at the finish, the final time slower by 14 fifths than Santa Anita's nine-furlong stakes par of 148⅖.

The track variant for the day, however, was Slow 17 at both the pace call and the wire. Bertrando had left the field behind in a manner that flattered his ability. This was a sensational performance. The older, mature Bertrando looked very much the horse to beat for the remaining eleven months of the year.

So simulcast handicappers, local handicappers too, seeking clues to the stakes caliber of southern California 4YOs should examine the San Fernando Stakes. Watch for a pace figure and speed figure unmistakably higher than the older stakes pars. Whenever handicappers find that combination, the winner might be an important horse.

The first Grade 1 event of 1993 was the Santa Monica Handicap, a sprint for fillies and mares 4UP. None of the entries displayed a Grade 1 title. None even had entered a Grade 1 contest.

Following a two-week siege of rain, the track had stayed muddy, but remarkably fair. I was eager to play against the 4–5 favorite and had spotted the solid alternative, a 5YO certain to be a co-favorite. I wanted 5–2.

The race contains a lasting lesson about relative class. Examine the records of the top pair:

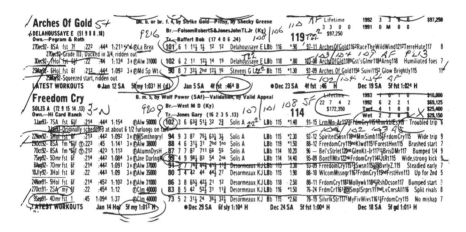

Arches Of Gold clearly has been classier. Just as clearly, today she would be vulnerable.

On December 27, Arches Of Gold had risen from a romp versus nonwinners of one allowance race to a Grade 3 sprint limited to 3YOs, same distance as today's. Despite Arches Of Gold's fast numbers, the class jump appeared steep. In the field was Race The Wild Wind, a well-documented stakes commodity, and a splendid sprinter. Race The Wild Wind had gone to the post on December 27 at 8–1, odds that left me salivating.

Arches Of Gold would confront a contested pace and better horses on December 27, and I had bet against her with confidence. Pressed strongly nearing the quarter pole by Race The Wild Wind, Arches Of Gold had responded. The filly, forced to dig deep, proved classy enough. She demonstrated, not just speed, but also dogged determination against a very talented foe.

Now, three weeks later, the outcome might be different. Away since May 25, Arches Of Gold had delivered two top efforts, the second extreme, and might be vulnerable to the "bounce." She had never competed in mud. Although Arches Of Gold does not need the lead to win, three additional front-runners in the field should compromise her early foot.

A former claimer, Freedom Cry had never won a stakes, let alone a graded stakes, not to mention a Grade 1 title. Yet the mare approached the Santa Monica's seven furlongs in the finest form of her career and she was undefeated (two for two) on wet surfaces. She was also exiting a troubled trip against a Grade 1 winner, Laramie Moon, where she had recorded competitive speed and pace figures, probably should have won, and was being returned today by leading trainer Gary Jones, who is hot.

If Arches Of Gold bounced, or disliked mud, Freedom Cry figured to win. Handicappers were offered 7–2 on her chances. I grabbed it.

Arches Of Gold shot to the front after a quarter-mile, but toward the quarter pole stopped cold. Freedom Cry dispensed her biggest race and recorded her highest speed figure ever. She paid $9. In a two-horse showdown, a key bet to win netted $750.

Two comments on this predictable outcome: As many handicappers might have intuited, January at Santa Anita qualifies as an especially kindly month for "bounce" patterns. The reason is obvious. Many horses will be coming back from lengthy layoffs.

Second, whenever two contenders in small fields form the brunt of the competition, take the odds—every time. No doubt Arches Of Gold is the superior sprinter, probably Grade 1. Six months along in the calendar, if the same two contenders form the guts of a graded sprint, Arches Of Gold probably will win. But whenever a young, still-developing filly is moving ahead in class, looks vulnerable on certain fundamentals, will be overbet, and in the same situation a good but less classy individual is arriving at a peak performance while underbet, the conclusion follows absolutely. Play for the upset. Take the overlay.

* * *

In late January, Best Pal resurfaced from a May 9 layoff under Grade 2 conditions at a middle distance. As many handicappers understand, since Best Pal represented the finest of Grade 1 specimens, a true champ during 1992, he figured to lose in his comeback.

The principle bears up remarkably well. The established multiple Grade 1 winners (4UP) returning from long layoffs in races below Grade 1 figure to disappoint from the moment the names appear in the entries. Chasing larger objectives, an all-out assault in a lower-grade race makes no sense and is not happily indulged. Best Pal's winter objective would be the million-dollar Santa Anita Handicap, not a Grade 2 stakes of late January.

The question is whether an attractive alternative at a decent price figures to upset. Against Best Pal, another horse did figure this day, and that horse's past performances contained a scarcely understood aspect of class evaluation. Examine the respective records on page 32:

Best Pal 🐎

DESORMEAUX K J (—)
Own.—Golden Eagle Farm

B. g. 5, by Habitony—Ubetshedid, by King Pellinore
Br.—Mabee Mr-Mrs John C (Cal)
Tr.—Jones Gary (20 3 3 5 .15)

	Lifetime	1992	5				$1,672,900
124	23 12 6 1	1991	:0	2	5	1	$1,107,500
	$3,805,695	Turf	1	0	1	0	$30,000

Jovial-En 🐎

WALLS M K (65 4 7 0 .06)
Own.—Jackson & Swift

B. h. 6, by Northern Jove—Rensaler, by Stop The Music
Br.—Cheveley Park Stud Ltd (Eng)
Tr.—Jackson Bruce L (5 2 0 0 .40)

	Lifetime	1993	1	1	0	0	
115	16 5 0 0	1992	4	0	0	0	
	$267,200	Turf	9	3	0	0	

Best Pal's special dimensions cannot be denied.

But what of Jovial?

Before smashing classified horses on January 1, the 6YO had not won in two and a half years. But suddenly, a tremendous performance, yielding a Beyer Speed Figure of 111. Is the huge effort an aberration? Or should a repeat performance be expected?

A repeat performance is almost assured.

Remember this: Whenever Grade 1 standouts snap out of doldrums that might have persisted for months or years with an undeniably super performance, they must be expected to retain the razor sharpness for a time. The horses boast extraordinary back class and now they feel spry again. Jovial fit the category, its best races no longer visible.

As mysterious as the resurgence may appear, the horses are

wired to run wild again and handicappers should anticipate nothing less. Workouts following the resurrection will be fast. In the afternoons, the horses will be jumped steps ahead in class by optimistic stables and they will fire real bullets against all foes. Only a truly top horse in excellent form can thwart them. The positive form lasts for a time—three months, six months, nine months perhaps—and just as suddenly disappears again. Just as quickly as handicappers should support the improvement, they should desert the decline.

Best Pal boasted maximum class, of course, but hardly excellent form. At even money, Best Pal can be tossed. Jovial, a firm second choice at 5–2, warrants a prime bet. The result chart documents the expected outcome extremely well, and is flattering to both horses.

EIGHTH RACE	1 ¹⁄₁₆ MILES. (1.39) 56th Running of THE SAN PASQUAL HANDICAP (Grade II). $150,000
Santa Anita	Added. 4-year-olds and upward. By subscription of $100 each to accompany the nomination, $1,000 additional to start, with $150,000 added, of which $30,000 to second, $22,500 to third,
JANUARY 24, 1983	$11,250 to fourth and $3,750 to fifth. Weights, Monday, January 18. Starters to be named through the entry box by the closing time of entries. A trophy will be presented to the owner

of the winner. Closed Wednesday, January 20, 1983, with 14 nominations.

Value of race $158,500; value to winner $91,400; second $30,000; third $22,500; fourth $11,250; fifth $3,750. Mutuel pool $496,465. Exacta pool $406,818.

Last Raced	Horse	M/Eqt.A.Wt	PP	St	¼	½	¾	Str	Fin	Jockey	Odds $1
1Jan83 7SA1	Jovial-En	L	6 115	6	7	52½	4½	43	2hd	12½	Walls M K	2.50
9May92 10Pim4	⑤Best Pal	LB	5 124	3	2	31½	3½	3hd	1hd	2½	Desormeaux K J	1.00
310ct92 10GP11	Marquetry	LB	6 118	5	3	22	23	2½	3½	3hd	Delahoussaye E	4.00
9Jan83 10BM1	Provins	LB	5 115	7	6	6½	6³½	6³½	62	4hd	Hawley S	21.50
9Jan83 8SA3	Excavate	LB	5 115	1	4	41½	54	54	52	51½	Valenzuela P A	28.20
1Jan83 7SA2	Memo-Ch	LB	6 114	2	1	11½	1½	1hd	43	6no	Atkinson P	15.90
6Dec92 8Hol4	Reign Road	LBb	5 117	4	5	7	7	7	7	7	Flores D R	10.60

⑤—Best Pal Disqualified and placed fifth.

OFF AT 4:23. Start good. Won ridden out. Time, :234, :47 , 1:11 , 1:35², 1:41⁴ Track fast.

$2 Mutuel Prices:	6–JOVIAL-EN _____	7.00	4.20	3.60
	1–MARQUETRY _____		4.20	3.20
	7–PROVINS _____			6.00

$2 EXACTA 6–1 PAID $30.20.

B. h, by Northern Jove—Rensaler, by Stop The Music. Trainer Jackson Bruce L. Bred by Cheveley Park Stud Ltd (Eng).

JOVIAL-EN, outrun early after breaking a bit awkwardly, moved up steadily to reach contention before going a half without being hustled, raced wide down the backstretch, advanced readily to engage for the lead five sixteenths out while four wide, came into the stretch four wide, battled for command in the upper stretch while under some right handed encouragement and was shown the whip in the final sixteenth while drawing away. BEST PAL lurked in an easy striking position early after a good start, raced along the inner rail going into the backstretch, angled to the outside approaching the five-eighths pole, advanced readily to engage for the lead nearing the five sixteenths marker, was under left handed pressure in the stretch, battled for command early in the drive, then could not match the response of JOVIAL-EN in the last sixteenth. Following a stewards' inquiry and a claim of foul by the

POSTSCRIPT Jovial's speed and pace figures were 109–114. With a speed figure of 111 (Quirin-style), Best Pal ran roughly six lengths below his 1992 form, both at the pace call and at the wire. Following a second race to bolster current form, Best Pal will be primed for his main objective of winter.

Most handicappers lamented January for its two weeks of downpours, but yours truly found continual sustenance in the stakes races. It had been a very good month indeed, but it wasn't over, paraphrasing Yogi, until the very end.

On the final day of the month, a Grade 2 sprint for 3YO fillies at seven furlongs presented class handicappers with another generous winner, and several pointers on their specialty.

The race is highly instructive. Consider the four fillies at the center of an eight-horse field.

  7 FURLONGS. (1.20) 42nd Running of THE SANTA YNEZ BREEDERS' CUP STAKES (Grade II). $100,000 Added (*$75,000 added, plus $25,000 Breeders' Cup Fund). Fillies. 3–year–olds. (Foals of 1990). By subscription of $75 each to accompany the nomination and $750 additional to start. with $75,000 added and an additional $25,000 from the Breeders' Cup Fund for Cup nominees

This is not just a stakes sprint. Not altogether dissimilar from the seven-furlong Cal-bred stakes at the top of the month, this race is open to all comers in the 3YO filly division. Here are its special elements:

- It's a long sprint.
- It's limited to January 3YOs.
- It carries the Grade 2 class designation.
- The purse is $100,000-added, top money for 3YO sprinters.

The winner, therefore, will likely be quite a good horse. Other handicapping implications should not be missed:

1. Best bets at seven furlongs have won shorter and longer. High early speed carried at least six furlongs in a route

also counts, notably preceding a finish of some merit.

2. Three-year-olds of January typically will have revealed neither their best speed figures nor highest class levels. So improvement patterns should be much admired.

3. Under Grade 1 and Grade 2 conditions, competitive seasoning in open stakes should be greatly preferred. Extended or exhaustive stakes battles will have alerted young horses of high potential as to the exhaustive new experiences upcoming. Conversely, lack of stakes seasoning defeats numerous talented 3YOs on the first attempt in top-grade stakes.

4. Step-ups among nonclaiming 3YOs might be aggressive, but should also be realistic. Allowance to open stakes is acceptable. The same advance to Grade 1 or Grade 2 stakes is improbable.

5. Juvenile performances do not transfer reliably to the 3YO season, but the preferred pattern should be of improvement—faster, stronger, better.

Now to the past performances:

Of the four contenders, Blue Moonlight can be readily discounted. Two short workouts in forty-three days does not a sharp 3YO produce. Unlike older horses, youngsters exhibiting form defects, however slight, are unlikely to prevail in a Grade 2 sprint. Graded sprints should be hotly debated at every call.

Set Them Free went postward here at 4/5. A definite underlay. No play.

Set Them Free does not dominate on class. The Pasadena is a Listed stakes, purse of $75,000-added, but the filly galloped in the mud. The Beyer Speed par today is approximately 94, four lengths faster than Set Them Free's Pasadena figure.

The filly had never negotiated seven furlongs. She had

trained once, in sharp fashion, since December 29. After winning the Bay Meadows Debutante at two, Set Them Free was trounced in the Breeders' Cup Juvenile Fillies, not exactly a ringing endorsement of her talent or potential.

Regarding the Beyer Speed Figure of 101 versus maidens, young horses notoriously record inflated figures when coasting wire to wire against ordinary rivals. Discount speed figures earned in that manner. Set Them Free might be talented enough to annex a Grade 2 sprint, but the evidence supporting the goal is far from conclusive and 4/5 is far from fair.

Of Tour, this beautifully bred daughter of Forty Niner violates a fundamental tenet of class evaluation. She jumps from a nonwinners once allowance effort to a Grade 2 stakes. The class rise is not acceptable, unless (a) both the pace figure and speed figure of the allowance race are superior to today's stakes par (Tour's are not), (b) the horse won at the lower level with reserves of speed and power, and (c) the odds are attractive, not low.

Extended to win her initial allowance try, Tour was sent off in the Grade 2 Santa Ynez at 3–1. No thanks. The occasional successes cannot overcompensate handicappers for the more regular defeats.

What do handicappers know about Fit To Lead, who went to the post here at 8–1 and won going away by five-and-a-half lengths? Was the margin of victory predictable by class evaluation? Maybe not, but Fit To Lead presented the following credentials:

- Top speed figure last out, in a restricted stakes at a mile and one-sixteenth, nine days ago. The filly approaches today's encounter in improving form.
- Repeated stakes experience, short and long.
- Nicely suited to long sprints.
- The second-place last out occurred versus Likeable Style, so far the most impressive 3YO filly to appear. Fit To Lead had resisted Likeable Style as best she could, finishing six

lengths ahead of the third finisher. A big effort at a longer distance against a potential stakes star should not be underestimated by class analysts.

• An extra added attraction, trainer Caesar Dominguez has been sizzling.

The hesitation is Fit To Lead's pair of dull efforts under graded stakes conditions, August 28, at Del Mar (Gr. 3) and December 19, at Hollywood Park (Gr. 1).

Both setbacks can be explained satisfactorily. The Balboa at Del Mar was a long sprint against males following a single allowance score. Not only is the class rise premature (Why males?), at 23–1 Fit To Lead bled while forcing the pace and next appeared with Lasix.

The Grade 1 Hollywood Starlet offers a half-million dollars to the finest fillies in southern California. Eligible at the moment for nonwinners twice allowances, Fit To Lead did not fit a Grade 1 description.

She did fit the Grade 2 January sprint stakes snugly, as the result chart testifies. Equally persuasive to handicappers as the authority of Fit To Lead's victory, should be how badly the favorites disappointed. Set Them Free could not handle the unfamiliar class and distance requirements simultaneously, and fell back haplessly.

Value of race $187,500; value to winner $62,500; second $28,800; third $15,000; fourth $7,500; fifth $2,500. Mutuel pool $314,791. Exacta pool $334,551.

Last Raced	Horse	M/EqI.A.Wt	PP St	¼	½	Str	Fin	Jockey	Odds $1
22Jan93 8SA2	Fit To Lead	LB	3 116 4 5	3 1½	2hd	1 1½	1 5½	Nakatani C S	8.60
19Dec92 7Ho14	Nijivision	B	3 114 5 8	8	8	4hd	2nk	Solis A	7.90
13Jan93 8SA2	Booklore	LB	3 114 6 7	7 2½	7½	5 1½	3 3½	Black C A	21.30
19Dec92 7Hol5	Blue Moonlight	LB	3 123 2 2	2½	3 3½	2 3	4 3	Valenzuela P A	13.70
29Dec92 8SA1	Set Them Free	LB	3 121 3 1	1hd	1hd	3 1½	5 3½	Delahoussaye E	.80
13Jan93 8SA4	Borneastermorn	LB	3 116 1 6	6 6	6 5	8	6 1½	Flores D R	29.70
23Jan93 7SA3	Angie's Treasure	LBb	3 115 7 3	4½	5 2½	6 1	7 3	McCarron C J	25.30
23Jan93 7SA1	Tour	B	3 116 8 4	5hd	4½	7½	8	Stevens G L	3.40

OFF AT 4:23. Start good. Won ridden out. Time, :22², :44⁴, 1:09², 1:22² Track fast.

$2 Mutuel Prices:	4-FIT TO LEAD	19.20	9.60	6.00
	5-NIJIVISION		8.40	4.40
	6-BOOKLORE			7.40

$2 EXACTA 4-5 PAID $102.60.

Dk. b. or br. f, (May), by Fit to Fight—Islands, by Fortl. Trainer Dominguez Caesar F. Bred by Laura Leigh Partners L P (Ky).

FIT TO LEAD attended the early pace, raced wide most of the way down the backstretch, battled for the lead around the far turn, drew clear in the upper stretch, then extended her advantage in the final furlong for a decisive win. NIJIVISION, far back while last early after breaking slowly, rallied after a half, failed to pose a threat to FIT TO LEAD in the last furlong but edged BOOKLORE for the place. BOOKLORE, far back early, also rallied after a half, came into the stretch four-wide and was edged for the place by NIJIVISION. BLUE MOONLIGHT vied for the lead to the top of the stretch, then weakened. SET THEM FREE, wide most of the way down the backstretch, vied for the lead until nearing the top of the stretch, then gave way. BORNEASTERMORN was five-wide into the stretch. ANGIE'S TREASURE, in contention early, faltered and brushed with TOUR at the head of the stretch. TOUR, also in contention early, raced wide down the backstretch, and faltered while brushing with ANGIE'S TREASURE at the top of the lane.

POSTSCRIPT Was Fit To Lead a class bonanza here? In a strict sense, no. None of the contenders could be classified certifiably. Perhaps none would prove to be the authentic Grade 2 article, winning a second Grade 2 title.

In a broader sense, however, Fit To Lead measured up to the best. Her stakes experience and the much-improved performance last out, at a longer distance against fancy opposition, carries the cause.

Developing 3YOs of January and beyond will be moving ahead in class. Many of them can accomplish realistic objectives and most of them cannot satisfy unreasonable demands. Handicappers having a high regard for those distinctions will not often be misled.

FEBRUARY

Did I say Bertrando had exhibited sheer, unadulterated brilliance?

Did I suggest Bertrando's tour de force in Santa Anita's San Fernando Stakes at nine furlongs marked him as southern California's dominant 4YOs, and therefore among the most dominant 4YOs in the country?

Well, in the upset of the week, month, and perhaps the year, Bertrando lost the ten-furlong Strub Stakes (Gr. 1) at 30 cents on the dollar.

He finished a labored second to Siberian Summer, a non-stakes winner who paid $34.40.

I thought Bertrando would win the Strub as he pleased, as did the battalions of bettors who plunged. The selling points are worth a review:

- Except Bertrando, none of the eight horses entered had won either a Grade 1 or Grade 2 stakes.
- In the weakest Strub stakes in memory, only two of Bertrando's opponents could qualify for a second look.
- Bertrando had just recorded speed and pace figures enormously high for a 4YO of January.
- Bertrando would be the lone front-runner in the field.
- Bertrando had just whipped the same horses he met in the Strub by nine to thirty lengths.

Do handicappers admit to a real difference between middle distances and classic distances? I never considered a wager against Bertrando in the Strub, *but* posthumously I recollected that Bertrando possessed an unusually high dosage index. His D.I., in fact, is 7.70, a tremendous imbalance of speed and stamina.

Why horses that can dominate so undeniably at middle distances so often cannot duplicate the feats at classic distances qualifies as one of the sport's mysteries. The extra furlong, from nine to ten, separates virtually all pretenders to the thoroughbred throne.

No matter what its staunchest critics believe about dosage, they might entertain a basic conclusion of the research:

- When winners of open stakes up to nine furlongs are considered, the proportion of having dosage indexes above 4.0 is approximately 40 percent.
- When only winners of open stakes at ten furlongs or longer are considered, the proportion of D.I.s above 4.0 drops to approximately 5 percent.
- The populations of stakes winners are significantly different.

The most provocative aspect of the 1993 Strub Stakes occurred in its aftermath. On his local TV show five days later, the excellent southern California handicapper Jeff Siegel insisted Bertrando had lost the Strub because he had been held (rated) by the jockey (Chris McCarron) early.

"Bertrando is a pure one-dimensional speed horse," argued Siegel. "Speed horses cannot be held. They must be allowed to run free."

If speed horses are rated, theoretically, other front-runners, pressers, and stalkers can stay close without undue exertion, gaining striking position, even while the more brilliant speed horse has been tugging away, losing energy. That kind of unhappily restrained speed demon will be vulnerable late.

If permitted to run freely, without restraint, the speed demon separates himself readily from his closest pursuers, relaxes eventually into a comfortable stride, and finishes well enough to win.

Other respectable handicappers of southern California regurgitated Siegel's argument, so that Bertrando's defeat at 3/10 in the Strub was placed squarely on jockey McCarron.

My spin on the issue differs significantly and applies to races similar to the Strub Stakes. At a mile, a mile and one-sixteenth, and a mile and one-eighth, speed horses who outclass the opposition can run away and hide, and usually should be permitted to do so.

At some point, inevitably, even the most talented speed horses must be guided in the quest to capture Grade 1 titles at ten furlongs. To imagine simply that Bertrando can outrun classy opponents across ten furlongs time after time assumes too much. Even if Bertrando had lasted in the 1993 Strub Stakes, where the opposition were patsies, in later, more definitive Grade 1 contests, with championships at stake, stronger and comparably talented rivals would surely pass him late. It happens all the time.

In fact, the ideal circumstance in which to rate Bertrando was the 1993 Strub Stakes. The opposition was plainly inept. The favorite did not have to show his best to prevail. All other considerations aside, that Bertrando flopped in this spot altered my fundamental perception of the horse.

Reflecting objectively on the race, Siegel and others might concede that Bertrando should have survived nonetheless. McCarron had taken hold early, all right, but lightly, and Bertrando had responded well enough. No fighting, climbing, or the conventional tug-of-war had ensued. On the backside, moreover, Bertrando relaxed nicely, reacting kindly to McCarron's handling, as the jockey insisted afterward.

Bertrando raced in the clear passing the quarter pole, and no one suspected an upset was brewing. Trevor Denman's call suggested Bertrando was breezing and would win waltzing. When Bertrando was asked to respond in the stretch, however, he could summon little. As Siberian Summer challenged, Bertrando persisted, but he was outrun to the wire.

If McCarron had allowed Bertrando to run freely at the outset, setting faster fractions for Siberian Summer to chase, the 4YO probably would have tired just the same. And I'm certain Bertrando then would have been more likely to squander subsequent Grade 1 contests at the classic distance against authentic Grade 1 opposition.

Not to be forgotten, on Strub day I had lunched alongside Scott Finley and other officials of *Daily Racing Form,* who were visiting Santa Anita for the weekend. Just as Finley and I had reminisced smugly on the El Atroz mutuels and Scott was noting how much he relished the daily simulcast of Santa Anita racing to Suffolk Downs, one of his associates, relatively new to horse racing, wondered aloud whether this favorite Bertrando might lose. If so, which horses might win — at a price. A brief discussion suggested Siberian Summer and Star Recruit as the only sane alternatives, but I did not take either horse seriously.

Finley had landed on Siberian Summer by his own devices. He even had bet the colt to win, played it atop Bertrando in multiple exactas ($86.20) and hooked it to three contenders in the late double, one of which naturally won ($388.80). Finley scooped $3,200 from the assorted pools, unconvinced, I suppose, that Bertrando would not lose.

Stunned at the outcome, I relegated Bertrando to the bullpen, persuaded he could not redeem himself in the Santa Anita Handicap. I felt just as confident I would get an overlay opportunity on the brilliant 4YO at a shorter distance later in the season.

February dragged on mercilessly, its historical significance amounting to a siege of rain unseen in southern California in many years.

A week following the Strub Stakes, our 3YO filly acquaintance Likeable Style took the Grade 1 Las Virgenes Stakes at a mile. She paid even money. The more interesting result was Likeable Style's speed figure. It matched par; no better. The media liked the race big time, but par figures do not distinguish 3YO division leaders very much. Figure analysts prefer to see something special, such as speed figures comfortably above par following a decent pace.

I filed Likeable Style in the Horses To Beat category, an intriguing twist on handicappers' more familiar Horses To Watch lists. In tracking the 3YOs, and young 4YOs, simulcast handicappers should consider each Santa Anita stakes a preliminary to the next event. The guiding principle should sound familiar. Overrated horses will be underlays. Underrated horses will be overlays.

It's February, and Likeable Style has a right to improve.

But I prefer to imagine that someday, not far away, the filly will be a conspicuous underlay. Par means average, and is not to be confused with the best of the best.

In a slight variation of the theme, on February 17, southern California's leading 3YO colt Personal Hope wired the restricted Bradbury Stakes by four lengths. The speed and pace figures barely toppled par. Nothing special, yet the colt had won in hand. He might have run faster. With rougher stakes upcoming, should Personal Hope be considered on course for the Kentucky Derby? It's too soon to know. But, why not? Maybe; maybe not?

In late February, the performance I had been awaiting came crashing down. It came unexpectedly, a bolt of a surprise.

It was a flat mile, the Grade 2 San Rafael Stakes for 3YOs. Despite backing the eventual winner, because he became an overlay, I felt no firm leanings prior to the running. A few hours following the race, after assigning the speed and pace figures, I got quite excited.

The past performances contained as well a fine point regarding the class evaluation of nonclaiming 3YOs, a circumstance overlooked consistently by handicappers, and in particular by figure handicappers.

Scan the records of the five leading principals:

First, I typically eliminate nonstakes winners under Grade 1 and Grade 2 conditions, unless (a) their speed and pace figures have matched or exceeded today's par or (b) they have finished close in good time at today's level. Exceptions would be predicated upon price. That procedure pared Union City from serious consideration.

Art Of Living looks tempting, shows solid figures, and boasts faultless connections and workouts, but is also the crowd's favorite. He exits a restricted stakes. Whenever a nonclaiming 3YO is moving ahead by multiple jumps in the stakes division following big wins where he was uncontested in the late stages, beware. Lower level races, including stakes, will frequently be decided early (2nd call), but better stakes more frequently will be decided late. The figures may be praiseworthy, but the intangibles of class may be missing.

Forced to exhibit perseverance, competitive spirit, determination, and maybe a long protracted stretch run while tiring against better horses, what will Art Of Living do? As favorites, co-favorites, and low-priced contenders, the presumption must hold that untested 3YOs will disappoint.

In figure handicapping, pace analysts will be wary enough to discount any nonclaiming 3YO stepping up too aggressively in class while carrying pace figures below par by more than two lengths. Forced to attend a more rapid pace against better for longer, too many youngsters cannot duplicate previously impressive speed figures.

Competitive demands throughout the late stages of races, however, are not as obligingly recognized. In the allowances, as well as in restricted, open, listed, and Grade 3 stakes, those later competitive demands may or may not be severe and prolonged. In Grade 2 and Grade 1 events, they normally will be. Even when best, any 3YO stakes candidate that has not experienced a rugged struggle in the late stages of top-class stakes competition can be discounted, certainly at a paltry price.

A 3–1 shot, Art Of Living was plastered in the Grade 2 stakes under discussion.

Now consider Stuka, a 3–5 shot, no less, in today's Grade 2 test.

At two, the colt drew off in sprints, including the Grade 3 Prevue at Hollywood Park, and so impressively it was hammered to 6–5 in the Grade 1, $500,000-guaranteed Hollywood Futurity, its first route. Handicappers should have avoided Stuka in the Hollywood Futurity and should view the 3YO as the conspicuous underlay it represents today. Stuka may be a top sophomore, but why take 3–5 when the matter has not been resolved.

A sensible alternative to the overbet favorites was Devoted Brass, playable at 5–1. After stomping maidens when favored at Stampede Park, the colt broke last at odds–on in that track's leading race for juveniles. Still, Devoted Brass won going away. Nice!

The gelding next appeared at Santa Anita in the care of high-percentage trainer Noble Threewitt. The horseman is an old hand. He saddled horses on opening day at Santa Anita in 1934.

Dismissed at Santa Anita (32–1) in the Grade 3, seven-furlong San Vincente Stakes, from six lengths behind Devoted Brass completed the second fraction in 22²⁄₅ seconds and finished a strong-rallying third. He ran the final three-eighths in 36³⁄₅, with obvious reserves. The *Daily Racing Form* tagline provided by the chartist declared, "closed strongly," an infrequent comment. The Beyer Speed Figure was 89, a marginally competitive figure.

Devoted Brass can contend in the Grade 2 field and he might just win by outkicking the others. A jockey change from Martin Pedroza to Kent Desormeaux qualified as an extra added attraction, though it also depressed the odds.

After breaking awkwardly, from six behind again Devoted Brass accelerated sharply on the far turn and quickly came abreast of the leaders in the upper stretch. He looked a handy winner at that juncture.

But Union City dug in determinedly and a stretch-long dogfight continued. When Devoted Brass was headed inside the sixteenth pole, I imagined he was done. Yet the gutty gelding dug in harder, found renewed energy, and was edging clear at the wire. He paid $12.20.

EIGHTH RACE

Santa Anita

FEBRUARY 27, 1993

1 MILE. (1.33²) 13th Running of THE SAN RAFAEL STAKES (Grade II). $150,000 Added. 3–year–olds. (Foals of 1990). By subscription of $100 each to accompany the nomination, $1,800 additional to start, with $150,000 added, of which $30,000 to second, $22,500 to third, $11,250 to fourth and $3,750 to fifth. Weight, 121 lbs. Non–winners of $78,000 at one mile or over allowed 3 lbs.; of a race of $40,000 at any distance, 6 lbs. Starters to be named through the entry box by the closing time of entries. A trophy will be presented to the owner of the winner. Closed Wednesday, February 17, 1993 with 15 nominations.

Value of race $157,500; value to winner $90,000; second $30,000; third $22,500; fourth $11,250; fifth $3,750. Mutuel pool $472,262. Exacta pool $473,386.

Last Raced	Horse	M/Eqt.A.Wt	PP St	¼	½	¾	Str	Fin	Jockey	Odds $1
7Feb93 7SA³	Devoted Brass	B	3 115 5 5	6	6	5¹¼	1ʰᵈ	1½	Desormeaux K J	5.10
6Feb93 6SA¹	Union City	LB	3 115 2 2	5⁵	4ʰᵈ	4ʰᵈ	2⁶	2¹²	McCarron C J	7.10
20Dec92 8Hol²	Stuka	Lb	3 118 6 3	3¹	3¹½	3ʰᵈ	4¹	3ⁿᵏ	Valenzuela P A	.70
7Feb93 7SA⁶	Lord Of The Bay	LB	3 121 1 1	1½	1ʰᵈ	1ʰᵈ	3½	4⁵	Black C A	27.00
27Jan93 8SA¹	Art Of Living	LBb	3 118 4 4	2ʰᵈ	2ʰᵈ	2ʰᵈ	5¹½	5¹¼	Stevens G L	3.60
7Feb93 7SA⁵	Joyofracing–GB	L	3 115 3 6	4½	5⁴	6	6	6	Walls M K	22.10

OFF AT 4:46. Start good. Won driving. Time, :22², :45¹, 1:10 , 1:22², 1:35 Track fast.

$2 Mutuel Prices:	5–DEVOTED BRASS	12.20	5.40	2.60
	2–UNION CITY		6.00	2.60
	6–STUKA			2.20

$2 EXACTA 5–2 PAID $67.80.

B. g. (Mar), by Dixieland Band—Royal Devotion, by His Majesty. Trainer Threewitt Noble. Bred by Phillips Mr–Mrs James W (Ky).

DEVOTED BRASS, off a bit awkwardly and bumped in the initial strides, trailed early while unhurried, raced wide down the backstretch, advanced quickly to engage for the lead a quarter of a mile out while five-wide, battled for command all the way down the stretch while to the outside of UNION CITY, was roused when the whip twice left-handed early in the stretch run, lugged in a bit leaving the furlong marker with the rider losing his hold of the right rein briefly approaching the sixteenth marker before he could regain his hold of it, brushed lightly with UNION CITY a sixteenth out and was under aggressive handling late to prevail in a hard drive. UNION CITY, patiently handled early while in an easy striking position, cruised up to engage for the lead nearing the quarter pole while four-wide, battled for command all the way down the stretch while to the inside of DEVOTED BRASS, was under left-handed pressure in the drive, was in rather tight quarters much of the final furlong, brushed lightly with DEVOTED BRASS a sixteenth out and grudgingly had to settle for the place. STUKA, bumped and checked in the opening strides when he veered inward, dueled for the lead for a little more than six furlongs, gave way and was lugging inward in the stretch. LORD OF THE BAY raced along the inner rail throughout, also dueled for the lead for a little more than six furlongs and gave way. ART OF LIVING dueled for the lead for a little more than six furlongs and faltered. JOYOFRACING–GB, close up early after breaking slowly, faltered and was four wide into the stretch.

POSTSCRIPT What had registered at the moment as impressive would be transformed to outstanding a few hours later. The Quirin-style figures for the Grade 2 mile stunned me: Pace 116, Speed 110.

Personal Hope had run 106–107, five lengths in arrears of Devoted Brass at the second call and three lengths back at the finish.

A lengthy thoughtful experience has instructed me how to recognize each season's 3YOs truly qualified to win the Kentucky Derby. They must record figures that approach the older stakes par at the finish after staying within a few lengths of the older stakes par after six furlongs. Santa Anita's older stakes par (Quirin-style) at the route is 113. Devoted Brass had qualified as a Kentucky Derby prospect.

When the Beyer Speed Figure for the San Rafael Stakes winner was published, it was 105, by several lengths the fastest race for a 3YO so far in 1993.

I had discovered my Kentucky Derby hopeful in February. I wanted immediately to convert my advantage. On Monday, March 1, I attempted to get 50–1 in the Las Vegas Future Books. The best offer was 30–1. With the Santa Anita Derby five weeks away, I decided to wait. If Personal Hope won another stakes, the Vegas lines should move, with Devoted Brass going up.

Regarding the long march to the Kentucky Derby, handicappers might ponder the speed and pace figures of a few interesting 3YOs of southern California. All of them had exited the Santa Anita Derby as winners.

KENTUCKY DERBY PROSPECTS

		PACE	SPEED
1992	A.P. Indy	112	107
1991	Dinard	107	111
1990	Sunday Silence	111	115
1988	Winning Colors	113	116

The four were southern California division leaders, nationally recognized as Kentucky Derby contenders. Two won at Churchill Downs. Neither A.P. Indy nor Dinard got to the gate in Louisville, but their figures can be accepted as characteristic of impressive 3YOs that are not quite impressive enough. As soon as 3YOs of winter have posted numbers similar to Sunday Silence and Winning Colors, handicappers can hurry to the nearest Future Book. But not before.

At 106–107, Personal Hope faced an uphill climb. Devoted Brass had almost arrived.

MARCH

Believe it or not, two weeks following the exhaustive Grade 2 San Rafael triumph, trainer Threewitt, notwithstanding fifty years of experience, entered Devoted Brass in the Grade 2 San Felipe Stakes, at $200,000-added and a mile and one-sixteenth the major prep to the Santa Anita Derby.

I was stunned, and chagrined. Wayne Lukas bypassed the San Felipe with Union City. The main contenders would be Personal Hope and Corby, southern California's two division leaders of the moment.

As mightily as Devoted Brass had impressed in the San Rafael, the smallish gelding would be highly susceptible to a performance "bounce." The gelding's Beyer Speed Figure had leaped from 89 to 105. My figures were stronger still. Devoted Brass had been severely extended to win; overextended. He was being wheeled back in fourteen days! A "bounce" was virtually preordained. I had expected to make a sizable wager on Devoted Brass in the Santa Anita Derby, but not today.

Then something unanticipated, and unprecedented, happened.

Caesars Palace erected a future-book line on Santa Anita's San Felipe Stakes. Personal Hope, Corby, and River Special controlled the lion's share of the action. So much so that on Friday, the day before the race, Devoted Brass was brandished at 30–1. I'm disciplined, but not chained. Unable to get 50–1 on the gelding in the Kentucky Derby, I'm handed 30–1 on a regional prep. I took $200 worth, confident the odds tomorrow at Santa Anita would be roughly 90 percent shorter.

At 7–2, and predictably, Devoted Brass floundered in the San Felipe, unable to sustain his roundhouse punch. He had rallied as before, but at the end trailed the winner Corby by two and a half lengths and runner-up Personal Hope by another length.

In advance of the San Felipe, a few analysts discounted Devoted Brass, not because he should "bounce," but because of his late-running style. They argued that Devoted Brass had won the San Rafael Stakes by overtaking a fast pace. In the San Felipe, they insisted, the pace should not be as swift, and in any event should not back up.

But Devoted Brass was not a one-run closer. In winning the San Rafael, the gelding had surged quickly into the fast pace around the far turn, before fighting furiously against Union City throughout the stretch. His victory had required two moves, and Devoted Brass had delivered both impressively.

The distinction can be considered crucial, an essential aspect of pace analysis, applicable frequently to closers in stakes races. As pace analyst Tom Brohamer has emphasized, to dominate on pace, and regardless of running style, horses must have demonstrated the ability to control two pace segments. Horses able to dominate only a single fraction are held to possess a pace weakness. Sprinters, and many routers, typically dominate the first two fractions, or the early pace. Leading stakes horses, obviously closers that come from behind the early pace, more often dominate the two closing fractions.

Pace analysis can vary sharply when analyzing the stakes. In overnight sprints, of horses that can control just one fraction, the notorious case is the sprinter who dominates the first call, slackens during the second fraction, before winning in decent time anyhow. Few of those sprinters will survive in a stakes sprint. The second fraction, or turn time, buries them.

Of late pace, the notorious weakness belongs to the one-run closer, the kind that "picks up the pieces." The horses control just one pace segment. In stakes competition at the route, the front-runners, pressers, and stalkers usually will not be falling apart. Only closers that can cut into the pace strongly on the far turn, gaining striking position, before rallying strongly, winning two fractions, should be expected to succeed.

Devoted Brass fit the latter description. To cement the point, let's fast-forward briefly to July and a Devoted Brass that has been restored to good health and positive form. In familiar style, the gutsy gelding won Hollywood Park's Swaps Stakes (Gr. 2) at a mile and a quarter. He had notched his second Grade 2 title, proving he belonged.

After waiting for four months, did I back Devoted Brass in the Swaps Stakes? I intended to, but the 3YO appeared in front-tendon wraps. So I passed. Wrong again. As a final twist in this tortuous tale, shortly after the Swaps Stakes I read that Devoted Brass, of Stampede Park, by way of Santa Anita, had been sold — to Saudi Arabia!

He was no longer the same, but following a perfect second-place prep in the Grade 1 San Antonio Stakes, I believed Best Pal would clobber a lackluster field in the 1993 version of the Santa Anita Handicap, at $1 million guaranteed, the richest and most definitive winter stakes in the nation.

After all, the mile and one-quarter of the race, so hostile to so many thoroughbreds, had been Best Pal's private domain. Even as a 3YO, Best Pal had performed significantly better at the classic distance than at middle distances, quite an unusual circumstance.

Instead, at 7–5 (no bet) Best Pal succumbed without a challenge. Look closely at the gelding's record. Do handicappers recognize a pattern here?

Best Pal
Own: Golden Eagle Farm
BLACK C A (133 17 16 11 .13)

B. g. 5
Sire: Habitony (Habitat)
Dam: Ubetshedid (King Pellinore)
Br: Mabee Mr–Mrs John C (Cal)
Tr: Jones Gary (27 4 3 4 .15)

L 122

Lifetime Record:					
1993	3	0	0	1	$103,750
1992	5	4	0	0	$1,672,000
Hol Ⓣ	1	0	1	0	$30,000

10Apr93-8OP	fst	1⅛	:464	1:102	1:353	1:483	Oaklawn H-G1	107	2	7	812	710	65	32½	Desormeaux K J	L 123	2.80	90–19	Jovial1171¼ Lil E. Tee1231¼ Best Pal1231½	
6Mar93-5SA	fst	1¼	:471	1:11	1:351	2:002	S Anita H-G1	105	1	8	76½	73¾	74¾	55	Desormeaux K J	LB 124	*1.40	88–13	Sir Beaufort119no Star Recruit117hd Ma	
Wide, climbing, lost shoe																				
24Jan93-8SA	fst	1$\frac{1}{16}$	:234	:47	1:11	1:414	Sn Psql H-G2	102	3	3	33½	3½	1hd	22¾	Desormeaux K J	LB 124	*1.00	92–15	Jovial1152¾ [D]Best Pal124½ Marquetry111	
Came out, impeded foe 5/8 Disqualified and placed 5th																				
9May92-10Pim	fst	1$\frac{3}{16}$	:473	1:112	1:354	1:544	Pim Specl H-G1	104	7	3	31½	31	22	44¼	Desormeaux K J	L 126	*.60	84–23	Strike the Gold114¾ Fly So Free1161¼ T	
11Apr92-8OP	fst	1⅛	:46	1:094	1:351	1:48	Oaklawn H-G1	121	6	5	55	53¼	1½	11½	Desormeaux K J	L 125	*.70	96–20	Best Pal1251½ Sea Cadet120½ Twilight A	
7Mar92-5SA	fst	1¼	:46	1:094	1:34	1:59	S Anita H-G1	123	4	5	53¼	1½	13	15½	Desormeaux K J	LB 124	*1.70	99–10	Best Pal1245½ Twilight Agenda1242¼ De	
9Feb92-8SA	fst	1¼	:463	1:102	1:35	1:594	C H Strub-G1	119	5	3	31	1hd	11½	11¼	Desormeaux K J	LB 124	*1.20	95–11	Best Pal1241¼ Dinard1208 Reign Road11	
Four wide backstretch, steadied near 3/8 pole																				
18Jan92-8SA	fst	1⅛	:47	1:111	1:353	1:481	Sn Fernando-G2	121	4	7	73¾	4¾	1½	13½	Desormeaux K J	LB 122	2.80	89–21	Best Pal1223½ Olympio1225½ Dinard1200	
30Nov91-8Hol	fm	1⅛ Ⓣ	:472	1:111	1:342	1:454	3↑ Citation H-G2	104	5	3	32	42	52¼	21¾	Desormeaux K J	LB 119	4.80	99–07	Fly Till Dawn1191¾ Best Pal119nk Wolf	
Run in divisions																				
9Nov91-8SA	fst	1⅛	:471	1:103	1:354	1:49	3↑ [S]Ca Cp Clsc H	100	2	3	31	2hd	1hd	2hd	Valenzuela P A	L 124	*.40	85–18	Charmonnier112hd Best Pal1247 Elega	

WORKOUTS: ●May 26 Hol 7f fst 1:253 H 1/4 May 21 Hol Ⓣ 6f fm 1:15 H (d) 1/2 May 16 Hol 6f fst 1:122 H 5/21 May 11 Hol 5f fst 1:004 B 3/21 May 6 Hol Ⓣ 4f fm :502 B (d) 4/7 Acc

Examine the Beyer Speed Figures. The supreme handicap horse in the United States at four during 1992, Best Pal had been injured in May at Pimlico and rested until January of 1993. Running eight to ten lengths below his 1992 form, Best Pal is no longer a champion.

The proof resides in the speed figures, a salient aspect of class evaluation. When prominent stakes horses 4UP return for another season, handicappers should pay attention to their figure patterns. If they have fallen below last season's marks after a couple of warm-ups, the horses have declined. Routinely, each will need a drop in class to win. Until the horses are lowered in class, no play. At the same class levels as before, the horses belong on the Horses To Beat list.

More broadly, as standard operating procedure, year to year comparisons of Beyer Speed Figures apply to all stakes divisions. Three-year-olds should earn better speed figures than they managed as juveniles. Lightly raced 4YOs should break through 3YO barriers. Stakes candidates 5UP should replicate last season's top marks. Because they compete at low prices against only the best, the best of the best, à la Best Pal, should be held strictly to duplicating former standards.

Following the Santa Anita Handicap, I dismissed Best Pal as a Grade 1 contender for 1993. The outcome of the million-dollar handicap was not exactly wholly reassuring regarding the merits of southern California's handicap horses. As the result chart shows, the first three finishers were rank outsiders.

FIFTH RACE
Santa Anita
MARCH 6, 1993

1 ¼ MILES. (1.57⁴) 56th Running of THE SANTA ANITA HANDICAP (Grade I). Purse $1,000,000 Guaranteed. 4-year-olds and upward. By subscription of $2,000 each (regular nomination) due on or before Tuesday, December 1, 1992, fee to accompany the nomination. A sustaining payment of $2,500 each is due on or before Thursday, January 14, 1993. For any horse not previously nominated and sustained, $5,000 will be due by Friday, February 26 with

Value of race $1,000,000; value to winner $550,000; second $200,000; third $150,000; fourth $75,000; fifth $25,000. Mutuel pool $1,251,519. Exacta pool $823,502. Trifecta pool $685,782.

Last Raced	Horse	M/Eqt	A.	Wt	PP	¼	½	¾	1	Str	Fin	Jockey	Odds $1
14Feb93 8SA2	Sir Beaufort	LB	6	119	2	3^{hd}	3^{hd}	4^{1}	3^{hd}	$2^{1\frac{1}{2}}$	1no	Valenzuela P A	11.80
7Feb93 8SA4	Star Recruit	LBb	4	117	10	2^{1}	$2^{\frac{1}{2}}$	2^{1}	$2^{1\frac{1}{2}}$	1^{hd}	2^{hd}	Pincay L Jr	59.20
7Feb93 8SA3	Major Impact		4	114	8	6^{1}	6^{3}	6^{4}	5^{1}	4^{1}	$3^{1\frac{3}{4}}$	Stevens G L	16.30
24Jan93 8SA1	(S)Jovial-En	L	6	117	7	$7^{1\frac{1}{2}}$	8^{1}	7^{hd}	6^{hd}	$5^{1\frac{1}{2}}$	4^{3}	Walls M K	3.70
24Jan93 8SA2	Best Pal	LB	5	124	1	$8^{\frac{1}{2}}$	$7^{\frac{1}{2}}$	8^{1}	$7^{3\frac{1}{2}}$	$7^{2\frac{1}{2}}$	$5^{1\frac{1}{4}}$	Desormeaux K J	1.40
14Feb93 8SA1	Marquetry	LB	6	118	9	4^{1}	$4^{1\frac{1}{2}}$	3^{hd}	4^{1}	$6^{\frac{1}{2}}$	6^{2}	Delahoussaye E	a-2.40
14Feb93 8SA3	Reign Road	LBb	5	115	3	11	11	11	10^{2}	$9^{3\frac{1}{2}}$	7^{1}	Flores D R	9.80
27Jan93 3SA4	El Trenzador-Ar	LB	5	113	5	5^{1}	$5^{\frac{1}{2}}$	$5^{1\frac{1}{2}}$	8^{4}	8^{4}	$8^{\frac{1}{2}}$	Nakatani C S	60.50
7Feb93 8SA2	Bertrando	LBb	4	120	4	$1^{\frac{1}{2}}$	1^{1}	1^{1}	1^{hd}	3^{hd}	9^{10}	McCarron C J	a-2.40
14Feb93 8SA6	Tel Quel-Fr	LB	5	116	6	$9^{2\frac{1}{2}}$	9^{4}	9^{5}	$9^{2\frac{1}{2}}$	10^{6}	10^{12}	Solis A	86.90
7Feb93 11TuP7	June's Reward	LB	5	114	11	$10^{3\frac{1}{2}}$	10^{3}	10^{hd}	11	11	11	Black C A	149.10

a-Coupled: Marquetry and Bertrando.
(S) Supplementary nomination.

OFF AT 2:50 Start good for all but TEL QUEL-FR Won driving Time, :23², :47¹, 1:11 , 1:35¹, 2:00² Track fast.

$2 Mutuel Prices:				
	3-SIR BEAUFORT	25.60	11.20	8.00
	9-STAR RECRUIT		32.00	12.80
	8-MAJOR IMPACT			7.00

$2 EXACTA 3-9 PAID $916.60 $3 TRIFECTA 3-9-8 PAID $6,286.60.

Gr. h, by Pleasant Colony—Carolina Saga, by Caro (Ire). Trainer Whittingham Charles. Bred by Buckland Farm (Va).

SIR BEAUFORT, away in alert fashion and brushed in the initial strides, sat within close attendance of the early pace while along the inner rail, was boxed in on the far turn until angling to the outside of BERTRANDO and STAR RECRUIT approaching the quarter pole, came on readily to engage for the lead nearing the furlong marker, battled for command thereafter under aggressive handling and was game as can be to prevail by an extremely slim margin. STAR RECRUIT, off in good order and just off the early pace, engaged for the lead five sixteenths out, battled for command the rest of the way, was under left handed pressure through the final furlong, also was game as can be only to lose by an extremely slim margin and was reported to have lost his left front shoe. MAJOR IMPACT, outrun early but not far back, raced wide early, advanced to loom menacingly turning into the stretch, came into the stretch five wide, continued to come on through the drive when resolutely keeping to his task, was gaining strongly in the closing strides but could not quite get up in an excellent try. JOVIAL-EN, devoid of early speed, rallied on the far turn to loom dangerous turning into the stretch, was fanned six wide into the stretch, continued to gain in the drive but did not have the necessary late punch. BEST PAL, away in good order and also devoid of early speed, brushed with TEL QUEL-FR approaching the clubhouse turn when the rider was seeking to move to the outside, got to the outside going into the clubhouse turn, raced five wide all the way down the backstretch while climbing, also rallied on the far turn to loom dangerous turning into the stretch, was fanned seven wide into the stretch, drifted in a bit briefly in the upper stretch, lacked the needed kick in the drive and was reported to have lost his left front shoe. MARQUETRY lurked within close range of the pace through the early stages, entered the stretch four wide and weakened. REIGN ROAD, far back early, steadily improved his position after going six furlongs but failed to threaten. EL TRENZADOR-AR, in contention early, gave way. EL TRENZADOR'S RIDER dropped his whip a sixteenth out. BERTRANDO, away alertly and brushed in the opening strides, established the pace through the early stages, vied for the advantage from the five sixteenths marker to the top of the stretch, then faltered. TEL QUEL-FR, rank early after breaking awkwardly, brushed with BEST PAL approaching the clubhouse turn, raced wide down the backstretch and was not persevered with late. JUNE'S REWARD broke slowly, trailed through the final four furlongs and also was not persevered with late.

Owners— 1, Calantoni Victoria; 2, DanDar Farm; 3, Glen Hill Farm; 4, Jackson & Swift; 5, Golden Eagle Farm; 6, Engelson & Engelson & Frankel; 7, Cooke Jack Kent; 8, Gamel & Haras Sonoita; 9, 505 Farms & Nahem; 10, Darley Stud Management Inc; 11, Porter Ken.

Trainers— 1, Whittingham Charles; 2, Fanning Jerry; 3, Proctor Willard L; 4, Jackson Bruce L; 5, Jones Gary; 6, Frankel Robert; 7, Robbins Jay M; 8, McAnally Ronald; 9, Frankel Robert; 10, Whittingham Charles; 11, French Neil.

Overweight: Star Recruit 2 pounds; El Trenzador-Ar 1; June's Reward 2.

$3 Triple (2 or 5-3-3) Paid $533.70. Triple Pool $525,413.

The 1993 Santa Anita Handicap Out of Town

Cross-track wagering usually favors simulcast bettors with higher odds, but not automatically. Under certain circumstances, horses that are underbet at the local track may be overbet at out-of-town simulcast sites.

When Sir Beaufort won the 1993 Santa Anita Handicap by a nose, he paid $25.60 at Santa Anita Park and at that track's intertrack satellite-wagering sites. At simulcast sites out of town, the payoffs were curiously lower:

Aqueduct	$15.00
Laurel	15.80
Philadelphia Park	15.20
Gulfstream Park	15.20
Oaklawn Park	17.80

What did simulcast bettors know that local bettors did not? Or, what did local bettors know that simulcast bettors did not?

Local bettors knew that Sir Beaufort had surrendered a short stretch lead to Marquetry three weeks ago in the San Antonio Stakes, a prep to the Santa Anita Handicap, and could not show his best at a mile and one-quarter.

Simulcast bettors did not know either fact, but they knew that Sir Beaufort was trained by the legendary Charlie Whittingham.

Local bettors fastened on the horse, and simulcast bettors fastened on the trainer. Since the trainer had greater appeal than the horse, the simulcast payoffs were lower.

The lesson is plain. Where horses and racetracks will be relatively unfamiliar, leading trainers and jockeys will be correspondingly overbet. Something to think about . . .

With the three prerace favorites, Best Pal, Bertrando, and Jovial, finishing up the course, the trifecta of Santa Anita's signature race paid $6,286.60. Jovial had run well enough, but the result here hardly signified a rosy spring and summer for older southern California handicap horses. Bertrando again had set the pace, but again had faltered badly. He was no mile and one-quarter specialist.

Ironically, earlier in the meeting I had determined that the winner, Sir Beaufort, would enjoy a banner season. At 2–1, with my support, he had ripped apart a strong stakes field going seven furlongs. Up to a mile, Sir Beaufort looked untouchable.

Beyond a mile, Sir Beaufort had always been extended. Three weeks before, in the Grade 1 San Antonio Stakes across nine furlongs, Sir Beaufort actually had wrestled the advantage into the stretch from Marquetry, but had lost his short lead, and the duel that followed, when that crack fought back inside the sixteenth pole. No one expected therefore that Sir Beaufort would rebound to win the Santa Anita Handicap. When he did, the upset gave grand-master Charles Whittingham his ninth Santa Anita Handicap trophy, a remarkable achievement.

I retreated meekly from the Santa Anita Handicap, with no Horses To Watch and no future bets up my sleeve. A few days later trainer Bobby Frankel announced that Bertrando would be rested and aimed at New York's Metropolitan Mile on Memorial Day. My spirits were lifted. I was thinking the Metropolitan Mile might be my biggest bet of the year. And I planned to place the bet somewhere outside of Southern California.

Although I did not realize it until later, soon enough I would benefit from another graduate of the Santa Anita Handicap.

On Tuesday, March 16, I flew to Miami for the Florida Derby. Other than wanting an up-close personal view of the Florida 3YOs, I had no special interest in the race. Santa Anita had provided no simulcasts from Florida or anywhere and I was itching to begin a probe of stakes races at other places. Three support stakes on the Florida Derby program interested me, notably a turf race to which Bobby Frankel would be sending an obscure French import.

Only a sprint stakes would be carded on Friday of the big weekend, but that might prove interesting as well.

On landing late, I drove to Hallandale, bought a *Racing Form* for Wednesday, and by midnight was seated comfortably in a dimly lit diner directly across from Gulfstream Park.

While surveying a roundup piece telling how Devil His Due had upset the previous Saturday's $500,000-added Gulfstream Handicap, paying $28.00, I came upon the kind of haunting information I had promised myself to avoid in 1993. The news immediately soured my mood. I became irritated too at how it might sound when I recounted the blunder in this book:

> Latin American, a 23–1 shot, took command at the top of the stretch to win the $150,000 New Orleans Handicap at the Fair Grounds.
>
> The 5YO . . . clear at the eighth pole . . . went unchallenged . . . the rest of the way . . . running the mile and one-eighth in 149⅕, two-fifths of a second off the track record. . . . Latin American paid $48.60, $21.00, and $10.20. . . .

How did this happen? I had sworn it would not. I had backed Latin American in each of his prior two starts at Santa Anita; two losses. The horse had been claimed from leading trainer Gary Jones by the competent but unknown Robert Marshall for $100,000 in 1992, precisely the sort of handicap hombre that might find softer spots outside of southern California.

I had been dutifully checking the entries at the various racetracks in *Daily Racing Form*, but missed this Fair Grounds feature. Pickings had been slim outside of southern California and actually I had been scouting for action. Wrapped up in Devoted Brass last weekend, I had been caught napping. The miscue cost me a couple of thousand. The win mutuel was $48.60.

A couple of months later Latin American would win the Grade 1 Californian, the second most prestigious dirt stakes at Holly-

THE HANDICAPPER'S STAKES FESTIVAL

wood Park's spring-summer meeting. The New Orleans race was a Grade 3 handicap featuring an undistinguished cast and an overbet local favorite. The situation virtually defines the notion of a Handicapper's Stakes Festival. This was exactly what it's about. Stealing outrageous value from the best horse at a track where bettors might be unfamiliar with the shipper's class edge. The first great overlay on the simulcast circuit in 1993 and I'm looking the other way.

Gulfstream Park offered handicappers playing conditions currently unrivaled at other major tracks. Full fields. Even the also-eligible lists were jammed. I encountered one six-horse field during the entire week. High quality, competitive racing. Outstanding grass racing. Leading stables, trainers, and jockeys. An excellent stakes program, filled with unfamiliar shippers from New York, Kentucky, and other outposts from the East and Mideast.

The contrast with Santa Anita—small fields, bad races, short prices, underlays galore, so many noncompetitive nonclaiming races and stakes—could not have been sharper. More than occasionally the wistful notion of changing shores swept over me. Andrew Beyer has described the winter racing in Florida as a handicapper's paradise. He gets no rebuttal from me.

After Latin American it helped restore my equilibrium when on my first bet at Gulfstream I converted an even-money shot under Julie Krone into a trifecta ($5) worth $1,200. The payoff startled me. In southern California, where the Pick-6 and serial triple predominate, the trifecta has been a weak sister among the exotics. The pools are shallow, the payoffs typically poor, and I've only dabbled in the bet.

On Thursday night I was a guest on a Miami sports-talk radio show hosted by Ed Kaplan. Talk-show hosts, even ones impressively informed on a wide array of sports, rarely can discuss thoroughbred racing intelligently, not to mention astutely. Kaplan proved the exception to the rule. Intelligent, informed, even contemporary, he lobbed bright, penetrating questions my way and contributed pointedly to the discussion, which persisted beyond a preplanned fifteen minutes for two hours. After all, as Kaplan advised his listeners, it was Florida Derby week.

When I conceded to callers that despite a cursory review of the past performances I did not have a clue as to the probable outcome of the Florida Derby, but strongly recommended bettors avoid the favorite and other low-priced contenders, Kaplan extended the response into a rumination on the importance of getting value.

Other segments covered in amazing detail the rise of figure handicapping (Kaplan pushed me for a critique of The Sheets and Thoro-Graph), the state of affairs among the 3YOs in the West (I conceded, I had not seen even one that looked like a Kentucky Derby winner), the contemporary emphases on pace ratings (I gave unbridled support to the use of pace figures and speed figures in combination), money management and betting strategies (I confessed my weaknesses), and the current malaise in the sport and industry (instead of other forms of gambling, I blamed management). I did enjoy it all.

On Friday, the sprint stakes proved uninviting; no shippers, no overlays, and no selection. I did learn that the odds-on favorite, the Phipps-owned, McGaughey-trained Furiously was no great shakes. I put Furiously on my Horses To Beat list.

Saturday's twelve-race Florida Derby program presented no claiming races and four stakes, a mini-festival. Frankel's French import in a Grade 3 turf stakes was listed at 6–1. As I had anticipated, for me it would be the bet of the day.

An hour before post time, a thunderous, torrential downpour soaked south Florida. The rain lasted forty-five minutes. The track was labeled sloppy — so sloppy and wet the four grass races were shifted to the main track. There would be eighteen scratches. Good-bye, key bet.

When the first two races were stolen wire to wire by speed horses on the inside, neither favorites, a number of press-box analysts declared an inside-speed bias would predominate. The third race was promptly won from behind on the outside. Ditto, the fourth. The inside did remain favorable, but not decisive.

My position on the Florida Derby remained vague and unformed, except that the front-running Storm Tower was certain to be overbet in relation to real chances. Storm Tower had won a division of Florida's Fountain of Youth Stakes (Gr. 2) in ordinary time following a dull pace. The Beyer Speed Figure was 94. The other half of the Fountain of Youth had proceeded in slower time, at a slower pace. The winner was Duc d'Sligovil, but what's in a name? The Beyer Speed Figure was 88, ugh! I had discounted both halves, but could isolate no appealing alternative on Gulfstream's board.

Thoro-Graph handicappers conducted a heavy campaign for Wallenda, a 15–1 shot. Wallenda was exiting a second in an allowance race, shooting immediately for the Grade 1 moon. As pitiful as the field looked, I afforded Wallenda a longshot's chance, but the colt possessed little fundamental appeal.

The winner (on the favorable inside) was Bull Inthe Heather, a maiden graduate, no more. The colt had run second in the tardier division of the Fountain of Youth at 35–1. Nobody's choice in the Florida Derby, he paid $60.80. Bull Inthe Heather approached the Grade 1, $500,000-added Florida Derby presenting these credentials:

Was it second Lasix? A biased track surface? An improving 3YO? Please.

Reviewing the big race on the playback, I consoled myself that the trip had not been in vain. Now I could dismiss the Florida 3YOs, not only in the Kentucky Derby, but in other derbies. This was a nondescript group. Storm Tower (2nd) was best of the bunch, but California's Personal Hope would smother him within four furlongs. I would leave Florida with no future bets and no Horses To Watch.

But not before I became the beneficiary of an unexpected, atypical tip on a live one. With roughly five minutes left in the betting before the twelfth race, Andrew Beyer approached me and inquired whether I had an opinion. Happily, I did not. Whereupon Andy trumpeted the charms of Number one.

He was short and sweet. "Competitive fig, hidden trip, has the inside. . . ." Beyer turned and walked back to his chair. At a mile and one-sixteenth, the race was an allowance for nonwinners once other than maiden or claiming.

Thinking that Beyer rarely touts, I glanced at the tote. Number one was 35–1. I walked to a window and deposited $50 to win.

Then I looked at the past performances again. Here are the records for Beyer's tip and the 6–5 favorite I had imagined should win. As the horses loaded into the gate, the observation I could not shake was that eleven days ago, Secret Negotiator had run at the same class at Gulfstream at 173–1.

From the midpoint of a twelve-horse pack *along the rail* on the far turn, Secret Negotiator began to move up noticeably. He continued to advance. In the upper stretch, now a factor, Secret Negotiator angled outside and unleashed a powerful late surge. The outcome was settled quickly. Beyer's tip won by four. He paid $77.

Delighted I had sojourned to Florida for a week and hoping I could return for Gulfstream's winter season soon, I collected $1,925 and a dinner check for three.

SPRING

APRIL

Three days into April the speedy Personal Hope took the Santa Anita Derby (Gr. 1) gang wire to wire. The pace was rapid, but the final three-eighths were completed in 38⅘ seconds. Personal Hope's figures confirmed my impression that I had not yet seen the Kentucky Derby winner:

BEYER SPEED	QUIRIN SPEED AND PACE	
98	114	106

I did not bet on Santa Anita's Derby, but had been keenly interested in two contenders.

Poised in striking position at the head of the stretch, and following a perfect trip, Union City seemed coiled to snap the necks off the leaders and would have no excuse if he did not. He did not. I eliminated Union City.

Spicing the Santa Anita Derby was the belated entry of the juvenile filly champion Eliza. In her comeback, Eliza had crushed the Santa Anita Oaks (Gr. 1) opposition on March 7, and she was a stickout among the 3YO fillies of southern California. Owner Allen Paulson understood the filly as special. He easily envisioned her winning the Kentucky Derby.

In winning the Oaks, Eliza earned the following figures:

BEYER SPEED	QUIRIN SPEED AND PACE	
98	107	107

The leading filly at Santa Anita looked very much like the leading colt. The question was whether Eliza could run a few lengths faster to the pace call when pressing talented colts and still run a few lengths faster to the wire.

Nothing much changed as a result of the Santa Anita Derby, an exciting race in which Eliza forced the early pace, gained command briefly by accelerating on the far turn, and was defeated by a length after a long determined drive. It was a fair test of ability and spirit. Eliza's figures would be: Beyer, 98; Quirin, 114–105. I eliminated Eliza as a serious threat for the roses.

To be fair to Personal Hope, his pace figure had been impressively strong and after surrendering the advantage on the far turn to the filly, he had regained it resolutely. In a feasible scenario, Personal Hope might control a slower pace at Churchill Downs, take the lead into the long stretch, and hold.

On the other hand, Personal Hope had been fully extended to win the Santa Anita Derby. In doping the Kentucky Derby, handicappers might remind themselves it's the toughest, roughest race on the American calendar. Still-developing 3YOs are required to travel a distance they have never attempted on a track surface few of them have experienced. It's a rugged experience and test. No horse "steals" the Kentucky Derby, and only a few have inherited the roses on the cheap, by picking up tiring horses from far behind.

Personal Hope's speed and pace configuration (Fast-Average) indicated the colt could not finish strongly enough following a rapid pace. Although a slower pace would help, the evidence suggests Personal Hope's basic class settles at a cut below what normally is demanded in Kentucky.

With three major preps to go and the leading colts of Florida dull and of southern California average, the 3YO division had begun to resemble a poor crop. Could there be anything in New York or Arkansas that might brighten the horizon? I suspected not. If the colts in the key preliminaries persisted in running par and below-par, not only would the Kentucky Derby be unpredictable, but also the customary well-disguised overlays in other derbies at other tracks would never materialize. Attempting to find the least slow among a below-par bunch is fool's play.

New York form was confirmed as below-par when Storm Tower lasted in the Wood Memorial and the undistinguished California shipper Tossofthecoin rallied to finish second. Despite copious study, I could not find a decent wager in the Wood Memorial.

The best, or worst, was still to come.

At Oaklawn Park, Dalhart had trounced the Grade 2 Rebel field wire to wire in fast time. The speed figure was high. Dalhart approached the Arkansas Derby (Gr. 1) as an even-money standout. Was Dalhart the one?

On the morning of the Arkansas Derby, Andrew Beyer was interviewed on a southern California radio show. A local analyst pressed him for an opinion, after insisting that Dalhart should win the Arkansas Derby hands-down and now must be rated the horse-to-beat in Kentucky.

"I'll book any action you want on Dalhart," shot back Beyer, with characteristic flair. "Dalhart's biggest figures have come when he's alone in front. Those horses are always overrated. I don't even like Dalhart in Arkansas."

Dalhart promptly blew the Arkansas Derby. The winner rocked the tote at 108–1, the famous Rockamundo, and now the road to the Kentucky Derby was becoming a carnival.

Had I fancied Rockamundo in the slightest, I could have backed him, as the Arkansas Derby was simulcast to Santa Anita and I did not want Dalhart. Rockamundo paid $435 to win at Santa Anita, twice the payoff at Oaklawn Park, and the second-richest-win-payoff in the track's storied history.

Not betting, I nevertheless experienced the Arkansas Derby with a wave of regret. In the $500,000 derby, the southern California shipper Diazo had rallied strongly into a hot pace around the far turn, before flattening. Diazo had continued on gamely, and finished evenly, beaten just a couple of lengths.

I would have doubled down on a key bet on Diazo in any 3YO stakes in the country below Grade 2. After Devoted Brass, Diazo had qualified as my favorite among the Santa Anita 3YOs.

Diazo was not yet a stakes winner. On March 21, however, Diazo had smashed a nonwinners once allowance field at a mile and one-sixteenth (1st route), staying close to a par pace before running off effortlessly in the stretch. In winning, Diazo had delivered the fastest allowance clocking by a 3YO at Santa Anita. The figures can be considered prototypical of the potentially exceptional 3YO:

BEYER SPEED	QUIRIN SPEED AND PACE	
105	105	110

By both methods the speed figures were five lengths faster than par. Diazo had won convincingly, with obvious reserves of speed and power. Diazo might be unfashionably late for the Kentucky Derby party (six weeks away), but he was a good one. I put him at the top of my Horses To Watch list. I desperately wanted to see Diazo next in a nice open stakes out-of-town.

Instead, trainer Bill Shoemaker had picked the Grade 2, $500,000-added Arkansas Derby, one of the major stepping-stones to the Kentucky Derby, and a level of stakes competition for which Diazo was not ready. Do untested winners of local tennis tournaments play next at Wimbledon? How many amateur golfers have won the U.S. Open?

I trust handicappers will no longer miss the point. A premature rise from preliminary nonwinners allowances to top-grade stakes almost invariably begs defeat for lightly raced, unseasoned threes, no matter how talented. Competitive seasoning does count. As soon as Diazo's entry was announced, I knew he would lose the Arkansas Derby. Not only that, he would be over-bet in the simulcast to Santa Anita besides.

To pursue the matter, seasoning in open stakes competition can be considered a prerequisite to winning the Grade 1 and Grade 2 sophomore stakes of spring and summer. A rugged, prolonged confrontation against Grade 1 or Grade 2 opposition typically requires a previous similar experience in lower-grade stakes to prevail. Handicappers should rarely be dismissive about adequate seasoning. If inexperienced in stakes, even leading 3YOs will be vulnerable at Grade 1 or Grade 2 levels.

If that is so, handicappers want to know, how do I explain Bull Inthe Heather's ascent as a maiden graduate in the Florida Derby, or Rockamundo's taking apart the Arkansas Derby?

The explanation is that neither horse figured to win. Each won by default, because the opposition was lackluster. Grade 1 and Grade 2 stakes for 3YOs usually will not be lackluster. Horse racing is not a parlor game. Handicappers seek to support horses that fit the race. It's fundamental to repeated success.

In the aftermath of the Arkansas Derby, trainer Shoemaker praised his colt's performance, noted the colt should benefit tremendously from the encounter, and announced Diazo would be a starter in the Kentucky Derby. More nonsense.

In the background loomed the fabulously rich owner Allen Paulson, who runs a hundred horses and earlier had lost the pre-Derby favorite Gilded Times to injury. Paulson's Corby had emerged as a Derby prospect too, but with lots to prove. Diazo became a Paulson substitute. Paulson's decision to run Diazo in the Derby erased my thoughts of scoring heavily on the colt's abundant talent—until later.

In the radio conversation where he had unmasked Dalhart, Beyer had leaned to Prairie Bayou as his Derby choice. He cited the gelding's consistency and running style, a latecomer with punch. Prairie Bayou had just won the Grade 2, $500,000-added Jim Beam at Turfway Park, a major stepping stone. A New York shipper, Prairie Bayou had won two ungraded stakes at Aqueduct during the winter. I respected Prairie Bayou, without getting excited about him. He promptly annexed the Grade 2 Bluegrass Stakes at Keeneland, another major prep, looking more powerful than ever, and at last the Kentucky Derby had found its favorite.

When the Beyer Speed Figure for the Bluegrass Stakes emerged, however, it was an unfashionable 96. The favorite for the 1993 Kentucky Derby would be eminently beatable, which, I suppose, had been apparent all along.

Back at Santa Anita, the stakes program and an unremittingly difficult season for handicappers was winding down. The unending downpours had washed out the turf program, a personal domain. My fast start of January had been stalled for two months.

In early April, at last, two opportunities popped up on the grass, the first routine, the second atypical.

The conditions of the Providencia Stakes, $75,000-added, for 3YO fillies, restricted eligibility to nonwinners of $30,000 (first money) at a mile or over in 1993. On examining eligibility conditions handicappers should form mental images of the horses best suited to today's race. Suitable horses do not always win, but they are always contenders, and their presence or absence provides the race analysis with a logical structure.

In a restricted stakes limited to 3YOs that have not won a specified amount at a route, class handicappers can favor the following:

1. Fillies that have finished close in open, listed, or graded stakes at a route, without winning. The better the race, the better.
2. Winners of sprint stakes stretching out under favorable conditions, i.e., stakes winners of routes have been effectively barred.
3. Lightly raced impressively improving 3YOs that have completed preliminary nonwinners allowance conditions and are entering the stakes against restricted competition.

As usual, 3YOs that have been tested repeatedly and found lacking can be discounted. So can claiming horses. Three-year-old claiming races are leagues removed from the 3YO non-claiming races. Handicappers cannot afford to be tolerant.

With that mental set, examine the fillies in the Providencia Stakes. The handicapping is rudimentary. (See page 70.)

None of the entrants had finished close in a listed or graded stakes. Two, however, had won minor stakes, Amal Hayati as a juvenile at Aqueduct and On The Catwalk as a juvenile in Ireland. Amal Hayati had won a minor event called the Jr. Champion Stakes at a mile at Monmouth Park as well, a sign of distance capability, but inconclusive as to relative class. The winner's share did not surpass $30,000, or Amal Hayati would not be eligible today.

On The Catwalk warranted the handicapper's main interest. After facing males repeatedly, and beating them, On The Catwalk entered a listed stakes at seven furlongs at Leopardstown and surprised again at 6–1.

More important, in any restricted stakes barring horses that have won meaningful money at a mile or longer, a first priority goes to impressive sprinters stretching out following winning sprints. The race, if you will, has been written with those horses in mind. If winners of listed stakes can stretch out effectively, they regularly can outrun routers who have looked unimpressive.

Handicappers who pared the Providencia Stakes to Amal Hayati and On The Catwalk would probably prefer the charms of the sprinter, a listed stakes winner. I backed On The Catwalk to win at 7–2 and boxed the pair of stakes winners, nonfavorites both, in multiple exactas. When On The Catwalk won going away and Amal Hayati easily held second, the exacta paid 14.9 to 1, or $31.80.

The favorite at 8–5 was Voluptuous, presumptively because the filly had won at a mile and one-sixteenth as a 2YO and had finished second sprinting March 17, in the listed La Habra

71

Stakes, beaten only a length. Amal Hayati had finished fourth in that race.

On ability, neither 3YO can be classified reliably, but Amal Hayati has accomplished more, winning two open stakes in New York and New Jersey. In her only start of 1993, Amal Hayati had rallied in the unrestricted La Habra Stakes. Stretching out to a more comfortable middle distance for Wayne Lukas, and a snug eligibility fit, Amal Hayati might be the horse to beat.

On the other hand, Amal Hayati's speed figures have remained slightly below par for 3YO fillies of March-April. If On The Catwalk can exceed par, she deserves the nod. Imports as a group should be regarded as superior to their American counterparts, and this filly comes ashore as a listed stakes winner who has also beaten males (twice). The profile outclasses restricted stakes conditions.

On The Catwalk won convincingly at 7–2, and Amal Hayati held second. The win bet and an exacta combination proved attractive, and the pair completed a successful double play.

A few days later lightning struck suddenly. It came hurtling out of an interesting Grade 3 event. I preferred one horse at first, but would soon change my mind. Let's examine the past performances together.

8

TURF COURSE
1 MILE
SANTA ANITA

1 MILE. (Turf). (1.32³) 6th Running of THE SANTA ANITA BUDWEISER BREEDERS' CUP HANDICAP (Grade III). $150,000 added ($50,000–added plus $100,000 Breeders' Cup Fund). Fillies and mares. 3-year-olds and upward. By subscription of $100 each which shall accompany the nomination, $250 to pass the entry box and $250 additional to start with $50,000 added and an

Visible Gold
Ch. m. 5, by Deputy Minister—Fit and Fancy, by Vaguely Noble
GONZALEZ S JR (73 3 8 7 .04)
Br.—Due Process Stable (Ont-C)
Own.—McCaffery & Toffan
Tr.—Gonzalez J Paco (37 6 10 4 .16)
115
Lifetime 17 5 2 3 $179,675
1993 1 0 0 0 $1,250
1992 9 4 1 1 $146,325
Turf 9 5 1 1 $164,075
Wet 1 0 0 0

7Mar93- 7SA fm *6½f ⓣ:212 :434 1:123 ⒻB ThoutfulH 85 3 4 31½ 41½ 43 58 Gonzalez S Jr LBb 117 11.20 87-08 HrtOfJy1212WrldlyPssssn1161¾CrtmDMy114 Weakened 10
24Dec92- 8Hol fm 1⅛ ⓣ:464 1:103 1:412 3+ⒻDahlia H 92 8 1 11½ 1½ 1hd 75¾ Pincay L Jr LBb 117 4.80 82-17 Kostroma-Ir124nk Vijaya1142 Guiza116 Weakened 8
24Dec92-Grade II
1Nov92- 8SA fm 1 ⓣ:463 1:092 1:343 3+ⒻL R RowanH 97 1 1 12½ 12½ 11½ 1¾ Pincay L Jr LBb 117 *.70 90-10 Visible Gold117¾ Vijaya1163 Fortissima-Ch116 Driving 6
12Sep92- 8Dmr fm 1⅛ ⓣ:464 1:102 1:413 3+ⒻⓇOsunitas H 96 4 1 12 11½ 12 1½ Desormeaux KJ LBb 116 *1.10 98-06 VisibleGold116½NowShowing1162¾Vijaya120 Just lasted 7
9Aug92- 5Dmr fm 1⅛ ⓣ:463 1:102 1:42 3+ⒻAlw 40000 96 7 1 17 16 14 13½ Pincay L Jr LBb 118 2.60 96-03 VsblGold1183½SouthrnTrc1163½QnSz-NZ116 Ridden out 9
17Jly92- 5Hol fm 1⅛ ⓣ:463 1:101 1:402 ⒻAlw 34000 93 10 1 12½ 13 15 13½ Pincay L Jr LBb 119 4.00 93-12 VsblGld1193½RrPtrl-GB1192½BllCntn-NZ116 Ridden out 10
19Jun92- 6Hol fm 1 ⓣ:451 1:083 1:34 ⒻAlw 34000 84 4 1 14 13 1½ 31¾ Pincay L Jr LBb 119 8.30 93-04 Cntfy-NZ116½LittlByLittl1161¼VisiblGold119 Weakened 10
17May92- 6Hol fst 6½f :213 :443 1:163 3+ⒻAlw 32000 59 1 4 32 31½ 55½ 811 Pincay L Jr LBb 122 4.70 78-11 Laursi1151Gmbit'sIceLdy1191SilentlySundy107 Faltered 12
9Apr92- 8SA fm *6½f ⓣ:213 :433 1:14 ⒻAlw 32000 81 6 1 11½ 12 1½ 23½ Delahoussaye E LBb 120 7.00 85-11 Zigaura1203½ Visible Gold1203½ DixieDerby117 Held 2nd 8
3Jan92- 7SA sly 1 :451 1:104 1:364 ⒻAlw 35000 — 6 1 11½ 712 721 — Pincay L Jr LBb 120 3.30 — — Common Threads11715StormBerry120¾Eaglet117 Eased 7
LATEST WORKOUTS Apr 7 SA 4f fst :484 H Apr 1 SA 7f fst 1:253 H Mar 27 SA 6f gd 1:134 H Mar 21 SA 5f fst 1:003 H

Gold Fleece
Ch. m. 5, by Deputed Testamony—Go Solo, by Riverman
SOLIS A (358 40 65 50 .11)
Br.—Lil Stable (Md)
Own.—Alvarez & Ham
Tr.—Sadler John W (98 14 16 13 .14)
115
Lifetime 15 6 5 0 $237,375
1993 3 1 1 0 $48,750
1992 3 2 1 0 $85,100
Turf 11 5 4 0 $210,975
Wet 1 0 1 0 $8,800

14Mar93- 3SA fm 1 ⓣ:48 1:12 1:36 ⒻAlw 55000 99 4 2 2½ 1hd 1½ 1¾ Solis A LB 114 *.60 85-15 GoldFleec114¾Grvrs-Fr1141¼WddingRing-Ir116 Gamely 4
21Feb93- 8SA gd 1 ⓣ:463 1:103 1:361 ⒻBna Vista H 97 7 3 34½ 36½ 43 44¼ Solis A LB 115 3.70 82-16 MrblMidn-GB118hdSuivi1171¼PrtyCitd116 Always close 7
21Feb93-Grade III
5Feb93- 8SA fm 1 ⓣ:462 1:102 1:342 ⒻAlw 55000 100 5 1 1½ 1hd 1hd 2½ Solis A LB 115 2.80 92-07 Exchnge119½GoldFleece115hdPrtyCitd116 Brushed start 6
23Feb92- 5SA fm 1 ⓣ:453 1:092 1:332 ⒻBna Vista H 106 2 2 22 1½ 11½ 11 Solis A LB 114 4.60 96-06 Gold Fleece1141 Elegance1153½ Danzante114 All out 9
23Feb92-Grade III; Run in divisions
30Jan92- 8SA fm 1 ⓣ:471 1:104 1:341 ⒻAlw 44000 98 9 1 1½ 1½ 11½ 11¾ Solis A LB 114 3.40 92-08 GoldFlec1141¾BrisDMr114hdRglPc-GB117 Bobbled start 10
3Jan92- 8SA sly 1 :464 1:11 1:362 ⒻAlw 44000 100 5 2 2½ 2hd 2hd 21 Solis A LB 118 2.60 84-17 SilvrButy-Ar1161GoldFlc1185HighIndTd115 Good effort 6
3Jan92-Originally scheduled on turf
7Dec91- 8Hol fm 1⅛ ⓣ:471 1:11 1:404 ⒻⓇAllez FraH 93 4 2 21 21 2½ 21¼ Solis A LB 116 10.10 90-07 Exchnge1171¼GoldFlec116nkStinFlowr122 Forced issue 9
19Oct91- 5SA fm 1 ⓣ:462 1:10 1:34 3+ⒻAlw 34000 90 5 2 21 2½ 11 12 Valenzuela P A LB 116 2.20 93-06 Gold Fleece1162 Assombrie1131LocalLass-Ir117 Driving 8
25Aug91- 8Dmr fm 1⅛ ⓣ:482 1:131 1:492 ⒻDmr Oaks 83 6 3 32½ 41½ 54½ 58¼ Pincay L Jr LB 120 6.30 83-09 Flwlssly1202SttlSymphony120½Fowd120 4-wide stretch 6
25Aug91-Grade III
10Aug91- 8Dmr fm 1 ⓣ:463 1:102 1:344 ⒻSn Clmnt H 93 4 3 43 51¾ 32 21¾ Desormeaux K J B 114 15.40 96-04 Flwlssly1201¾GoldFlc1142½MissHighBld117 Boxed in 3/8 9
LATEST WORKOUTS Apr 8 SA 4f fst :481 H Apr 2 SA 7f fst 1:263 H Mar 27 SA 5f gd 1:042 B Feb 16 SA 5f fst 1:011 H

Party Cited
B. f. 4, by Alleged—Dream Play, by Blushing Groom
STEVENS G L (385 75 70 53 .19)
Br.—Rogers Trust (Ky)
Own.—Bull Market Stable & Tanaka
Tr.—Rash Rodney (54 5 6 10 .09)
118
Lifetime 15 3 2 4 $170,565
1993 3 0 1 2 $53,250
1992 8 3 1 1 $83,856
Turf 15 3 2 4 $170,565

13Mar93- 8SA fm 1⅛ ⓣ:453 1:091 1:461 ⒻSanta Ana H 102 2 2 31½ 31½ 31½ 2¾ Delahoussaye E LB 116 4.20 87-12 Exchange120¾ Party Cited116½ Villandry116 Game try 5
13Mar93-Grade I
21Feb93- 8SA gd 1 ⓣ:463 1:103 1:361 ⒻBna Vista H 99 5 5 54 44 32½ 31¼ Valenzuela P A L 116 8.50 83-16 MrbleMidn-GB118hdSuivi1171¼PrtyCitd116 Good effort 7
21Feb93-Grade III
5Feb93- 8SA fm 1 ⓣ:462 1:102 1:342 ⒻAlw 55000 100 6 2 2½ 2hd 2hd 3½ Stevens G L LB 116 8.60 92-07 Exchnge119½GoldFleece115hdPrtyCitd116 Brushed start 6
18Oct92- 4WO yl 1¼ ⓣ:492 1:421 2:074 3+ⒻE P Taylor 94 11 12 121 1121 10 58 55 Solis A 118 :25.20 57-45 Hatoof1181½ Urban Sea1181¼ Hero's Love123 Late bid 12
18Oct92-Grade II
11Sep92♦4Goodwood(Eng) gd 1¼ 2:122 ⓣ AbrustSelectStks(Gr3) 32½ Williams J 116 16.00 — — Knifebox126½ Jeune1222 PrtyCited116 Bid then evenly 10
12Aug92♦3Salisbury(Eng) gd*1¼ 2:073 ⓣⒻUpavon Stks 21 Williams J 131 *1.00 — — Delve 1261 Party Cited13110 NeverACare117 Bid, hung 5
31Jly92♦2Goodwood(Eng) gd 1¼ 2:072 ⓣ Spitfire Hcp 1hd Williams J 130 12.00 — — PrtyCited130hd WildFire111no Mutbhi114 Bid, led, held 8
6Jly92♦6Windsor(Eng) gd*1¼ 2:064 ⓣ Staines Stks 13½ Williams J 121 4.00 — — PrtyCited1213½ FlmingArrow1302 Yildiz114 Going away 15
24Jun92♦2Kempton(Eng) gd 1 1:364 ⓣⒻFunfairGraduationStks 1¾ Williams J 120 6.50 — — Party Cited 120¾ Pelagonia 1204 Enaya 126 Led fnl 3f 15
30Apr92♦3Newmarket(Eng) gd 1¼ 2:053 ⓣⒻPrettyPollyStks(L) 514½ Quinn T R 122 33.00 — — AllAtSe1225 Armrm1222½ MysteryPly122 Prominent 8f 6
LATEST WORKOUTS Apr 9 SA 3f fst :363 H Apr 4 SA ⓣ 6f fm 1:171 H (d) Mar 30 SA 4f fst :492 H Mar 9 SA 5f fst 1:011 H

Gravieres–Fr
Dk. b. or br. m. 5, by Saint Estephe—Gay Spring, by Free Round
DESORMEAUX K J (232 63 40 30 .27)
Br.—Baer & de Balanda & Powell (Fra)
Own.—Frankel & Gann
Tr.—Frankel Robert (65 19 14 10 .29)
115
Lifetime 16 4 3 2 $316,060
1993 3 0 1 0 $15,125
1992 2 1 0 0 $84,900
Turf 16 4 3 2 $316,060

14Mar93- 3SA fm 1 ⓣ:48 1:12 1:36 ⒻAlw 55000 98 1 4 42½ 31 32 2¾ Desormeaux K J L 114 3.60 84-15 GldFlc114¾Grvrs-Fr1141¼WddngRng-Ir116 Boxed in 3/8 4
21Feb93- 8SA gd 1 ⓣ:463 1:103 1:361 ⒻBna Vista H 84 2 6 75 74½ 74½ 75¼ Nakatani C S LB 117 4.40 75-16 MrbleMiden-GB118hdSuivi1171¼PrtyCitd116 Rank early 7
21Feb93-Grade III
5Feb93- 8SA fm 1 ⓣ:462 1:102 1:342 ⒻAlw 55000 96 3 6 56½ 53½ 53½ 42¼ Delahoussaye E LB 116 2.80 90-07 Exchnge119½GoldFleece115hdPrtyCitd116 Broke slowly 6
19Apr92- 8SA fm 1 ⓣ:462 1:102 1:342 3+ⒻBd Br Cp H 77 5 5 54½ 53½ 67 612¼ Stevens G L LB 119 *.50 79-12 DncO'MyLf116½OnlyYrs-GB117nkCrstlGng118 Wide trip 7
19Apr92-Grade III
14Mar92- 8SA fm 1⅛ ⓣ:48 1:12 1:473 ⒻSanta Ana H 104 3 8 89 75¾ 43 1½ Stevens G L LB 116 3.00 81-19 Gravieres-Fr116½ Appealing Missy117¾ExplosiveEle115 8
14Mar92-Grade I; Off slowly, angled out 4-wide, bumped 1/8, drifted in 1/16
23Nov91- 8BM fm *1⅛ ⓣ:474 1:122 1:481 ⒻCarmel H 97 3 7 59 43½ 11½ 1¾ Nakatani C S 117 *.70 89-13 Grrs-Fr117¾MssHhBld1171OldElc112 Hard ridden, game 9
5Oct91- 8SA fm 1 ⓣ:454 1:102 1:332 ⒻH C Rmsr H 102 7 9 94¾ 1½ 1hd 2½ Flores D R 117 26.20 95-09 Fllssly123½Grvrs-Fr1174½ZmHmmr117 Rough start,wide 10
14Aug91♦5Deauville(Fra) gd*1 1:434 ⓣⒻPrix de la Calonne 53½ Gillet T 126 5.00 — — ShaTha1211½ Metamorphose1211 Saraposa121 Mild bid 10
3Aug91♦4Deauvielle(Fra) gd*1 1:371 ⓣⒻPrix d'Astarte(Gr2) 73 Mongil W 119 7.50 — — Leariv1291 CrystlPth119nk OnceInMyLife122 No threat 12
4Jly91♦4Evry(Fra) gd*1⅛ 1:541 ⓣⒻPrix Chloe(Gr3) 31¾ Boeuf D 123 2.50 — — La Carene 1211½ Sha Tha 121nk Gravieres 123 Late bid 7
LATEST WORKOUTS Apr 5 SA 7f fst 1:271 H Mar 30 SA 5f fst 1:021 H Mar 23 SA 4f fst :483 H Mar 9 SA 5f fst 1:014 H

Wedding Ring–Ir
Ch. f. 4, by Never So Bold—Fleur d'Oranger, by Northfields
DELAHOUSSAYE E (334 64 47 56 .19)
Br.—Aubert R M & Strauss R C (Ire)
Own.—V H W Stables
Tr.—McAnally Ronald (139 27 28 21 .19)
115
Lifetime 18 5 2 5 $179,877
1993 1 0 0 1 $9,900
1992 13 4 2 3 $108,540
Turf 18 5 2 5 $179,877

14Mar93- 3SA fm 1 ⓣ:48 1:12 1:36 ⒻAlw 55000 95 2 1 1½ 2hd 2½ 32 Delahoussaye E 116 2.10 83-15 GldFlc114¾Grvrs-Fr1141¼WddngRng-Ir116 Broke slowly 4
17Oct92- 9Lrl fm 1⅛ ⓣ:481 1:13 1:494 3+ⒻAll Along 95 3 7 74 74½ 22½ 22¾ Krone J A 112 10.10 79-09 MrblMd-GB1142¾WddR-Ir1122½SbDcr-Fr114 Bore in 1/8 7
17Oct92-Grade II
4Oct92♦6Longchamp(Fra) sf*1⅛ 2:022 ⓣⒻPrix de l'Opera(Gr2) 73¾ Boutin M 121 34.00 — — Hatoof 126½ La Favorita 1211 Ruby Tiger 128 In close 12
25Sep92♦3StCloud(Fra) yl*1 1:421 ⓣⒻPrix Coronation(L) 1½ Boutin M 121 18.00 — — WeddingRing121½ Alieria122nk Urmia121 Prom, up late 14
9Jly92♦4Evry(Fra) gd*1⅛ 1:522 ⓣⒻPrix Chloe(Gr3) 73¾ Boutin M 121 20.00 — — FormdblFlght1211 SrtogSorc121nk Frbol121 Stride late 10
25Jun92♦5Longchamp(Fra) gd*1 1:453 ⓣⒻPrix des Tuileries(L) 44½ Black C 123 8.00 — — Manureva1232 Shannkara1232 LFvorit123 In close late 11
8Jun92♦6Mulheim(Ger) sf*1⅜ 2:272 ⓣⒻPreis der Diana(Gr2) 33 Black C 123 5.50 — — Longa1232½ Arstou123½ WeddingRing123 Finished well 12
31May92♦6Longchamp(Fra) yl*1¼ 2:14 ⓣⒻPrix de la Seine(L) 32½ Jarnet T 123 11.00 — — Urban Sea 123½ SnsEscle 1232 WddingRing 123 Rallied 9
12May92♦4Longchamp(Fra) gd*1 1:45 ⓣⒻPrix de Bagatelle(L) 73¾ Boutin M 123 12.00 — — MrbleMidn1231 PolishStyl123nk BttlQust123 No threat 10
4Apr92♦6Dusseldorf(Ger) sf*7½f 1:363 ⓣ Preis der Dreijahrigen 22 Boutin M 123 6.20 — — Pltx1282 WddngRng1232½ Montplcno123 Finished well 9
LATEST WORKOUTS Apr 5 SA 6f fst 1:124 H Mar 30 SA 5f fst 1:00 H Mar 23 SA 4f fst :47 H Mar 7 Hol 7f fst 1:271 H

Because Grade 3 stakes tend to be inferior by a clear margin to the Grade 1 and Grade 2 kind, class handicappers know to favor stakes contenders on that drop. Otherwise, they consider the purse sizes and quality of opposition of good efforts in Grade 3 and listed stakes.

The wrinkle here does not concern stakes races, however, except by implication.

Visible Gold. Fast, but probably outgunned. Reeled off four front-running victories last spring and summer at Hollywood Park and Del Mar. Moves from turf sprint to route with high pace figures. Has won two stakes, but neither is listed or graded. Favorable post for flat mile, but inexperienced rider, of the type that infrequently wins on grass.

Gold Fleece. Solid, Grade 3 stakes winner exiting a win in a highly restricted classified race. Pace figure below Visible Gold's by five lengths. Cannot control front. Unlikely to outrun stakes closers late.

Party Cited. Just placed in the Grade 1 Santa Ana stakes to division leader Exchange. Drop to Grade 3 is clearly a money run. Top figure in last. Barn cold, but acceptable, and leading rider up. Class, form, speed, all systems go. Class of field, and probable favorite.

Gravieres. Grade 1 winner 13 months ago, but nothing since. Exits highly restricted classified race (non-winners of $18,000 twice at a mile or over since March 15) in which he could not run down Gold Fleece. Troubled trip, but had dead aim at stretch call. Current form shaky, thus trainer Frankel's drop to classified conditions in last. Lost. May return to top form, but why bet on it?

Wedding Ring. Third in the classified event won by Gold Fleece, but no threat to win. Needed race, and fits Grade 3 conditions well. Listed stakes winner on yielding course in France, in race limited to 3YOs (Coronation). So-so record in listed and graded company of France, but good second in Grade 2 all along last October at Laurel. Contender.

Of class evaluation, I have never liked stakes horses exiting highly restricted classified races which they have lost, unless the race is clearly a warm-up. Gravieres can be tossed on the standard, notably at low odds. Wedding Ring needed the classified race, but her overall record against 3YOs is hardly distinctive.

Gold Fleece fits Grade 3 races, but faces an unusually swift pacesetter in Visible Gold. A faster pace for pressers and stalkers on grass normally translates to a slower finish.

Anyway the race is sliced, Party Cited figures to win.

The odds a few minutes before post proved provocative:

Visible Gold	25–1
Gold Fleece	7–2
Party Cited	2–1
Gravieres	2–1
Wedding Ring	3–1

The odds impelled me toward Visible Gold and I quickly revisited his record. With the top pace figure and the inside post at a mile, a distance the mare favored, Visible Gold had tactical advantages that might upend the class.

I had one horse to beat. Party Cited hardly qualified as the quintessential miler. I now explored Visible Gold's backlog of speed & pace figures, and found this comparison:

Party Cited	118	111	Last race
Visible Gold	118	110	September 12, DMR

What should handicappers do?

The huge odds on Visible Gold might be explained by the raw apprentice (3 for 73 at the meeting, or 4 percent), but raw apprentices do fit best on lonesome front-runners. I bet Visible Gold to win and covered with multiple exacta boxes coupling Visible Gold and Party Cited.

Visible Gold darted to the front, raced freely and relaxed, and scampered all the way. No horse got close enough to challenge. The longshot paid $48.80. Party Cited ran poorly; no excuse.

Coinciding with the final weeks of Santa Anita's winter/spring meeting is Oaklawn Park's ten-day Festival of the South. The most traditional, and best established, of the stakes festivals, the fascinating track in Hot Springs, Arkansas, presents handicappers with a series of stakes that includes three Grade 1s: the Apple Blossom Stakes for fillies and mares, 4UP; the Oaklawn Handicap, 4UP; and the Arkansas Derby, an outstanding test for 3YOs.

I have never played at Oaklawn Park. Until recently, the track lacked not just grass racing but also exotic wagering, powerful disincentives for me. Oaklawn Park does feature a bustling stakes program, one loaded with shippers (and overlays) from tracks to the east and west. Day to day, the racing is fine. The history, culture, and ribald small-town mystique of Hot Springs spices the trackside action.

Because important local horses have shipped to Oaklawn Park regularly, Santa Anita usually takes the Grade 1 simulcasts from the Festival of the South. I do not recall a serious wager from prior simulcasts, but in 1993 I had an ace in the hole and I intended to play it. But not at Santa Anita.

My ace was entered in the Oaklawn Handicap, among the last legs of the American Championship Racing Series (ACRS), in 1993 featuring the handicap division's two leaders, Best Pal and Lil E. Tee. I preferred a third horse, and I knew the price would be right.

The betting advantage was framed by three converging circumstances. First, as the Santa Anita Handicap had rendered painstakingly clear, Best Pal no longer was a top horse. Sometime during the season, Best Pal might deliver a knockout blow, as ex-champs occasionally can, but I felt confident it would not land at Oaklawn Park.

Lil E. Tee provided a sterner test. In Las Vegas during March, I had witnessed the 4YO's comeback performance at Oaklawn Park, home base, in a seven-furlong sprint. To be sure, I had wagered against the 1992 Kentucky Derby winner that day, who had appeared in front tendon wraps, had not raced in 10 months, and resembled a multiple Grade 1 winner warming up in a minor contest.

But Lil E. Tee had slaughtered the seven-furlong foes with a devastating late run, recording a monstrous speed figure. He had followed that display with a sensational romp in Oaklawn's Grade 2 Razorback Stakes, at a middle distance. The pair of victories were so dominant, if he held together, no small qualification, Lil E. Tee should not only head the handicap division, but also he might be first in line for Horse of the Year.

So, what might be the knock on Lil E. Tee?

Conceivably, Lil E. Tee could "bounce" following a lengthy layoff and a duo of sensational efforts. If ordinary horses can be expected to "bounce" after a single overexertion, exceptional horses sometimes require two taxing races.

I gladly discounted Lil E. Tee in the Oaklawn Handicap, although I experienced pangs of doubt. Besides, I could cover the downside against Lil E. Tee's best race in exactas.

Factor three, and the third-rated horse in the race, was my ace, Jovial, a southern California shipper trained by low-percentage Bruce Jackson, to be ridden by the great Eddie Delahoussaye. Delahoussaye's presence in Arkansas was reassuring, in part because Jovial is a closer, Delahoussay's specialty, in part because Jackson frequently relies upon Danny Jackson or another low-percentage rider. At Santa Anita, during winter, before the horse began to fire, Jackson had used Mickey Walls on Jovial. The Canadian had handled Jovial splendidly, but the switch to Delahoussaye reflected positive trainer intentions. The change would prove timely.

If Lil E. Tee regressed even slightly, he should be hard-pressed to withstand Jovial's late rush. Revisit the 6YO's past performances closely:

Jovial will be no Horse of the Year candidate and the Breeders' Cup Classic will go without him, but he's an authentic high-grade stakes competitor who in April of 1993 fit a performance pattern extremely dangerous to any horse in his path.

In the two races he had won at Santa Anita, Jovial's speed and pace figures looked tremendous:

	PAR	PACE	SPEED
Classified Alw	111	116	115
San Pasquale (Gr. 2)	113	108	114

A former stakes star, Jovial had not won for more than two seasons. Suddenly, he's ultra sharp again. The phenomenon occasionally arises in an older horse's record. When it does, the horses can be ferociously sharp and fast for a time; for months. During that period the horses attack like tigers. Until they disintegrate again, they are extremely difficult to beat.

Since January 24, Jovial had finished fourth in the Santa Anita Handicap (beaten two lengths after a wide rally) and he had missed a stakes later at Santa Anita due to a virus. Inactive since March 6, a loss, Jovial would be less appetizing to the Oaklawn bettors. Good!

In preparation for the Oaklawn Handicap, Jovial's workouts

had looked fabulous, the times sharp, the splits and final fractions the fastest on the tabs. Jovial had retained his winter form.

To Santa Anita simulcast bettors, Jovial might be as bettable, or more bettable, than Best Pal, but at Oaklawn Park the handicappers would be preoccupied with Lil E. Tee and Best Pal. A key bet to win was placed on Jovial in Las Vegas. Exacta boxes coupling Jovial and Lil E. Tee provided protection. I ignored Best Pal.

I got 7–2 on Jovial at Oaklawn Park.

Jovial lagged far back under Delahoussaye. As the race proceeded around the far turn, I got a service break. Jockey Pat Day moved (uncharacteristically) early. He sent Lil E. Tee to the front midway on the far turn, just as Best Pal could be seen lugging out toward the rear and offering no threat. I imagined that Day wanted first run and a clear margin against Best Pal.

Out of the picture even as the horses approached mid-stretch, Jovial had not received as much as a courtesy call from the track announcer. Watching on a TV monitor, I was perplexed (and discouraged) that Jovial would not even supply the thrill of the chase. Lil E. Tee now was running low on energy, going evenly at best, but several lengths clear.

Suddenly, near the finish, the announcer picked up a flying object on the far outside and suddenly, loudly, barked out one of those late wake-up calls that intimates the onrushing horse will not be denied. In a brilliant, beautifully judged ride that has been his signature piece for fifteen seasons, Eddie Delahoussaye had saved Jovial for a late run through the stretch. In high gear on the outside, Jovial glided by Lil E. Tee and won comfortably by a couple of strides.

Jovial paid $9.40. Lil E. Tee finished second, the exacta paying $39.60. It was textbook perfect, and a fitting wrap to what I believed had been my shrewdest play of the young season. Cross-track betting may not be the antidote to the small fields and low prices of contemporary racing, but it helps handicappers balance the books.

* * *

Santa Anita elapsed on a succession of downbeats. In a misguided effort to cope with the tax laws of California, on the Thursday prior to the Oaklawn Handicap, track officials announced they would be suspending all simulcasts. The change of policy had no ill effects on my plans, but the irony (the track explained it could not afford the excess betting) did arouse my appreciation of the humor.

During the final days I consulted my Horses To Watch and Horses To Beat lists, checking for connections to the future. The exercise revealed how thin the track's 1993 stakes divisions had been.

	HORSES TO WATCH	HORSES TO BEAT
Handicap horses, 4UP	Bertrando Jovial	Best Pal
Fillies and mares, 4UP	None	Paseana Jolypha
3YO colts	Diazo Gilded Times	Personal Hope Corby
3YO fillies	Eliza	Likeable Style
Grass horses, 4UP	Kotashaan Bien Bien	Star Of Cozzene

On the Horses To Beat list, Paseana, the defending champion, recently had won Oaklawn Park's Grade 1 Apple Blossom, but at Santa Anita she had lost stakes battles to a reformed claiming horse (Southern Truce). Her figures, à la Best Pal's, had declined by irreversible lengths. Now losing to fillies and mares she would have crushed in 1992, Paseana would be an upset candidate for me for the rest of the year.

Before the curtain closed on Santa Anita handicappers were given a notice from leading trainer Bobby Frankel, who was currently dominating the grass divisions with the turf cavalry of Prince Khaled Abdullah's Juddmonte Farm. Frankel announced that Juddmonte had imposed upon him for just one favor in 1993.

The Prince would like to win the Breeders' Cup Classic with his 4YO filly Jolypha. Jolypha had finished third in the 1992 Classic, as a 3YO filly, no less, so the step from third to first in America's bellwether race did not appear to be a giant step to Prince Abdullah, or presumptively, to his southern California trainer.

Shortly after the comments had left Frankel's mouth, I put Jolypha on the Horses To Beat list. I knew (a) Jolypha would not be primed to win preliminary events, (b) she would be relentlessly overbet regardless, (c) the 1992 Breeders' Cup Classic would not be remembered as the alltime best, and (d) Jolypha was superior on grass, but unclassified on dirt.

Frankel had not even entered Jolypha at Santa Anita during winter, citing the rains and the resulting interruptions in her training regimen. The trainer noted he had plenty of time to prepare Jolypha to win it all. Yet matters had not been proceeding smoothly. In addition, Frankel, as talented a horseman as he is, had never trained a champion.

With Santa Anita done, the Kentucky Derby has arrived.

MAY

On that hallowed day, the first Saturday in May, beyond all expectations, with no firm opinions, and without having tallied once in the preliminary rounds, I backed the winner of the Kentucky Derby, raking in $695 when Sea Hero paid $27.80 at Churchill Downs.

The explanation probably will sound as inadvertent as the bet itself. Certain races just treat certain handicappers especially well, the way certain baseball batters hit certain pitchers well. Two major American classics have been kind to me, the

Kentucky Derby and the Arlington Million. On the first Saturdays of May I've benefited from Sunday Silence, Winning Colors, Ferdinand, Swale, Spend A Buck, and even Gato Del Sol, nonfavorites all.

I nailed Gato Del Sol on my first attempt utilizing Steve Roman's dosage index, an unforgettable introduction. Now comes Sea Hero, another improbable long shot. On the day before the Derby, furthermore, I had not intended to bet.

On that day before the roses, however, I relished a fantastic betting opportunity, an exacta, that I did not expect to lose. The race I wanted was the Early Times Handicap, a grass route bringing together the classiest grass miler in the country and a southern California shipper who was surely second best in the field.

The one-two punch was Lure and Star Of Cozzene. I advised associates on the scene in Louisville to buy me a $200 one-way exacta at 4–1 or better. No horse could beat Lure at his favorite game. He had daylighted the Breeders' Cup Mile last November, thrashing the best grass milers in the world at 5–1 as a 3YO. Star Of Cozzene had bested Kotashaan twice at Santa Anita, early, when the turf star of the meeting was rounding into peaked form. Star Of Cozzene was very good, but he wasn't Lure.

Lure won, but only by three-quarters, which surprised me. Star Of Cozzene got second, and had threatened the top horse. The most predictable exacta of the season paid $13.60.

I received the results by telephone on Friday night. My associates asked if I wanted to wager on the Derby at Churchill Downs. I declined. I was coaxed, prodded, even jeered. So I capitulated.

"Okay, bet fifty dollars to win on Sea Hero at ten to one or up," I said.

"Sea Hero?" came a retort. "Why Sea Hero?" the caller repeated, in a tone intended to straighten me out on the merits of the Derby prospects.

I explained, patiently, that I had been searching for a

stranger and an overlay, and Sea Hero fit on a few important counts: a Grade 1 winner, beautifully bred, admirable dosage, and best of all, the colt represented a provocative trainer pattern.

Despite working for Paul Mellon's Rokeby Stable forever, trainer Mack Miller, a no-nonsense conservative, had not bothered to try the Kentucky Derby for two decades. He was going with Sea Hero in 1993. If Miller gave Sea Hero a sniff at the roses, so did I.

Miller's style also appealed to me in a way that made Sea Hero more bettable on this special day than in his other 1993 races. Like Charlie Whittingham in the west, Miller can be inordinately patient and planful with young horses, bringing them to a pitch only for the main objectives. As does Whittingham, Miller does not aim particularly straight at preliminary objectives. He stays focused on number one.

So, I mused, handicappers probably can discount several of Sea Hero's 3YO stakes, which were awful. His last had shown marked improvement, however, and Sea Hero had won New York's Grade 1 Champagne as a juvenile. Today was D-Day. If Sea Hero possessed a best effort, it probably would materialize on Derby Day.

On Sunday night, six days before the Derby, I had dispensed the same logic on Jack Rubin's national radio talk show, out of Las Vegas, *Rubin on Racing*.

I had begged off, but Rubin pressed me later in the show for a Derby pick. Another guest, *Daily Racing Form* trackman Steve Feldman, had just delivered an amazingly multilayered and forcefully stated argument by which he had concluded (I kid not) that Florida Derby winner Bull Inthe Heather was a standout.

When prompted by Rubin to respond, I could not contain myself. I dissented as vehemently as Feldman had insisted. Bull Inthe Heather had followed a sluggish, bias-aided Florida Derby upset with a discouragingly slow second in Florida's Flamingo Stakes. Really, he was a pretender. I felt Bull Inthe

Heather had virtually no chance to win the Kentucky Derby, and said so.

Now Rubin demanded I provide an alternative. I confessed to harboring interests in a trio of colts, with Sea Hero the first of three.

I watched the Kentucky Derby in living-room comfort. When Sea Hero exploded at $27.80, I imagined I might have wagered at the Santa Anita satellite, now taking Hollywood Park's signal. Sea Hero might be 30–1 in the southern California pools. Later that afternoon, I visited Santa Anita to play the local races. Sea Hero had not been 30–1 at Hollywood Park. He paid $33 there.

In the postscripts to Sea Hero's Derby, several distinguished analysts, figure handicappers notably, insisted the colt could not have been taken seriously and accepted the outcome as conclusive evidence the 1993 3YO crop was tainted.

My reaction remains strikingly dissimilar. In the Kentucky Derby of 1993, no colt figured on figures. Under those circumstances, which arise more than occasionally, a figure analysis becomes the wrong analysis.

More fascinating than the Kentucky Derby was Friday's Kentucky Oaks, a stakes I expected to win, but did not. Determined to take advantage of Eliza's excruciating effort versus colts in the Santa Anita Derby, which I believed would set her back, I had dismissed Eliza to begin.

Tripping through the past performances of the others, three fillies stood out as classiest. I had not expected the Oaks to spread itself out so neatly. Unable to separate the three, I keyed one of them top and bottom to the other pair in multiple exactas. And I "baseballed" the three in trifectas.

Emphasizing class evaluation, handicappers should find the same three contenders. Scan the past performances now:

9 Churchill

1 1/8 MILES. (1.482) 119th Running KENTUCKY OAKS (Grade I.) $250,000 Added. Fillies. 3-year-olds. By subscription of $100 each on or before February 20, 1993 or by supplementary nomination of $25,000 each by time of closing Wednesday, April 28, 1993, $1,500 to pass the entry

Cormorant's Flight

Dk. b. or br. f. 3(Apr), by Cormorant—Double Suez, by Double Zeus
Br.—Double Suez Partnership (Md)
Own.—Marathon Farms
Tr.—Cartwright Ronald (—)
121
Lifetime 10 5 0 0 $142,335
1993 4 3 0 0 $111,000
1992 6 2 0 0 $31,335
Wet 1 0 0 0

4Apr93-10Pim fst 1 1/16 :464 1:123 1:442 ⒻⓈCesrsWish 89 1 1 13 12½ 16 17 Luzzi M J Lb 119 2.20 83-26 Cormornt'sFlight1197HelloHnn114hdMiscibl114 Driving 8
6Mar93-10Lrl fst 7f :23 :462 1:244 ⒻⓈPolitey 74 7 2 15 11½ 12 13 Luzzi M J Lb 116 *.80 89-10 Cormorant's Flight1163Bocamis1141½Allepia116 Driving 8
30Jan93- 9Lrl fst 6f :22 :452 1:102 ⒻⓈJameela 93 1 1 1½ 11½ 16 19¾ Luzzi M J Lb 112 3.90 88-20 Cormornt'sFlght1129¾Bcms112½Crnrnbw121 Ridden out 5
9Jan93- 9Lrl sly 6f :223 :464 1:133 ⒻMarshuStks 64 2 2 2½ 2½ 22 62 Rocco J L 113 4.90 70-29 Crnrnbow120nkSntmntldmond114hdDshro112 Gave way 8
19Dec92-10Lrl fst 1 1/16 :483 1:133 1:45 ⒻCameo 62 7 3 1hd 3nk 44 48¼ Rocco J L 113 8.20 80-13 Winka1125½ Da'sMimi1122¼Carnirainbow118 Wide early 10
21Nov92-10Lrl fst 1 1/16 :463 1:113 1:443 ⒻⓈJuv'nlFilly 70 1 1 12 12 1½ 43 Rocco J L 119 8.80 87-14 BroadGains1192¼Carnirainbow119hdWink119 Weakened 9
3Nov92- 9Lrl fst 7f :23 :463 1:264 ⒻⓈWhtsmmr 33 5 1 1½ 2hd 47½ 518¾ Rocco J 116 2.80 55-27 Carnirainbow1194¼ Bocamis112nkMostarch114 Fell back 6
18Oct92- 8Lrl fst 6½f :23 :473 1:182 ⒻAlw 16500 74 1 4 1½ 11½ 13½ 16¾ Rocco J 116 2.20 85-18 Cormornt'sFlight1166¾NvyTights1132LostLf113 Driving 6
29Sep92- 8Pim fst 6f :234 :48 1:131 ⒻAlw 16800 36 2 6 31 2hd 33½ 611¾ Rocco J 119 *1.20 67-25 Cercid1161½NvyTights1144ApplingDr.Bick109 Gave way 7
19Sep92- 2Pim fst 6f :231 :47 1:123 ⒻMd Sp Wt 74 7 4 31½ 31 11½ 14½ Rocco J 119 3.50 82-23 Cormornt'sFlght1194½BuckRoll1192TsHooch114 Driving 10

LATEST WORKOUTS ●Mar 27 Pim 6f fst 1:132 H Mar 21 Lrl 6f fst 1:131 H Mar 17 Lrl 4f sly :50 B Mar 1 Lrl 5f fst 1:013 H

Sum Runner

Dk. b. or br. f. 3(Mar), by Summing—Juliac, by Accipiter
Br.—Elam R L (Ky)
Own.—Cohen S Solon
Tr.—Winfree Donald R (—)
121
Lifetime 8 6 1 1 $234,193
1993 4 3 0 1 $177,018
1992 4 3 1 0 $57,175
Wet 1 1 0 0 $17,810

28Mar93- 9FG fst 1 1/16 :461 1:11 1:434 ⒻF G Oaks 79 7 2 2hd 1½ 11½ 34¾ Fires E L 121 *.50 90-09 SlkyFthr1132¾Sh'sLttlShy1212SumRnnr121 Early speed 7
28Mar93-Grade III
8Mar93- 3OTC fst 1 1/16 :492 1:143 1:474 ⒻObsChmpion 93 7 1 12 14 16 19 Fires E L 122 —— 93-03 Sum Runner1229 Dasharoo122no Unlaced122 Hand ride 11
8Mar93-Fillies Division
3Feb93- 9GP fst 7f :221 :451 1:233 ⒻForward Gal 95 1 4 11 11 12½ 12½ Fires E L 118 *1.40 85-19 SumRunner1182½Boots'nJcki121½LunrSpook118 Driving 9
3Feb93-Grade II
18Jan93-10GP fst 6f :214 :444 1:101 ⒻOld Hat 92 3 5 12 12 14 16 Fires E L 114 3.00 90-15 SumRunner1146BestinSle114½HiddenFir116 Ridden out 9
5Dec92- 9TP fst 6½f :224 :471 1:203 ⒻThe Gowell 74 10 1 2hd 1hd 32½ 213 Melancon L LB 118 *1.90 64-29 S'sMmnt11413SmRnnr1181SpclAlrt116 Dueled 2nd best 10
27Nov92- 8CD fst 6f :214 :463 1:12 ⒻAlw 30100 77 4 2 3½ 3nk 11 11½ Day P LB 118 *.50 86-17 SumRunner1181½Amnuens1123Unlcd121 Veered in start 7
11Nov92- 7CD my 6½f :23 :462 1:183 ⒻAlw 27400 80 2 3 12½ 15 16 19 Melancon L LB 118 *1.00 87-16 SumRunner1189GoldenGoos113½SquwTlk121 Riddenout 6
10May92- 3Crc fst 4½f :222 :462 :524 Md Sp Wt 87 6 1 12½ 15 15½ Ferrer J C 113 6.20 —— SumRunnr1135½TotllyCool116¾CowboyBtch116 Handily 10
10May92-Bumped start, very convincingly

LATEST WORKOUTS ●Apr 18 CD 6f fst 1:121 H ●Apr 9 CD 6f gd 1:132 H

Boots 'n Jackie

B. f. 3(Jan), by Major Moran—Cherokee Ace, by Cherokee Fellow
Br.—Bee Bee Stables Inc & Equitor In (Fla)
Own.—Bee Bee Stables & TorteraToni
Tr.—Tortera Emanuel (—)
121
Lifetime 16 4 7 3 $646,910
1993 4 0 3 0 $67,000
1992 12 4 4 3 $579,820
Wet 1 1 0 0 $97,500

10Apr93- 8Spt fst 1 1/16 :473 1:123 1:45 ⒻN J Clb Oak 82 6 6 65 44 22½ 23¾ Arguello F A Jr 122 1.80 87-11 TrAffr1203¾Boots'nJck1224¾RssnBrd115 Clearly second 7
13Mar93-10GP fst 1 1/16 :491 1:14 1:433 ⒻBonne Miss 80 2 6 66½ 58½ 68½ 48½ Russ M L L 122 6.30 83-15 Dispute1148 SkyBeauty1143LunarSpook117 Belated bid 6
13Mar93-Grade II
28Feb93-10GP fst 170 :474 1:13 1:42 ⒻDavona Dale 90 2 5 45 3½ 22 25 Lee M A L 121 *1.10 86-18 LunrSpook1165Boots'nJckie1211InHerGlory112 Gamely 7
3Feb93- 9GP fst 7f :221 :451 1:233 ⒻForward Gal 90 6 9 97½ 79 45 22½ Lee M A L 121 2.10e 82-19 SmRnnr1182½Boots'nJck121½LnrSpook118 rallied inside 9
3Feb93-Grade II
21Nov92- 8CD my 1 1/16 :484 1:134 1:471 ⒻGolden Rod 79 3 6 63¾ 65 41½ 11¼ Lee M A LB 120 1.80 78-25 Boots'nJck1201¼MllCrk115nkDncAccnt113 Wide driving 6
31Oct92- 5GP fst 1 1/16 :47 1:103 1:424 ⒻBr Cp Juv F 89 7 10 107 88½ 65¾ 31½ Lee M A L 119 15.10 96-03 Eliz1191EductdRisk119½Boots'nJcki119 Wide,ang in str 12
31Oct92-Grade I
17Oct92-10Crc fst 1 1/16 :482 1:133 1:464 ⒻFl Stln 88 8 10 65¾ 54½ 22 12½ Lee M A L 120 *1.60e 93-11 Boots'nJcki1202½SuphGm1202½Sigrun120 Driving, 5-wd 13
17Oct92-The My Dear Girl Division
27Sep92-10Crc fst 170 :482 1:141 1:45 ⒻGardenia Bc 75 7 8 65¾ 64 23½ 22 Lee M A L 116 *.50e 86-12 SuphGem1142Boots'nJcki1166NrthEdg112 Rallied 7 wd 11
12Sep92-10Crc fst 7f :222 :46 1:25 ⒻⓇFlaStallion 85 3 7 76½ 73¾ 32½ 12 Lee M A L 118 6.20 90-14 Boots'nJcki1182Exrcising1182½Sigrun118 Driving inside 8
12Sep92-Susan's Girl Division

LATEST WORKOUTS Apr 27 CD 5f fst 1:023 B Mar 11 Crc 4f fst :50 B

Quinpool

B. f. 3(Jan), by Alydar—Squan Song, by Exceller
Br.—Skara Glen Stable (Ky)
Own.—Darley Stud Management Inc
Tr.—Mott William I (1 0 0 1 .00)
121
Lifetime 4 2 1 1 $32,190
1993 3 2 1 0 $29,310
1992 1 M 0 1 $2,880

16Apr93- 6Kee fst 1 1/8 :471 1:131 1:513 ⒻAlw 22800 77 2 3 36 31½ 11½ 14 Bailey J D 117 *1.00 77-25 Quinpool1174StyleSetter1152SettlFshion115 Ridden out 6
5Mar93- 6GP fst 1 1/16 :473 1:12 1:443 ⒻMd Sp Wt 80 3 2 22½ 22 2hd 1no Krone J A 120 *.70 87-22 Quinpool120noPrncssPolon1203½Urus120 Fully extended 12
7Feb93- 3GP fst 6f :222 :461 1:123 ⒻMd Sp Wt 73 2 8 54½ 32 23½ 21¾ Krone J A 120 1.80 76-21 Les Etoiles-Ir1201¾ Quinpool1204¾ PrincessPolonia120 11
7Feb93-Lugged in backstretch and drive rallied
3Jly92- 3Bel fst 5f :22 :453 :58 ⒻMd Sp Wt 76 1 4 65 2½ 3½ 32¾ Smith M E 117 *1.80 88-11 SkyButy1172PortofSilvr117¾Quinpool117 Bid, weakened 8

LATEST WORKOUTS Apr 26 CD 5f sly 1:052 B ●Apr 11 CD 6f fst 1:151 B Mar 23 GP 6f fst 1:18 B Mar 16 GP 5f fst 1:031 B

Dispute

B. f. 3(May), by Danzig—Resolver, by Reviewer
Br.—Phipps Ogden Mills (Ky)
Own.—Phipps Ogden Mills
Tr.—McGaughey Claude III (—)
121
Lifetime 5 4 1 0 $188,104
1993 3 3 0 0 $149,800
1992 2 1 1 0 $38,304
Wet 1 1 0 0 $14,400

13Mar93-10GP fst 1 1/16 :491 1:14 1:433 ⒻBonne Miss 95 3 1 11½ 11 1½ 1¾ Bailey J D 114 2.70 92-15 Dispute114¾ Sky Beauty1143 Lunar Spook117 Driving 6
13Mar93-Grade II
12Feb93- 5GP fst 170 :471 1:114 1:413 ⒻAlw 30000 94 1 2 22½ 21 2½ 1½ Bailey J D 112 *.40 93-07 Dispute112½HonstPrincss11213Misspitch114 Ridden out 4
22Jan93- 8GP fst 7f :222 :454 1:234 ⒻAlw 18000 83 8 3 31 2hd 11 14 Bailey J D 112 *.80 84-20 Dispute1124LostLeaf1131½BnsheeWinds114 Ridden out 8
22Oct92- 8Aqu fst 7f :231 :463 1:244 ⒻAstarita 80 4 6 1hd 2hd 23 25¼ Bailey J D 119 6.20 75-18 MissedtheStorm1195¼Dispute1196½Sttuette119 2nd best 6
22Oct92-Grade II
26Sep92- 6Bel sly 6f :221 :452 1:111 ⒻMd Sp Wt 73 7 5 31 2½ 1½ 11¼ Bailey J D b 117 *1.60 [illegible] Dispute1171¼ For My Jet1172¾ FleetingWays117 Driving 9

LATEST WORKOUTS Apr 27 CD 5f fst 1:03 B ●Apr 21 Kee 5f fst 1:001 B Apr 16 Kee 5f gd 1:031 B Apr 11 Kee 5f fst 1:041 B

Aztec Hill — B. f. 3(Mar), by Proud Truth—Tribal Hill, by Cox's Ridge — Lifetime 11 6 1 1 $294,920 — 1993 4 3 0 0 $235,680 — 1992 7 2 1 1 $49,240 — Wet 4 0 1 1 [illegible]

Own.—Loblolly Stable — Br.—Loblolly Stable (Ky) — Tr.—Bohannan Thomas (—) — 121

9Apr93- 9OP fst 1⅛ :471 1:124 1:441 ⓕFantasy 94 2 7 63 41½ 12½ 15 Smith M E 121 2.60 90-19 Aztec Hill1215 Adorydar1172Stalcreek117 Four wide 1/4 7
9Apr93-Grade II
21Mar93- 9OP gd 1⅛ :474 1:13 1:442 ⓕHoneybee 91 6 3 42½ 31 12 14½ Gryder A T 122 3.40 79-23 AztecHill12214½Avi'sShdow116nkLifIsDlicious112 Driving 8
21Mar93-Grade III
14Feb93- 8Aqu my 1⅛ ⊡:472 1:113 1:441 ⓕBusher Bc H 69 5 5 56 56 510 513 Smith M E 118 *1.10 71-18 TrueAffir1208½EnsignJonne1132½Wink113 Pinched back 6
14Feb93-Grade III
16Jan93- 8Aqu fst 170 ⊡:482 1:124 1:422 ⓕBusanda 89 4 3 31 3nk 11 14 Smith M E 112 1.50 96-14 AztecHill1124EnsignJonn1123½TruAffir121 Ridden out 5
20Dec92- 6Aqu fst 1⅛ ⊡:48 1:132 1:454 ⓕAlw 29000 90 5 5 43 33 11½ 16 Gryder A T 116 *1.00 79-24 Aztec Hill1166 Lovely Bid1163 MissouriBelle111 Driving 6
17Dec92- 7Aqu sly 170 ⊡:472 1:12 1:43 ⓕAlw 29000 71 3 6 69½ 69½ 59½ 37 Gryder A T 116 *1.50e 83-13 AllAbility1164½EnsignJoanne116½AztecHill116 Mild rally 8
10Oct92- 4Bel my 1 :463 1:111 1:363 ⓕFrizette 64 8 8 86 86 69½ 510½ Day P 119 11.20 76-13 EdctdRs1191½StndrdEpmnt1194½BlStrtBls119 No threat 8
10Oct92-Grade I
19Sep92- 5Bel fst 7f :222 :46 1:231 ⓕMatron 76 9 1 75½ 65 45½ 47½ Antley C W 119 11.10 81-11 SkyButy1192½EdctdRsk1192½FmlyEntrprz119 Mild rally 9
19Sep92-Grade I
20Aug92- 4Sar fst 7f :23 :461 1:244 ⓕMd Sp Wt 67 7 3 64½ 64 2½ 14 Antley C W 117 *.60 81-14 AztecHill1174CrsDncr1176GoodWitchGlind117 Drew off 9
24Jly92- 4Bel my 6f :221 :461 1:12 ⓕMd Sp Wt 62 3 4 44 41½ 3nk 21½ Antley C W 117 2.00 78-15 Life'sWlk1171½AztcHill1171½SkiAtDwn117 Rallied inside 8
LATEST WORKOUTS Apr 28 CD 3f fst :36 B — Apr 21 CD 4f fst :512 B — Apr 3 OP 5f fst 1:033 B — Mar 15 OP 4f fst :51 B

Eliza — B. f. 3(Mar), by Mt Livermore—Daring Bidder, by Bold Bidder — Lifetime 7 5 1 1 $1,012,200 — 1993 2 1 0 1 $204,200 — 1992 5 4 1 0 $808,000

Own.—Paulson Allen E — Br.—Paulson Allen E (Ky) — Tr.—Hassinger Alex Jr (1 0 0 0 .00) — 121

3Apr93- 5SA fst 1⅛ :464 1:101 1:49 San Anta Dy 96 1 2 2½ 1½ 2hd 31 Valenzuela P A LB 117 3.20 84-12 Personal Hope122½ Union City122nk Eliza117 Game try 7
3Apr93-Grade I
7Mar93- 8SA fst 1⅛ :471 1:11 1:424 ⓕS A Oaks 99 7 2 2½ 12 15 12½ Valenzuela P A LB 117 1.80 90-14 Eliza1172½ Stalcreek1171 Dance For Vanny117 Driving 9
7Mar93-Grade I
31Oct92- 5GP fst 1⅛ :47 1:103 1:424 ⓕBr Cp Juv F 92 9 3 3nk 11 11½ 11 Valenzuela P A L 119 *1.20 90-03 Eliz1191EductdRisk119½Boots'nJck119 Strong handling 12
31Oct92-Grade I
17Oct92- 8Kee fst 1⅛ :461 1:10 1:431 ⓕAlcibiades 99 3 2 21 11½ 11 14 Valenzuela P A LB 118 *.80 88-23 Eliza1184Avie'sShadow1185TrueAffir118 Eadily in hand 6
17Oct92-Grade II
19Sep92-10AP fst 1 :463 1:122 1:392 ⓕArl Wsh Las 84 2 1 12 13 18 112 Valenzuela P A L 119 *.90 69-35 Eliza11912 Banshee Winds1193 Tourney119 Stumbled 6
19Sep92-Grade II
19Aug92- 8Dmr fst 7f :214 :441 1:223 ⓕSorrento 80 7 2 1½ 11½ 1hd 23½ Valenzuela P A B 117 *1.10 83-12 Zoonaqua1173½ Eliza1171 Medici Bells117 Held 2nd 11
19Aug92-Grade III
9Aug92- 6Dmr fst 5½f :211 :44 1:03 ⓕMd Sp Wt 87 6 6 3½ 1hd 11 12½ Stevens G L 117 1.90 96-05 Eliza1172½ Set Them Free1175 Nijivision117 Handily 10
LATEST WORKOUTS ●Apr 23 CD 5f fst 1:00 H — Apr 18 CD 5f fst 1:034 B — Apr 12 CD 3f fst :363 B — Mar 25 SLR tr.t 6f fst 1:14 H

Dream Mary — Dk. b. or br. f. 3(Apr), by Marfa—Dream Dream, by Wajima — Lifetime 10 3 2 0 $52,089 — 1993 6 2 2 0 $41,829 — 1992 4 1 0 0 $10,260 — Turf 6 2 2 0 $30,309

Own.—Welohan T R — Br.—Ross Valley & Thunderhill (Ky) — Tr.—Sonnier J Bert (—) — 121

16Apr93- 8Kee yl 1⅛ Ⓣ:483 1:134 1:522 ⓕPalisades 75 3 4 21½ 21 67½ 58½ Sellers S J Lb 113 6.50 66-25 HrlnHn1192NrthrnEmrld1121½Hnlnss117 Checked, tired 8
24Mar93-10GP fm 1⅛ Ⓣ:50 1:144 1:51 + ⓕSwtstChnt 85 3 7 64 63½ 31½ 22½ Sellers S J Lb 114 9.30 74-23 O. P. Cat1142½ Dream Mary114hd Misspitch114 Rallied 9
2Mar93- 8GP fm *1⅛ Ⓣ 1:54 + ⓕAlw 24000 81 4 5 75½ 75 41½ 1½ Guidry M Lb 115 4.20 76-20 DrmMry115½Rin'sMlt115½LitchfildInn117 Drivng 5 wide 9
19Feb93- 8GP fm *1⅛ Ⓣ 1:52 + ⓕAlw 23000 75 5 4 45½ 44 3½ 23 Guidry M Lb 117 12.50 83-14 O. P. Cat1153 Dream Mary117½ Debbie'sBliss114 Rallied 10
7Feb93- 7GP fst 1⅛ :47 1:12 1:461 ⓕAlw 22000 57 5 7 713 812 713 718½ Guidry M Lb 115 7.30 60-26 InHrGlory1151½TochOfLv1154½ScrittO'M112 No threat 9
24Jan93- 5GP fst 1⅛ :482 1:132 1:462 ⓕAlw 19000 74 3 5 52½ 73½ 3nk 13½ Guidry M Lb 113 13.30 78-24 Dream Mary1133½ T. V. Maud112½ Star Jolie114 Driving 8
15Dec92- 5Crc fm *1⅛ Ⓣ 1:471 ⓕMd Sp Wt 63 1 6 63½ 41½ 11½ 11 Castillo H Jr Lb 119 2.70 76-16 Dream Mary1191 Jicarilla1193½ Little Zip119 Driving 7
2Dec92- 3Crc fm *1⅛ Ⓣ 1:471 ⓕMd Sp Wt 49 7 6 64½ 53 33½ 411½ Castillo H Jr Lb 119 4.90 65-21 CngQn1192½ShrpTrcy1190½C.U.LtrSl119 Wide gave way 8
30Oct92- 2GP fst 6f :212 :443 1:102 ⓕMd Sp Wt 45 7 6 910 913 712 712½ Solis A b 118 9.20 79-06 CircleCommnd1180Filimint1182½LittleZip118 No threat 11
21Oct92- 5Kee fst 6½f :223 :46 1:183 ⓕMd Sp Wt 51 1 6 4½ 41½ 31½ 43½ Miller D A Jr LBb 118 9.60 80-08 LtfClss1181½EclsvSmbl1182Asfrppl118 No late response 12
LATEST WORKOUTS Apr 27 CD 4f fst :482 B — Apr 14 Kee 3f fst :36 H — Apr 8 Kee Ⓣ 7f fm 1:283 H (d) — Apr 4 Kee 3f fst :36 H

Avie's Shadow — Dk. b. or br. f. 3(Jan), by Lord Avie—Gold Shadow, by Mr Prospector — Lifetime 8 2 3 0 $208,245 — 1993 3 0 2 0 $70,475 — 1992 5 2 1 0 $137,770 — Wet 1 1 0 0 $10,170

Own.—Nichols Tom & Maxine — Br.—Viking Group IV (Ky) — Tr.—Smith Thomas V (1 0 1 0 .00) — 121

17Apr93- 8Kee fst 1⅛ :483 1:122 1:432 ⓕAshland 91 2 4 41½ 41½ 32 22½ Gomez G K 115 11.00 84-19 LnrSpk1212½Av'sShdw115½RmnRchl115 Drft out,fnl fur 7
17Apr93-Grade I
21Mar93- 9OP gd 1⅛ :474 1:13 1:442 ⓕHoneybee 83 2 6 67 62½ 33 24½ Day P 116 3.10 74-23 AztcHll1224½Av'sShdow116nkLflsDlcs112 Four wide 1/4 8
21Mar93-Grade III
7Mar93- 9OP fst 1 :464 1:111 1:373 ⓕMagnolia 79 6 8 89½ 79½ 77½ 77½ Day P 119 *1.00 81-17 ProprRflction119nkMri'sKy1155Vctor'sPrz117 No threat 8
17Oct92- 8Kee fst 1⅛ :461 1:10 1:431 ⓕAlcibiades 92 1 4 49 49½ 21 24 Day P B 118 7.20 84-23 Eliz1184Avie'sShadow1185TrueAffir118 Driving 2nd best 6
17Oct92-Grade II
27Sep92-10TP fst 1 :454 1:111 1:374 ⓕClipstta 62 1 8 920 1091 712 513½ Bass S H B 118 10.40 74-20 TruAffr1141½JoyousMlody112nkSpclAlrt114 No threat 11
30Aug92- 9RD fst 6f :214 :454 1:133 ⓕBassinet 73 13 3 1110½ 69½ 42 1½ Bass S H L 122 18.30 80-25 Avie'sShdow122½DixieBnd1221Hono'sHoney122 Driving 14
21Jly92- 1ElP my 6f :223 :462 1:114 ⓕMd Sp Wt 59 5 6 42½ 54½ 3½ 11½ Bass S H B 121 *2.10 88-12 Avie'sShdow1211½Misbelif1213StylStr121 Steady drive 9
27Jun92- 6CD fst 6f :214 :462 1:111 ⓕMd Sp Wt 36 5 10 32½ 33 57 617 Bass S H 121 12.00 73-11 Angel Fever12111SaucyLyps1213Rindwell121 Weakened 11
LATEST WORKOUTS Apr 15 CD 4f sly :51 B — Apr 7 OP 1 fst 1:412 H — ●Apr 1 OP 5f fst 1:01 H — Mar 4 OP 4f fst :501 B

Lunar Spook — Gr. f. 3(Jan), by Silver Ghost—Rafael Luna, by Idle Minds — Lifetime 10 5 2 2 $349,118 — 1993 4 2 0 2 $232,273 — 1992 6 3 2 0 $116,845

Own.—Craig Sidney — Br.—Buchholz Barry T (Fla) — Tr.—Sonnier J Bert (—) — 121

17Apr93- 8Kee fst 1⅛ :483 1:122 1:432 ⓕAshland 95 4 3 21 2½ 1½ 12½ Sellers S J L 121 2.60 87-19 LnrSpook1212½Av'sShdw115½RmnRchl115 Driving, clear 7
17Apr93-Grade I
13Mar93-10GP fst 1⅛ :491 1:14 1:433 ⓕBonne Miss 89 5 3 32½ 34 34½ 33½ Guidry M L 117 2.00 88-15 Dispute114½ Sky Beauty1143 LunarSpook117 Lk'd resp. 6
13Mar93-Grade II
20Feb93-10GP fst 170 :474 1:13 1:42 ⓕDavona Dale 99 7 2 23½ 11 12 15 Guidry M L 118 3.20 91-18 LnrSpook1185Boots'nJck1211InHrGlry112 Convincingly 7
3Feb93- 9GP fst 7f :221 :451 1:233 ⓕForward Gal 89 2 5 32½ 33 33½ 33 Guidry M L 118 3.00 82-19 SmRmr1182½Bts'nJck121½LnrSpk118 Lacked response 9
3Feb93-Grade II
12Dec92-10Crc fst 1⅛ :49 1:144 1:471 ⓕBoca Raton 82 10 2 21 1hd 11 24 Guidry M L 120 *1.00 87-13 Sigrun1154 Lunar Spook1202 Supah Gem120 No match 10
16Nov92- 5GP fst 170 :46 1:11 1:41 ⓕGo ForWand 87 4 1 11 11 13 16 Day P L 116 *1.40 96-04 Lunar Spook1166 Flirting Miss1143Sigrun116 Hand ride 8
17Oct92- 8Haw fst 6½f :222 :452 1:171 ⓕMarica 84 8 2 11 13 16 111½ Hirdes R J Jr L 112 2.90 90-16 LnrSpok11211½MjstcLgh113½Clrwthflr112 Under wraps. 9
25Sep92- 5AP fst 6f :223 :461 1:113 ⓕAlw 23000 58 5 7 3½ 2hd 21 44 Pettinger D R L 119 *.70 81-15 TrueLuvJon113½Clrwithfire1131½MjesticLeigh113 Faded 8
3Sep92- 9AP fst 6f :221 :464 1:103 ⓕMd Sp Wt 85 5 1 11½ 13 17 110½ Pettinger D R L 119 9.20 90-16 LunarSpook11910½TwoStepsForwrd1191½Apjv119 Easily 10
6Aug92- 6AP gd 5½f :224 :472 1:064 ⓕMd Sp Wt 55 1 2 1½ 12½ 23 20 Torres F C L 118 6.10 74-27 SrtogShdows1180LnrSpok1184IrshMmnt118 Faded rail 12
LATEST WORKOUTS Apr 28 CD 3f fst :352 B — ●Apr 13 Kee 5f fst :590 H — Apr 6 Kee 5f fst :594 H — ●Mar 31 Kee 3f fst :35 H

Eliza apart, three fillies were exiting Grade 1 or Grade 2 stakes which they had won. None of the others could match those credentials. The three: Dispute, Aztec Hill, and Lunar Spook. Sometimes handicapping can be as deceptively simple as this, although none of the three yet had won *two* top-grade stakes.

Eliza ruined the plot. On the far turn, she rushed into the pace as strongly as did Dispute. The pair drew away, and waged a vicious stretch duel. As I discarded the exotic tickets, I interpreted the Kentucky Oaks as another occasion (consecutive) in which Eliza, who had lost, had engaged another division leader in a dragdown, allout fight. She would be vulnerable again next time, and I would be ready.

My trip to the Preakness was stimulated less by the middle leg of the Triple Crown than by the five support stakes on the Pimlico program. The day before, Friday, would be bolstered by two attractive stakes.

On two afternoons of racing in Maryland, handicappers would be presented with The Preakness (Gr. 1), The Pimlico Special (Gr. 1), The Black-Eyed Susan (Gr. 2), The Early Times Dixie Handicap (Gr. 3), the Maryland Million (restricted), the Sir Barton Stakes (Open), The Never Bend Handicap (Open), and the Maryland Breeders' Cup Handicap (Open). Is that a Handicappers' Stakes Festival? Simulcasts and cross-track betting would be part and parcel of the weekend package.

On Friday, The Early Times Dixie Handicap on the grass promised a reprise of the one-two finish at Churchill Downs between Lure and Star Of Cozzene. The exacta today, however, would pay peanuts. I never considered a wager. Lure won; Star Of Cozzene finished second.

The better part of Friday was the Black-Eyed Susan Stakes, successor to the Kentucky Oaks, for 3YO fillies, often the same 3YO fillies. The Black-Eyed Susan proved as elementary to decipher as its predecessor. Only one of the fillies I fancied in the Oaks bothered to enter the Black-Eyed Susan. A new wrinkle led me to suspect the odds would be fair. The morning line on Aztec Hill was attractive: 3–1.

Review her past performances, and those of two other fillies who merited respect:

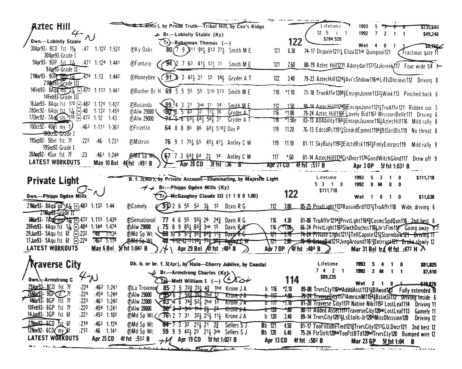

Aztec Hill fits a pattern I have exploited in graded stakes for years: an authentic top-grade horse swinging back under comparable conditions following an excusable disappointment. Fractious in the gate at Churchill Downs, Aztec Hill showed nothing. She since has trained at Belmont Park and vanned to Baltimore. Only two weeks have passed.

The record is undeniably strong. Four big wins in the last six, with a mud race and gate excuse explaining the losses. Her speed figures have continued to improve, and the smashing romp in the Fantasy Stakes (Gr. 2) looks definitive. This is a Grade 1/Grade 2 filly.

When Aztec Hill became an underlay at 9–5, Private Light and Traverse City begged greater inspection. I did not trust Private Light. Her Grade 2 Comely score occurred on an off-track. In the fifty-four days since, Private Light's workouts have been irregular, short, and slow. Despite the Phipps-McGaughey axis, I would take my chances Private Light was not prepared to annex her second Grade 2 title today.

Traverse City is a filly of a brighter color. Handicappers are urged to appreciate the pattern of development here, engineered by trainer Billy Mott, one of the nation's finest. It's as good as it gets with 3YOs.

Following her maiden win, Traverse City, a nicely bred daughter of Halo, is restricted to the allowances until two additional victories accumulate. The experience begs improvement, and Traverse City already has qualified as a bit of a terror at seven furlongs.

I like the next step. Mott selects an ungraded sprint for Traverse City's stakes debut. It's a seven-furlong listed stakes, purse of $50,000-added. Fully extended, the filly survives under familiar, comfortable conditions.

Not unimportantly, if Mott had tested Traverse City first in the Kentucky Oaks, or some similar graded stakes at a route, the filly probably would have lost, and might have been beaten badly. Many trainers, and owners, indulge that kind of hasty miscue. The horses may regress for weeks, or months. No wonder so few 3YOs develop to their maximum potential.

Traverse City had been carefully prepared for graded opposition. In combination with the class rise, the change from sprint to route means the filly will be attempting a double-jump. Few fillies can complete such a double-jump successfully. Traverse City, however, has been meticulously trained, and should render an excellent account of her abilities.

With the remainder of the field unattractive, I keyed Aztec Hill in multiple exactas with Traverse City and played each of them over Private Light. Aztec Hill won handily ($5.60), and

Traverse City got second. The exacta paid $37.40.

On Saturday's Preakness card, the Pimlico Special guaranteed a $600,000 purse to handicap horses 4UP, the horses also vying for a rich bonus in the last rendition of the ACRS. The money, bonus, and national television drew a ridiculous cast of six horses. Three of them had never won a Grade 1 stakes, and in a lamentable tradition that has veered out of control for several seasons, had been entered solely to salvage whatever minor shares they could.

A fourth horse, Pistols And Roses, had upset the Donn Handicap at Gulfstream Park in February at 44–1, and neither before nor since had looked like a threat to a decent horse.

The contention stopped abruptly at two deep. I preferred Devil His Due over Strike The Gold, who had returned three weeks ago from an October layoff, had won at a mile, and was facing a classic "bounce" pattern.

Was there a play? Not at Pimlico, where on the first click Devil His Due dropped to 6–5. I wanted 2–1. I got it, at Philadelphia Park, my hometown track, where Devil His Due returned $6.40. Not a spectacular example of the cross-track betting edge perhaps, but a happy ending.

The strategy generalizes well to stakes races having small fields and a couple of legitimate contenders. Handicappers can (a) set an agreeable line and (b) select the simulcast site likely to exceed that line. Make the play there. When the Pimlico Special proved bettable at Philadelphia Park, I knew I would be betting at Philadelphia Park again.

To summarize the 1993 Preakness, the slowest rendition on record, I wanted nothing in the straight pools, but did entertain a few exacta combinations. In the wake of the Kentucky Derby, when analyzing the Preakness and Belmont Stakes, I have adhered to a betting tactic that has yielded mixed results, including several overlays to win.

Unless a true-blue champion or authentic division leader has emerged, which has been unusual lately, I prefer a 3YO that has *not* won the Kentucky Derby. My rationale is basic. The Triple Crown races are so varied, idiosyncratic, and challenging that in the absence of a standout the final two jewels typically will be won by dissimilar horses, each of them well suited to a particular leg.

Nothing resembling a top colt had stepped forward during spring of 1993. Sea Hero would go without Lasix, a minor concern, but his style did not seem suited to the tight turns of Pimlico. He was hardly a gem of consistency. At 2–1, I did not want Prairie Bayou, the Derby runner-up, and a gem of consistency.

I had admired Personal Hope's effort in the Kentucky Derby, his finest performance so far. In a determined burst, the speedy colt had wrestled the lead into the Louisville stretch and he had held second near the shadow of the wire. The Preakness not only should permit a softer run near the front, but also Personal Hope would break from the inside.

Most of all, I liked a certain stranger. He looked like this:

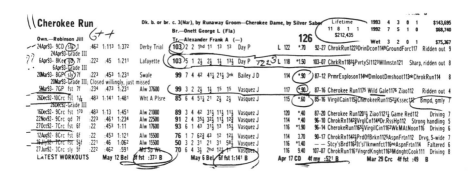

Unable to spot a dismal performance in the record, I judged Cherokee Run's last two races not only his best, but also a pair that should translate into an even better performance today.

A positive pattern among 3YOs is paired figures. Notice Cherokee Run paired 99s in Florida, first overnight and next in the Grade 3 Swale Stakes.

The colt next improved to a speed figure of 103 in the Grade 3 Lafayette at Keeneland. And in the Derby trial at Churchill Downs, another 103.

Paired figures by improving 3YOs intimate further improvement. If the pattern persists, Cherokee Run should record an even faster figure in the Preakness, perhaps a 105 or 106. Sea Hero earned a 105 in the Kentucky Derby. On their best afternoon, no other Preakness prospect had matched those numbers. Speed figures count more in predicting the Preakness outcome than the other Triple Crown races.

I backed Cherokee Run to win and boxed him in multiple exactas with Personal Hope.

Personal Hope faded quickly when the real running began. Cherokee Run, however, grabbed the lead authoritatively into the stretch and continued strongly all the way. But he was swallowed up within fifty yards by Prairie Bayou, who unleashed a tremendous run from the prestretch call to the wire. The favorite was mighty convincing.

I left Pimlico confident I would tag Cherokee Run at a decent price later. Alongside Diazo, I put Cherokee Run on the 3YO list of Horses To Watch during the second half.

On the Preakness undercard, in the support stakes, I benefited from a class overlay I managed to back intelligently. I was saved in another race from a best-bet loss by the price. Examine the past performances of my bet in the Never Bend Handicap, a $75,000-added stakes for 3UP at a mile and one-sixteenth:

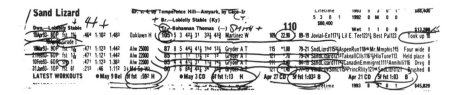

Exiting the Grade 1, $500,000-added Oaklawn Handicap, with a respectable fourth at 22–1 against the ranking handicap horses in the nation, Sand Lizard leapt off the paper in this $75,000 line-up. On Beyer Speed, Sand Lizard had recorded a dazzling 105 at Oaklawn Park.

The closest speed figure to Sand Lizard's in the Never Bend field was 100, which three horses showed, none in graded competition. Owned by Loblolly Stable, trained by Tom Bohannan (Prairie Bayou), Sand Lizard had trained for today's race like a colt on a mission. A jockey switch from W. Martinez to New York leader Mike Smith added the final touch.

Best of all, Pimlico's morning-line maker had listed Sand Lizard at 10–1! What's wrong with this picture?

At first click, naturally, Sand Lizard shrank from 10–1 to 6–5. No play. Sand Lizard did much better on the board than on the track, where he collapsed inexplicably. I revisited the past performances.

With speed figures clustered between 85 and 87, Sand Lizard suddenly dispensed a 105 in a Grade 1 stakes. The improvement translates to nine or ten lengths, a radical rise. The still-developing 4YO was susceptible to the performance "bounce." Brother, did Sand Lizard ever "bounce!" Overbetting at Pimlico had prevented a bet, but I might get Sand Lizard on the "bounce-back" pattern. I put the colt on the Horses To Watch list.

The stakes I managed to play cleverly was The Maryland Budweiser Breeders' Cup Handicap, extending $150,000.00, a rich pot, to sprinters 3UP traveling six furlongs. The handicapping proved unchallenging, conceding in the end two obvious co-favorites. The trick would be in the wagering, as so often.

Consider the pair of favorites.

Senor Speedy
Own: Perez Robert

VELASQUEZ J (28 1 3 4 .04)

B. h. 6
Sire: Fast Gold (Mr. Prospector)
Dam: Quality Endures (General Assembly)
Br: Lundy Robert A (Ky)
Tr: Callejas Alfredo (1 1 0 0 1.00)

135

Lifetime Record: 3[illegible]					
1993	7	1	1	2	$182,309
1992	5	2	1	0	$163,509
Bel	11	5	1	1	$223,720

15Aug93-9Sar	fst	7f	:221 :442 1:084 1:214	3↑ Forego H-G2	103	8	2	97¾ 99¼ 33½ 33¾	Velasquez J	117 fb	11.10	92-12	Birdonthewire117 1½ Harlan110 2¼ Senor S		
2Aug93-8Sar	sly	6f	:214 :443 :564 1:091	3↑ A PhenomenonG3	92	5	7	78¾ 76½ 54 46	Bailey J D	122 fb	*1.70	90-11	Gold Spring119 1¼ Friendly Lover122nk D		
25Jly93-9Lrl	fst	6f	:213 :443 :563 1:083	3↑ F Frncs MemCG3	106	3	9	915 913 98¾ 52	Bailey J D	119 fb	3.70	95-11	Montbrook112½ Lion Cavern117no Flami		
15May93-8Pim	fst	6f	:223 :444 :571 1:093	3↑ M-Lnd Bd B C 150k	110	1	6	77½ 47 43 12½	Bailey J D	117 fb	3.30	97-09	Senor Speedy117 2½ He Is Risen115no Wh		
2May93-8Aqu	fst	7f	:223 :46 1:093 1:223	3↑ Carter H-G1	102	7	8	86 53¼ 43½ 54¼	Chavez J F	116 fb	4.70e	87-21	Alydeed122no Loach112 4 Argyle Lake113		
13Apr93-8Kee	fst	7f	:223 :454 1:093 1:212	3↑ Cmnwlth B C-G3	103	2	6	65¼ 62¾ 62½ 32½	Chavez J F	115 fb	6.10	99-15	Alydeed115hd Binalong118 2½ Senor Spee		
15Feb93-10Lrl	fst	7f	:23 :454 1:094 1:223	3↑ Gen George-G2	101	6	5	67½ 46 25 22	Chavez J F	118 b	*1.20	94-20	Majesty's Turn118 2 Senor Speedy118 13		
26Nov92-8Aqu	sly	6f	:22 :45 :571 1:094	3↑ Sprt Page H-G3	100	4	6	67 46 33½ 21¼	Chavez J F	122 b	*1.40e	91-16	R. D. Wild Whirl114 1¼ Senor Speedy122 2		
31Oct92-4GP	fst	6f	:213 :433 :553 1:081	3↑ Br Cp Sprnt-G1	95	4	14	149¾ 107¾ 98¾ 88¼	Chavez J F	126 b	16.50	96 —	Thirty Slews126nk Meafara120 3 Rubiano		

Callide Valley
B. g. 5, by Slewpy—Pago Lady, by Pago Pago
Br.—Semple Lindsay (Ky)
Tr.—Glass Oris J Jr (—)
Own.—West Gary L & Mary E

119

Lifetime							
29 12 4 6 $321,015	1993	5	4	0	0	$151,808
	1992	16	4	4	5	$105,532
	Wet	2	0	0	0	$3,000

1May93-6CD	fst	7f	:221 :444 1:22	Chrchll D H	106	10	2	31½ 1hd 1hd 11	Stevens G L	L	116	15.80	100-01	CallideVlley116 1 Furiously117hd Oji11[illegible]	Dueled drvg gmly	11
1May93-Grade III																
15Apr93-9OP	sly	6f	:21 :444 1:093	Count Flt H	88	5	7	73¾ 87¼ 88½ 78	Smith M E	L	120	4.20	83-21	Approach116 1¼ Ponche113 1½ Never Wavering110	3 wide	13
15Apr93-Grade III																
21Mar93-10FG	fst	6f	:213 :45 1:092	Pelleteri H	103	2	3	34½ 33½ 1hd 1no	Pedroza M A	L	123	*.70	97-10	ClldVlly123no Glsspr116 1¼ SpdyCr114	Exchangd bmps st	6
13Feb93-9OP	fst	6f	:212 :443 1:09	Hot Springs	108	7	6	63¾ 63¼ 2½ 11	Romero S P	L	118	5.20	94-18	CallideVlley118 1 Potentility118nk Approch115	Four wide	8
17Jan93-9FG	fst	6f	:221 :453 1:102	3↑ Col Power H	100	6	2	4½ 1½ 1hd 1½	Romero S P	L	119	*.90	92-13	Callide Valley119½ Glasspro113 3 RamsFellow114	Driving	6
19Dec92-10FG	fst	6f	:213 :45 1:101	3↑ Gaudin MemH	94	1	5	33 32 1hd 21½	Romero S P	L	119	*1.40	91-15	Xray118 1½ Callide Valley119 1½ Glasspro115	Held place	10
26Nov92-10FG	fst	6f	:22 :444 1:091	3↑ Thansgvg H	97	7	4	2hd 1hd 11½ 11	Romero S P	L	117	*3.40	98-11	Callide Valley117 1 Sixcess114½ Kool Kasey116	Driving	14
29Oct92-6Kee	fst	6½f	:221 :444 1:152	3↑ Alw 27600	103	8	2	41¼ 31 21½ 2nk	Sellers S J	LB	117	*2.20	100-10	Hppomns115nk ClldVlly117 5 StllrTwr121	Carried out, 2nd	8
17Oct92-7Kee	fst	7f	:223 :45 1:221	3↑ Alw 27600	98	5	3	52¾ 42½ 3nk 32	Sellers S J	LB	117	3.50	96-09	BrtshBnr120 2 Sthdffrt117hd ClldVll117	No late response	9
7Sep92-9Wds	fst	6f	:214 :441 1:093	3↑ At Tpka S Fe	89	2	5	32½ 47 34½ 32½	Steinberg P W	LB	116	5.10e	91-16	DeLConcorde112 2 OurBuckwhet115½ CllidVlly116	Evenly	9

LATEST WORKOUTS Apr 4 Kee 5f fst 1:01 H

Which horse do handicappers prefer?

As a younger handicapper I followed a guideline I believed ordered the priorities correctly: when in doubt, go to the class.

On that basis, Senor Speedy gets the nod. The 6YO had been a Grade 1/Grade 2 late-running sprinter in New York for several seasons. He had been used sparingly of late. In his third try of 1993, Senor Speedy had finished fourth in the Grade 1 Carter Handicap, in arrears of excellent sprinters. His Beyer Speed Figure that day (102) was two lengths slower than Callide Valley's last. Six furlongs may be short for the New York closer; maybe not.

Senor Speedy fit another pattern hospitable to class handicappers season upon season. He finally would be treated to the class drop he needed. No longer the Grade 1 and Grade 2 sprinter he once had been, Senor Speedy still can pulverize the stakes types he encountered in the Maryland Million. Anyone who cares to dispute the assertion should examine the stakes races in Senor Speedy's record prior to the Maryland Million and following the Maryland Million. Consider the differences. The Maryland race sticks out as a relatively soft spot.

Callide Valley had been a wonderful sprinter from the beginning, and had looked outstanding in 1993. In the Churchill Downs Handicap on May 1, Derby Day, Callide Valley completed the second fraction of a seven-furlong sprint in 22⅕ seconds. He also equaled the three-year track record at the distance.

On the other hand, Callide Valley had never won a Grade 2 sprint. On May 1, at 15–1, he had outrun Furiously, the Shug McGaughey trained sprinter I had found overrated in Florida.

When the betting began, Callide Valley sunk immediately to 6–5. I sensed a ripening moment. Senor Speedy, however, was leveled at 2–1 — until late. He then drifted up to 5–2, and then to 3–1.

Several years ago, I had revised my personal dictum on betting two-horse races. Go to the class was replaced by go to the price. The ideal situation finds the two imperatives converging, which was happening at Pimlico. I bet enthusiastically. Abandoning Callide Valley, I also stuck Senor Speedy atop five overlays in exactas.

As if on cue, Callide Valley dispensed a clunker, dropping out before the field had reached the prestretch call. Senor Speedy loomed up boldly along the rail in the upper stretch. The outcome thereafter was never in doubt. Senor Speedy split rivals in midstretch and roared to the front. He won smoking, the rider unable to pull him up afterward.

When the longest price on the board got second, I missed a $137.40 exacta, a deep disappointment.

Preakness Day dragged into a long, long, long succession of eleven races extending from 11 AM past six o' clock. Our party of five had purchased reserved tickets for two days, both in the private boxes at track level to the right of the finish line and in The Palace, a decorous, comfortable, air-conditioned enclosure of dining tables and pleasant service.

On Friday, we had arrived before the first race at the boxes. Our view of the backstretch was blocked in its entirety by an array of carnival-sized tents corporate sponsors had erected for the weekend. I was flabbergasted. Sight lines from the boxes were obstructed. The view was awful — there's no softer adjective. Following the first we departed hastily for The Palace.

On Preakness Day, our host sold the reserved tickets to the boxes, but not before warning the buyers they would be unable to see the runs down the backside. They paid the cover price regardless.

With stretches of forty to fifty minutes between races, The Preakness program quickly lost its charm. This was my inaugural visit to a Triple Crown event. I feel no desire to return. This was a social occasion, of course, a gay joyous gathering for the swarms of revelers jammed into the infield and packed into the seats. Unhappily, the afternoon also became congested, tiresome, unexciting, and more than a fraction tedious.

Breeders' Cup Championship Day excepted, racing's ceremonial occasions manage to elicit amazingly negative reactions from numerous regular handicappers. Several have told me bluntly they have sworn off "live" attendance. I can understand why.

With the second jewel in place, it was convenient to forget these forgettable 3YOs for a time and concentrate on the stakes for older horses. The Metropolitan Mile at Belmont Park was only two weeks away. I had been anticipating the race with some excitement for two and one-half months.

The moment Bobby Frankel announced Bertrando would next start in New York's Metropolitan Mile, I planned a major wager. I hoped only that (a) Frankel would not change his mind, and (b) the horse would make the race. The Grade 1, $500,000-added stakes convenes the fastest milers in the land and I hadn't the slightest doubt Bertrando was the fastest and the best. He might also be a sweet price, not in southern California, but in New York, and in my home town, Philadelphia.

The most glamorous mile on the American calendar, the Metropolitan for me can be measured under one handicapping rule of thumb: Favor the fastest sprinter that simultaneously has been the fastest winner in Grade 1 and Grade 2 middle-distance stakes. That horse that is capable of running a mile, and a mile and one-sixteenth, and a mile and one-eighth in rapid time, beginning, middle, and end. That horse is difficult to thwart in a one-turn mile. The Metropolitan is a one-turn mile. The kind of horse I have in mind (Bertrando) can throttle full speed ahead all the way.

The Metropolitan Mile annually draws sprinters, milers, and middle-distance horses to the gate. In 1993, Bertrando fit all three distances. I intended a maximum bet of $1,000, and I expected decent odds: a long layoff, two consecutive losses just prior to the layoff, and no extraordinary mile times in the record. Bertrando's brilliance should be partially hidden.

In the prelude to the big race, I encountered nothing short of mounting enthusiasm, until the night before when I engaged in the actual routine of handicapping. Still liking the bet, I now admitted to two reservations: the front of The Metropolitan would be top-heavy with speed, high-class speed; and the Canadian export Alydeed was difficult to classify.

The guts of the competition spread out like this:

Ibero (Arg) · B. h. 6
Own: Whitman Frank E
Sire: Cinco Grande (Secretariat)
Dam: Derienne (Traviglio)
Br: Haras San Ignacio de Loyola (Arg)
Tr: McAnally Ronald (—)
PINCAY L JR (—) 119

Lifetime Record:	25 8 7 2	$923,183
1993	1 0 1 0	$11,000 Turf 5 2 2 0
1992	10 2 2 1	$702,250 Wet 2 2 0 0
Bel	0 0 0 0	Dist 5 2 2 0

Furiously
Own: Mill House
Sire: Danzig (Northern Dancer)
Dam: Whirl Series (Roberto)
Br: Mill House (Ky)
Tr: McGaughey Claude III (18 3 5 5 .17)
BAILEY J D (52 12 11 6 .23) 115
Dk. b or br c. 4

Lifetime Record:	11 5 1 1	$219,020
1993	3 1 1 1	$39,020 Turf 0 0 0 0
1992	8 4 0 0	$180,000 Wet 0 0 0 0
Bel	1 1 0 0	Dist 1 1 0 0

Alydeed
Own: Kinghaven Farms
Sire: Shadeed (Nijinsky II)
Dam: Bialy (Alydar)
Br: Anderson Farms (Ont–C)
Tr: Attfield Roger (—)
PERRET C (21 6 4 3 .29) 124
Dk. b or br c. 4

Lifetime Record:	14 9 2 1	$870,689
1993	3 3 0 0	$221,657 Turf 0 0 0 0
1992	10 5 2 1	$608,280 Wet 1 0 1 0
Bel	0 0 0 0	Dist 1 1 0 0

Bertrando
Own: Five O Five Farms
STEVENS G L (—)

Dk. b or br c. 4
Sire: Skywalker (Relaunch)
Dam: Gentle Hands (Buffalo Lark)
Br: Nahem Ed (Cal)
Tr: Frankel Robert (—)

121

Lifetime Record: 10 5 3 1 $1,034,46

1993	3 1 1 0	$227,800	Turf	0 0 0 0
1992	3 1 1 1	$235,800	Wet	1 1 0 0
Bel	0 0 0 0		Dist	1 1 0 0

6Mar93-5SA	fst	1¼	:471 1:11 1:351 2:002	S Anita H-G1	98	4 1 11 1hd 31½ 99¾	McCarron C J	LB 120 b	2.40e	83-13	Sir Beaufort119no Star Recruit117hd Major Impact1141¾	Brush
7Feb93-8SA	fst	1¼	:472 1:114 1:354 2:003	C H Strub-G1	112	1 1 11½ 11 1½ 21¼	McCarron C J	LB 122 b	*.30	91-11	Siberian Summer1181¼ Bertrando1222 Major Impact1183	Out
16Jan93-8SA	sly	1⅛	:46 1:103 1:364 1:511	Sn Frnando HG2	109	3 1 11 11½ 16 19	McCarron C J	L 120 b	*1.50	74-30	Bertrando1209 Star Recruit120¾ The Wicked North1164	Co
26Dec92-8SA	fst	7f	:222 :45 1:081 1:203	Malibu-G2	102	7 1 11 1hd 2hd 3¾	McCarron C J	LB 120 b	*1.40	99-09	Star Of The Crop118¾ The Wicked North116nk Bertrando1205½	G
4Apr92-5SA	fst	1⅛	:461 1:102 1:361 1:491	S A Derby-G1	92	1 1 11 11 1½ 21¾	Solis A	B 122 b	1.10	82-11	A.P. Indy1221¾ Bertrando122nk Casual Lies122	I
15Mar92-8SA	fst	1 1/16	:222 :454 1:101 1:423	San Felipe-G2	97	4 1 1hd 1hd 12½ 1¾	Solis A	B 122 b	*.40	90-13	Bertrando122¾ Arp1161¾ Hickman Creek116	Ha
2Nov91-6CD	fst	1 1/16	:231 :463 1:12 1:443	Br Cp Juv-G1	92	5 1 11½ 1hd 25 25	Solis A	B 122 b	2.50	87-09	Arazi1225 Bertrando1223½ Snappy Landing122	;
13Oct91-8SA	fst	1 1/16	:221 :454 1:102 1:424	Norfolk-G1	95	3 1 11½ 11½ 14 19	Solis A	B 118 b	*1.50e	89-16	Bertrando1189 Zurich118¾ Bag118	Ric
11Sep91-8Dmr	fst	1	:214 :45 1:102 1:362	Del Mar Fut-G2	84	4 1 11 11 14 13½	Solis A	B 114 b	8.70	84-18	Bertrando1143½ Zurich1144½ Star Recruit115	
25Aug91-9Dmr	fst	6f	:214 :444 :571 1:101	[S]Md Sp Wt	89	3 3 1½ 2hd 1½ 12	Solis A	B 117 b	4.00	88-12	Bertrando1172 Ebonair1171 Simple King112	

WORKOUTS: May 24 SA 7f fst 1:241 H 2/8 May 17 SA 7f fst 1:274 H 3/6 May 11 SA 7f fst 1:282 H 3/4 ●May 5 SA 6f fst 1:121 B 1/21 Apr 29 SA 6f fst 1:141 B 4/13 Apr 23 SA 5f fst 1:011 H 16/32

Loach
Own: Condren William J
DAVIS R G (95 11 16 14 .12)

B. h. 5
Sire: Lines of Power (Raise a Native)
Dam: Scarlet Rain (Rainy Lake)
Br: Paulson Allen E (Ky)
Tr: Zito Nicholas P (11 0 2 0 .00)

113

Lifetime Record: 21 5 4 4 $255,921

1993	5 1 2 2	$100,274	Turf	2 0 1 0
1992	10 3 0 1	$120,232	Wet	0 0 0 0
Bel	2 0 0 0	$2,820	Dist	1 0 0 1

2May93-8Aqu	fst	7f	:223 :46 1:093 1:223	3↑ Carter H-G1	111	2 6 11 2hd 2½ 2no	Davis R G	112	8.70	91-21	Alydeed122no Loach1124 Argyle Lake113hd	Gamely, brus
10Apr93-8Aqu	fst	1	:232 :452 1:084 1:343	3↑ Weschester HG3	103	6 2 41 22 2hd 32	Davis R G	113	3.80	89-26	Bill Of Rights110¾ Fly So Free1181¼ Loach1133½	V
19Mar93-9GP	fst	7f	:223 :453 1:101 1:221	3↑ Gufstream 100k	105	2 3 1hd 1hd 1hd 22	Santos J A	L 114	*1.60	90-19	Binalong1122 Loach1144 Richman1134	Best c
21Feb93-10GP	fst	7f	:22 :444 1:093 1:222	3↑ Dpty Mnstr H 50k	108	2 6 21 21 2hd 1½	Santos J A	L 114	3.70	91-18	Loach114½ Hidden Tomahawk1132 British Banker114nk	
28Jan93-9GP	fst	6½f	:214 :443 1:094 1:163	Alw 21000N4X	94	4 2 42 43½ 33 31	Bailey J D	L 117	3.00	93-19	Hold Old Blue117½ Nifty's Swifty114½ Loach117½	L
11Oct92-5Bel	gd	1 1/16	:233 :462 1:102 1:42	3↑ Alw 47000	80	1 1 1½ 2½ 34 411½	Perret C	115	2.50	80-09	Key Contender1191½ Polonium1126 Temper Time115	G
29Aug92-8Sar	fst	1⅛	:454 1:10 1:344 1:471	3↑ Whitney H-G1	81	9 1 12 2hd 910 918¼	Rojas R I	110	*1.60e	83 —	Sultry Song115no Out of Place1154 Chief Honcho116	Usec
8Aug92-8Mth	fst	1⅛	:453 1:09 1:341 1:464	3↑ Iselin H-G1	94	8 1 12 11½ 42½ 67½	Rojas R I	L 111	*1.70e	98 —	Jolie's Halo116hd Out of Place1131 Valley Crossing111	
3Aug92-8Sar	fst	6f	:221 :443 :562 1:083	3↑ A Phenmenon-G3	84	9 5 31 33 65 69½	Rojas R I	115	5.20	91-08	For Really115nk Burn Fair115nk Drummond Lane122	
18Jly92-8Bel	fst	1¼	:46 1:102 1:352 2:001	3↑ Suburban H-G1	98	3 1 17 2½ 46 59¼	Smith M E	113	*1.50e	81-16	Pleasant Tap1191½ Strike the Gold1191¼ Defensive Play115	Usec

WORKOUTS: May 24 Bel 5f fst 1:003 H 4/36 May 17 Bel 5f fst 1:03 B 8/10 May 11 Bel 5f fst 1:05 B 18/19 Apr 24 Bel 5f fst 1:01 B 8/25 Apr 5 Bel tr.t 5f fst 1:02 B 20/36 Mar 31 Bel tr.t 4f fst :471 H 3/55

Forever Whirl
Own: Reskin Alan
TORIBIO A R (—)

Ro. c. 3 (Apr)
Sire: Island Whirl (Pago Pago)
Dam: Forever Lady (Forever Sparkle)
Br: Santa Cruz Ranch (Fla)
Tr: Wolfson Martin D (—)

107

Lifetime Record: 9 4 1 2 $181,625

1993	6 3 0 2	$170,979	Turf	0 0 0 0
1992	3 1 1 0	$10,646	Wet	2 1 0 0
Bel	0 0 0 0		Dist	0 0 0 0

10Apr93-11Hia	fst	1⅛	:48 1:12 1:374 1:511	Flamingo 200k	95	5 1 13½ 16 14 1hd	Toribio A R	L 118	7.40	88-19	ForeverWhirl118hd BullIntheHether122hd PridePrvils1184	Fully
28Mar93-7GP	fst	7f	:222 :453 1:11 1:24	Alw 29000N2X	93	4 5 42½ 32 11 15½	Krone J A	L 115	*1.70	83-23	Forever Whirl1155½ Sweet Beast1151½ Chief Desire1154½	
			Driving six wide top stretch									
20Mar93-8GP	sly	7f	:223 :453 1:101 1:231	Swale-G3	62	6 1 73½ 74¼ 814 717½	Smith M E	L 112	12.00	70-12	PrmirExplosion114hd DmlootDmshoot113nk ChrokRun1142¼	Shc
3Mar93-7GP	fst	6½f	:22 :442 1:10 1:17	Alw 23000N2X	84	9 1 51¾ 3½ 32½ 31½	Bailey J D	L 117	2.00	90-13	World Island117no Midnight Cookie1121½ Forever Whirl1172	
			Lacked response four wide									
6Feb93-9GP	fst	7f	:222 :45 1:094 1:233	Hutcheson-G2	88	6 4 2hd 2½ 22 31½	Lee M A	112	21.50	83-18	Hidden Trick1141 [D]Demaloot Demashoot114½ [D]Forever Whirl11	
			Drifted out repeatedly 1/8;placed 3rd in dble disqualification Disqualified and placed third									
21Jan93-8GP	fst	7f	:221 :451 1:10 1:232	Alw 18000N1X	82	4 2 2hd 1½ 11½ 11½	Bailey J D	115	22.50	86-15	ForeverWhirl1151½ ChantingGoshawk1152 LivingVicariously114n	

In descending order of preference, I liked Bertrando, Ibero, and Alydeed. How good was Alydeed?

Three for three at three tracks in 1993, with the Beyer Speed Figures superb, Canada's best colt was coming to the race of his life. Trainer Roger Attfield, a winner and a realist, had made that clear in prerace headlines. Attfield had pointed Alydeed specifically to the Metropolitan Mile; his major objective. Until Alydeed had trailed off in 1992, the colt was toying with 3YOs, although he had surrendered a two-length advantage in the Preakness. I imagined a potential champ would have won that day.

What bothered me were Alydeed's vastly improved speed figures at four. The opposite of the top horse on the skids, this looked like a good horse scaling the heights. Maybe Alydeed's

4YO speed figures could be attributed to the shorter sprints, but I wasn't sure. Should I risk a grand to find out?

Finally, I depended upon Alydeed's last two races, the all-out seven-furlong victories over Binalong and Loach. Unfamiliar with Binalong, I knew Loach to be a speed horse who was nobody's champion. If Alydeed had been pushed to the outer limits to beat Loach and his kind, he should not handle Bertrando.

Alydeed aside, the probable pace was complicated. After an in-depth review of the past performances, I was convinced Bertrando not only should be the speed of the speed, but also the class of the field. But could Bertrando survive a suicidal pace that might extend towards seven furlongs, and still finish powerfully enough to prevail?

The benefactors of a multiple-horse pace duel should be Alydeed or Ibero. Ibero had earned the top Beyer Speed Figure at a mile (114) while winning the $500,000-guaranteed NYRA Mile in the fall of 1992. He had started once in 1993 for trainer Ron McAnally, on turf, and since had been trained carefully for today's big-ticket objective. McAnally's trump is a genius for spacing horses' races. Ibero would be ready to show his best. The 6YO is a fantastic miler. No problem. I would ensure the win wager in exactas with Ibero.

On Saturday morning I relayed win-bets to Las Vegas ($500) (plugging into the New York pools) and to Philadelphia Park ($400), places where Alydeed should be favored and Bertrando underbet. In New York, I also took a $50 exacta box ($100) coupling Bertrando and Ibero.

I watched the simulcast at Santa Anita. I was correct about the betting. When the gates opened at Belmont Park, the odds were:

Hollywood Park	2–1
Belmont Park	4–1
Philadelphia	7–1

Bertrando broke well and shot to the front. Loach pressed him. The other speed was outrun. The pair of front-runners went 22⅕, 44⅕, 109⅕, and approaching the head of the long Belmont stretch, Loach retired.

Alydeed, fourth down the backside, now moved up boldly along the rail. My hopes sank. Alydeed collared Bertrando nearing the eighth pole and he was going much the best.

Ibero, meanwhile, had moved into contention from mid-pack, swung out behind a wall of four horses, and under a daring rugged ride under the great Laffit Pincay, Jr., literally cut a path in the four-horse wall. Once clear, Ibero gained his best stride and by mid-stretch had sailed by the front line. He won smartly.

Headed at the eighth pole and still a quarter-length behind Alydeed inside the sixteenth pole, Bertrando kept to his task and regained second. Despite inheriting the advantage from a suicidal pace, Alydeed could not hold the place. Bertrando showed a gritty determination. His rebound to second meant a saving payoff to me. The exacta in New York paid $43.80.

NINTH RACE
Belmont
MAY 31, 1993

1 MILE. (1.32^3) 101st Running of THE METROPOLITAN HANDICAP. Purse $500,000. (Grade I) 3-year-olds and upward. By subscription of $1,000 each which should accompany the nomination; $2,500 to pass the entry box; $5,000 to start. The Purse to be divided 60% to the winner, 22% to second, 12% to third, 6% to fourth. Weights Wednesday, May 26. Starters to be named at the closing time of entries. Trophies will be presented to the winning owner, trainer and jockey. (Closed Wednesday, May 12)

Value of Race: $500,000 Winner $300,000; second $110,000; third $60,000; fourth $30,000. Mutuel Pool $388,704.00 Exacta Pool $437,987.00 Triple Pool $353,308.00

Last Raced	Horse	M/Eqt.	A.	Wt	PP	St	¼	½	¾	Str	Fin	Jockey	Odds $1
2Apr93 ^{8}SA^2	Ibero-AR		6	119	1	8	5^1	6^½	5^½	3^{1½}	1^{1½}	Pincay L Jr	3.10
6Mar93 ^{5}SA^9	Bertrando	b	4	121	7	1	1^½	1^½	1^{hd}	1^{hd}	2^{nk}	Stevens G L	4.00
2May93 ^{8}Aqu^1	Alydeed		4	124	3	7	3^½	3^{hd}	3^{hd}	2^{hd}	3^{2½}	Perret C	3.20
6May93 ^{8}Bel^1	Fly So Free		5	118	6	4	7^{1½}	7^{3½}	6^{1½}	4^{2½}	4^{3½}	Krone J A	6.20
24Apr93 ^{8}Aqu^3	Bill Of Rights		4	111	5	6	8^1	8^2	8^½	7^½	5^½	Velazquez J R	12.70
25Apr93 ^{9}CD^2	Excellent Tipper	f	5	112	4	5	9	9	9	6^½	6^{3½}	Smith M E	27.70
17May93 ^{8}Bel^1	Blare of Trumpets	b	4	112	9	3	6^½	4^{hd}	4^½	8^½	7^{1¼}	Antley C W	20.10
2May93 ^{8}Aqu^2	Loach		5	113	8	2	2^1	2^1	2^½	5^½	8^¾	Davis R G	24.70
1May93 ^{6}CD^2	Furiously	f	4	115	2	9	4^½	5^{1½}	7^1	9	9	Bailey J D	4.00

OFF AT 5:27 Start Good. Won driving. Time, :22^1, :44^1, 1:08^3, 1:34^1 Track fast.

$2 Mutuel Prices:			
1-(A)-IBERO-AR	8.20	5.00	3.00
7-(G)-BERTRANDO		5.40	3.40
3-(C)-ALYDEED			2.80

$2.00 EXACTA 1-7 PAID $43.80 $2.00 TRIPLE 1-7-3 PAID $147.00

B. h, by Cinco Grande–Iberienne, by Treviglio. Trainer McAnally Ronald. Bred by Haras San Ignacio de Loyola (Arg).

IBERO a bit slow away from the gate, rushed up along the inside, was rated in good position while saving ground for five furlongs, angled out on the turn, checked briefly while splitting horses four wide leaving the quarter pole, loomed a strong threat while lugging in slightly in midstretch, then drew clear under a vigorous hand ride. BERTRANDO away alertly, battled for the lead inside LOACH for six furlongs, shook off that one leaving the quarter pole, dug in when challenged by ALYDEED in upper stretch, relinquished the lead to the winner inside the furlong marker then continued on gamely to hold the place. ALYDEED, settled just behind the early leaders, while saving ground, waited patiently for room while continuing to save ground on the turn, split horses entering the stretch, drew on nearly even terms with BERTRANDO approaching the furlong marker then weakened slightly in the final sixteenth. FLY SO FREE, unhurried for five furlongs while racing well out from the rail, circled five wide at the top of the stretch, made a run to reach contention in midstretch but couldn't sustain his bid. BILL OF RIGHTS outrun for five furlongs, angled out while gaining on the turn, advanced six wide into the stretch then rallied mildly in the middle of the track. EXCELLENT TIPPER never reached contention. BLARE OF TRUMPETS allowed to settle early, stalked the pace while four wide leaving the backstretch, remained a factor while strung out five wide at the top of the stretch then steadily tired thereafter. LOACH battled heads apart outside BERTRANDO for six furlongs and gave way. FURIOUSLY, away slowly, raced in close contention between horses for five furlongs then faded. BILL OF RIGHTS and BLARE OF TRUMPETS wore mud caulks.

Owners— 1, Whitham Frank E; 2, Nahem Edward; 3, Kinghaven Farms; 4, Valando Thomas; 5, Boketo Stable; 6, Mack Earle I; 7, Ran-Dom Stable; 8, Condren William J; 9, Mill House

Trainers—1, McAnally Ronald; 2, Frankel Robert; 3, Attfield Roger; 4, Schulhofer Flint S; 5, Kelly Timothy D; 6, Tesher Howard M; 7, Sciacca Gary; 8, Zito Nicholas P; 9, McGaughey Claude III

Overweight: Blare of Trumpets (3).

Scratched— Forever Whirl (10Apr93 ^{11}Hia^1)

POSTSCRIPT When the Beyer Speed Figures for the Metropolitan Mile were released, Bertrando got a 110. I imagined he would run several lengths faster. Away eighty-six days, if handicappers want to remind me Bertrando might have been a touch "short," I agree.

The 1993 Metropolitan Mile would be remembered here for its simulcast to Philadelphia Park. If bettors there gave 7–1 on Bertrando in a one-turn mile, I had found my betting base for simulcast wagers. In a phone conversation a few days later, I was stunned even more.

"Midway through the betting, Bertrando was 13–1 here," said

my source. "Then the track's local analyst picked him to win, and the odds began to drop. . . ."

Pari-mutuel pools at Philadelphia Park and other medium-sized markets can be relatively small. The odds can be volatile. Favorites will be buried under the money. But if horses should not be favored, the odds can be extremely generous. Let the 1993 Metropolitan Mile be instructive to handicappers everywhere: simulcast bettors should take the trouble to locate watering holes like Philadelphia Park. It pays.

Later on that Memorial Day afternoon at the Santa Anita satellite, I cashed in when one of the two best grass horses in the nation demolished the Grade 1, $500,000-added Hollywood Turf Handicap. Before the race, I did not realize Bien Bien possessed special dimensions. After the race, I could not deny it.

By late May, the country had become enthralled by the grass battles between New York's Lure and southern California's Star Of Cozzene, the latter having the edge when the races were stretched beyond middle distances. Now I suspected this new development might give me an enviable edge, perhaps in the Breeders' Cup Future Book, perhaps in head-to-head combat. In longer races, Bien Bien was superior to Star Of Cozzene, and I knew it.

Examine the past performances Bien Bien carried into the Hollywood race:

A loser to Star Of Cozzene in January on the Santa Anita grass, if Kotashaan had been missing, by April Bien Bien would have been Santa Anita's grass horse of the meeting. On March 21, in the marathon San Luis Rey, Bien Bien had finished thirteen lengths ahead of the third finisher. On April 18, in the decisive San Juan Capistrano, the most prestigious grass race on the winter calendar, Bien Bien had beaten Fraise, winner of the 1992 Breeders' Cup Turf.

In the Grade 1 Hollywood Turf Handicap, trainer Paco Gonzalez, underrated, took the blinkers off, jockey Chris McCarron took Bien Bien back, and the 4YO rallied sensationally to make mincemeat of the opposition. Bien Bien was a fully mature 4YO at last. The closing style had served him well in the past, and it surely would again. Notice too that on December 13 of his 3YO season, Bien Bien had withstood a nose to nose stretch duel with ranking older horses (winning via disqualification). Not many 3YO grass males can accomplish that.

And here is the result chart:

EIGHTH RACE	1¼ MILES. (Turf, Chute) (1.58³) 25th Running HOLLYWOOD TURF HANDICAP (Grade I). Purse
Hollywood	$500,000. 3-year-olds and upward. By subscription of $500 each, which shall accompany the nomination, $2,500 additional to pass the entry box and $3,000 additional to start, with $275,000 to the winner, $100,000
MAY 31, 1993	to second, $75,000 to third, $37,500 to fourth and $12,500 to fifth. Weights, Monday, May 24. Starter to be

named through the entry box by closing time of entries. This race will not be divided. The field will be limited to 14 (fourteen) horses. In the event that more than fourteen horses pass the entry box preference will be given to high weights based upon the weight assigned to each horse, adjusted for scale weights and sex allowance (assigned weight). Total earnings in 1993 will be used in determining the preference of horses with equal assigned weight. Those horses not drawn into the body of the race will be placed on an also eligible list in order of preference as specified herein. In the event of a scratch in the body of the race prior to the announced scratch time for the race, horses on the also eligible list will be moved into the body of the race based upon their order preference. Failure to draw into this race at scratch time cancels all fees. Trophies will be presented to the winning owner, trainer and jockey. Closed Wednesday, May 19, with 13 nominations.

Value of Race: $500,000 Winner $275,000; second $100,000; third $75,000; fourth $37,500; fifth $12,500. Mutuel Pool $580,930.00 Exacta Pool $454,774.00 Trifecta Pool $213,359.00

Last Raced	Horse	M/Eqt. A.Wt	PP	¼	½	¾	1	Str	Fin	Jockey	Odds $1
18Apr93 4SA²	Bien Bien	LBbf 4 119	8	6²	5½	51½	3¹	1¹	13½	McCarron C J	3.00
10Apr93 8OP³	Best Pal	LB 5 122	6	51½	3¹	3¹	2hd	3hd	2nk	Black C A	7.40
9May93 8Hol¹	Leger Cat-Ar	LB 7 116	1	2¹	2¹	2hd	41½	41½	3hd	Nakatani C S	13.60
8May93 8GG¹	Val des Bois-Fr	7 120	7	3¹	4½	4½	5hd	5hd	41¾	Valenzuela P A	3.40
25Apr93 8Hol²	Lomitas-GB	LB 5 117	4	4½	62½	6¹	61½	61½	5½	Delahoussaye E	2.10
5May93 8Hol⁴	Corrupt	LB 5 114	3	11½	11½	1²	1¹	21½	6nk	Castaneda M	31.00
5May93 8Hol¹	Beyton	f 4 117	2	7¹	71½	7hd	7hd	7¹	71¼	Solis A	22.50
9May93 8Hol²	Rainbow Corner-GB	B 4 114	5	8	8	8	8	8	8	Garcia J A	6.40

OFF AT 5:30 Start Good. Won driving. Time, :23³, :47⁴, 1:11², 1:34³, 1:57³ Course firm.

$2 Mutuel Prices:	8–BIEN BIEN	8.00	4.60	3.60
	6–BEST PAL		8.00	5.60
	1–LEGER CAT–AR			6.80

$2 EXACTA 8–6 PAID $61.40 $2 TRIFECTA 8–6–1 PAID $369.00

Ch. c, by Manila–Stark Winter, by Graustark. Trainer Gonzalez J Paco. Bred by Farish W S & Kilroy W S (Ky).

BIEN BIEN, outrun early when he relaxed nicely under patient handling, advanced readily to threaten approaching the quarter pole, took the lead in the upper stretch, was roused with the whip once right handed early in the stretch run, drew away in the final furlong, was roused with the whip once left handed nearing the sixteenth marker, was roused with the whip twice more right handed in the last sixteenth and came home strongly to win with authority. BEST PAL, never far back, lurked within close range of the pace down the backstretch, pressed the issue around the far turn, was no match for BIEN BIEN in the drive but was game to gain the place. LEGER CAT sat within close range of the early pace, remained close up around the far turn, also was no match for BIEN BIEN in the drive but kept to his task well enough in the final furlong to gain the show. VAL DES BOIS, close up early, lacked the necessary response in the drive and was not quite able to get up for the show. LOMITAS, away in good order, was rank through the early furlongs while being outrun but not far back, raced wide down the way down the backstretch, looked dangerous going into the far turn, did not have the needed response in last quarter and was four wide into the stretch. CORRUPT went to the front at once, established the pace through the early stages while under a snug rating hold and weakened in the drive. BEYTON, devoid of early speed, failed to generate the required rally and was four wide into the stretch. RAINBOW CORNER, the early trailer, raced wide down the backstretch, also failed to generate the required rally and was five wide into the stretch.

Owners— 1, McCaffery & Toffan; 2, Golden Eagle Farm; 3, Allred & Hubbard; 4, Gann Edmund A; 5, Jacobs Walter J; 6, Sangster & Tanaka; 7, Gamel & Roberts; 8, Juddmonte Farms

Trainers— 1, Gonzalez J Paco; 2, Jones Gary; 3, Mandella Richard; 4, Frankel Robert; 5, McAnally Ronald; 6, Rash Rodney; 7, Mandella Richard; 8, Frankel Robert

Exactly how fast did Bien Bien run from behind the pace here? He ran the last two quarter miles in 22⅗ and 22⅘ seconds, respectively.

Only champions can do that.

JUNE

The day after Memorial Day, June 1, I called a professional handicapper in Philadelphia.

"I might like to make a few bets on simulcasts to Philadelphia Park," I began.

He guessed that I must have liked the odds on Bertrando in the Met Mile. We commiserated on the outcome.

"I'll carry any simulcast bets you want to make in Philly," he promised.

Philadelphia Park had begun taking full-card simulcasts from southern California. In return, I might alert my colleague to a few delicious overlays in the west.

The logistics of cross-track betting remain impractical, necessitating a bit of personal networking. A loosely formed network of colleagues and acquaintances, preferably professional handicappers, is the untenable state of the art. Making bets for associates becomes inconvenient and annoying; a definite imposition. Two-way channels are firmly recommended, so both parties can benefit. If complications arise, close the network.

Long-term, interstate telephone betting accounts may be activated at various racetracks. The teletheaters of Connecticut take virtually everything. Ultimately, interactive cable systems will take up the slack, with trackside computers supplying bettors with updated odds and assorted handicapping information, and personal computers relaying the bets to on-track pools. The future is bright.

On the first weekend of June, I drove south of Los Angeles, to the splendid satellite wagering amphitheater at Del Mar, a $15 million edifice, and by a wide margin the most comfortable, most accommodating off-track wagering site in southern California.

I had not surveyed the local card, but wanted to watch the

simulcast of the Belmont Stakes, a wide-open affair. Having a relaxed lunch with colleague Greg Lawlor, I reiterated my observation that in the absence of a champ or division leader, handicappers should expect the Triple Crown races to be won by a different 3YO at each station. Greg nodded.

Like me, Lawlor was shopping for overlays and value, which were plentiful on the tote. Unprepared, I suppose I deserved what happened. With ten minutes to go, and with Prairie Bayou the overwhelming favorite, I had pared my interests to four horses, including my Horse To Watch, Cherokee Run, and three newcomers.

I reviewed the odds:

Virginia Rapids	7–1
Colonial Affair	19–1
Arinthod	10–1
Cherokee Run	9–2

At the odds, Lawlor landed on Colonial Affair. Just as I had decided to split a win-wager on Cherokee Run and Colonial Affair, box the pair in exactas, and play each atop exactas having the other two on the undersides, a young handicapping friend of Lawlor's approached our table. He was spilling over with enthusiasm for the art of handicapping.

Making a rather formal introduction, quite nicely, Lawlor characterized our interloper as a serious handicapper who had asked to meet the author of *The Handicapper's Condition Book*, and politely excused himself. He left to bet.

I began to chat with Lawlor's friend, who trotted out a succession of queries about handicapping and wagering. I do not mind the give-and-take, but the timing stunk. Soon Lawlor was tapping my shoulder, advising me that three minutes remained in the betting. The lines had grown long.

I rushed to the betting areas. A good samaritan I vaguely

knew had noticed my plight and obligingly handed me a voucher for the Autotote machine. The screen informed me I had $13.50 to bet. I retreated to the rear of the line.

As I stood fifth in line, Colonial Affair left the gate as a 21–1 shot at the Del Mar satellite. When Colonial Affair won, one of us cashed, not only the win-bet ($44.80), but also a $330.00 exacta having Kissin Kris on the underside.

The Belmont Stakes supplied additional evidence the 1993 3YOs might be the slowest, most unappetizing in a long time. Under the outstanding Julie Krone, the first female jockey to win a Triple Crown event, the winner looked like this:

Handicappers cannot fail to notice that prior to the Belmont Stakes, Colonial Affair was a nonstakes winner. Increasingly, nonstakes winners triumph in listed and graded stakes, a trend that has invaded even America's classics. It's not a positive development.

On cold dope, Colonial Affair's second in New York's Peter Pan Stakes (Gr. 2) could not be ignored, yielding as it did the highest Beyer Speed Figure of the 3YO season.

My Horse To Watch, Cherokee Run, did well. He led by a head after a mile, by a length and one-half after a mile and one-quarter. He tired in the stretch, no unforgivable sin at a mile-and-a-half. I kept Cherokee Run on the Horses To Watch list.

Belmont Park, to be sure, had carded a festival of stakes races in support of its Triple Crown classic. But it had rained in New York on Saturday morning, and I lost interest.

A Classic Pick by an Impressive Insider

As seasons meld into seasons, season upon season, time after time, I have been bemused by the inability of famous insiders and public selectors to hit the marks in the Triple Crown races.

Horsemen—trainers—have been especially inept, latching on to prerace favorites reflexively, and rarely formulating an opinion having either substance or merit.

Figure handicappers have seemed only slightly less lost, notably in the Kentucky Derby, apparently expecting speed figures earned at middle distances will transfer reliably to a mile and a quarter. They do not.

If a nonfavorite or interesting overlay should enjoy a disarmingly vital chance to upset, virtually no one among the insiders seems to know about it.

It's therefore practically imperative to report on it when an insider has comprehended something about a 3YO classic not so obvious to everybody else. The impressive young *Daily Racing Form* handicapper Brad Free, of southern California, nailed the 1993 Belmont Stakes absolutely, and for all the right reasons. Beyond being agreeable, it's instructive to reprise Free's succinctly forceful analysis of the big race:

Brad Free

1. COLONIAL AFFAIR
2. SEA HERO
3. PRAIRIE BAYOU
Longshot: ARINTHOD

He is lightly raced and improving each start. He possesses tactical speed, often required to win at a mile and a half. He enters the Belmont as a fresh horse against a sorry crop of 3-year-olds.

For **COLONIAL AFFAIR**, the Belmont Stakes is a window to fame. Bred to run all day, Colonial Affair figures for a dream trip just behind the pace. The Belmont often is won by the horse who attacks into the far turn, and that is where Julie Krone probably will make her move. The colt comes off a strong second-place finish in the Peter Pan, and with just three starts this year, he looms fresh and dangerous.

I haven't a clue as to the profits Brad Free collected following the 1993 Belmont Stakes. But I hope he made a score. He certainly deserved it!

* * *

Following the Belmont Stakes, I took a two-week recess. Tracking the stakes entries routinely, I saw nothing to whet the appetite. Sure enough, I missed one of the most fantastic opportunities, completely unpredictable, of 1993.

I had noticed the Grade 2 Princess Stakes for 3YO fillies at Hollywood Park on June 19, would feature the return of Eliza, the division leader who had not raced since the Kentucky Oaks. She joined a five-horse field. On my Horses To Beat list, Eliza might be below a peak, but the four-horse opposition merely filled out a nonbetting race. Or so I thought.

Eliza set a sprinter's pace, and faded. She finished fourth of five. Do handicappers notice anything peculiar about the result chart?

EIGHTH RACE

Hollywood

JUNE 19, 1993

1¹⁄₁₆ MILES. (1.40) 28th Running of THE PRINCESS STAKES. Grade II. Purse $100,000 Added. Fillies, 3-year-olds. By subscription of $100 each which shall accompany the nomination, $1,000 additional to start with $100,000 added, of which $20,000 to second, $15,000 to third, $7,500 to fourth and $2,500 to fifth. Weight, 121 lbs. Non-winners of $30,000 twice at one mile or over since December 25, allowed 2 lbs. One such race in 1993 or $50,000 at a mile or over at any time, 4 lbs. $35,000 at any distance in 1993, 6 lbs. Starters to be named through the entry box by closing time of entries. Hollywood Park reserves the right not to divide this race. Should this race not be divided and the number of entries exceed the starting gate capacity; preference will be given to high weights based upon weight assigned as prescribed in the above conditions and an also eligible list will be drawn. Total earnings in 1993 will be used in determining the order of preference horses assigned equal weight. Failure to draw into this at scratch time cancels all fees. Trophies will be presentes to the winning owner, trainer and jockey. Closed Wednesday, June 9, with 10 nominations.

Value of Race: $106,000 Winner $61,000; second $20,000; third $15,000; fourth $7,500; fifth $2,500. Mutuel Pool $458,233.00 Exacta Pool $343,702.00

Last Raced	Horse	M/Eqt.	A.Wt	PP	St	¼	½	¾	Str	Fin	Jockey	Odds $1
29May93 8Hol²	Fit To Lead	LB	3 117	3	3	2hd	22	26	11	1hd	Delahoussaye E	4.20
29May93 8Hol⁵	Swazi's Moment	B	3 115	5	4	410	48	32½	3hd	2hd	Stevens G L	5.00
5Jun93 8Hol⁵	Passing Vice	LB	3 119	4	5	5	5	5	425	38	Desormeaux K J	15.30
30Apr93 9CD²	Eliza	LB	3 119	1	1	11	11½	12	23½	431	Valenzuela P A	0.30
29May93 8Hol⁸	Zoonaqua	LB	3 119	2	2	33½	34	42	5	5	McCarron C J	19.10

OFF AT 5:19 Start Good. Won driving. Time, :22³, :45², 1:09², 1:35⁴, 1:42² Track fast.

$2 Mutuel Prices:	3-FIT TO LEAD	10.40	4.60	30.40
	5-SWAZI'S MOMENT		5.20	31.80
	4-PASSING VICE			51.40

$2 EXACTA 3-5 PAID $44.40

Dk. b. or br. f, (May), by Fit to Fight-Islands, by Forli. Trainer Mandella Richard. Bred by Laura Leigh Stable (Ky).

FIT TO LEAD, near the early pace, responded on the far turn when asked to go after the leading ELIZA, was under steady left handed pressure all the way down the stretch, took the lead approaching the furlong marker, drew well clear between calls nearing the sixteenth marker, then held on to narrowly prevail. SWAZI'S MOMENT, outrun early, propped to break stride approaching the half mile pole, closed strongly in the stretch but could not quite get up. PASSING VICE lagged far back early, raced along the inner rail through the final quarter, also closed strongly in the stretch but also could not quite get up. ELIZA, away alertly, established the early pace, was keen to go on around the clubhouse turn, could not pull away FIT TO LEAD on the far turn, relinquished the lead to that opponent approaching the furlong marker and faltered in the final furlong. ZOONAQUA, near the early pace, stopped badly, lost contact aftear going six furlongs, entered the stretch four wide and was not perseveres with in the stretch when hopelessly beaten.

Owners— 1, Colbert & Hubbard & Sczesny; 2, Gordy Berry; 3, Iron County Farms Inc; 4, Paulson Allen E; 5, Moss Mr & Mrs J S

Trainers— 1, Mandella Richard; 2, Rash Rodney; 3, Lewis Craig A; 4, Hassinger Alex L Jr; 5, Mayberry Brian A

$3 Triple 4-2-3 Paid $2,980.20 Triple Pool $119,333.00

The Mysterious Plunger, the phantom of the racetrack, had risked a cool $100,000 on Eliza to show. Look at those show prices!

I cursed my two-week recess.

Had I been present, and paying attention, no small point, I would have bet $200 to show on Fit To Lead, the winner. When Eliza ran out, and to recall, she was primed for an upending, I could have strolled majestically to the window and collected a $3,040 windfall.

Handicappers might pause to reflect on the matter. Anytime someone wants six figures on a champion, or would-be champion, to show, handicappers should leap at the chance to back the likeliest alternative to show. Horses make mistakes, jockeys make mistakes, trouble occurs, and at times good horses choose not to run. Horse racing is a game having a sizable error factor. In a season seemingly prone to the phenomenon, Eliza would not be the last 1–20 shot to disrupt the best-laid plans of southern California's mysterious show plungers.

The next weekend, back in action, I noticed one of my Horses To Watch entered in the closing-day feature at Golden Gate Fields. An open stakes, the Golden Gate Fields Budweiser Breeders' Cup Stakes, nine furlongs, for 3UP, purse of $150,000-added, would be loaded with older horses that had not managed to win a graded or listed stakes on dirt, including my good thing. That is, with one highly notable exception.

The exception looked like this:

Desert Sun looked like this:

Maybe I would be squandering a key bet on an outclassed five-year-old? But I could not resist Desert Sun's race of April 29, the fastest 7½ furlongs ever at Hollywood Park! Coming from New York to San Francisco with an excusable trip, Desert Sun also boasted Bobby Frankel in his corner.

Casual Lies had finished second in the 1992 Kentucky Derby, third in that year's Preakness, and had been northern California's Horse of the Year in 1992 by unanimous acclaim. He also had won at Golden Gate and was absolutely the best horse in the field.

Yet Casual Lies had not raced in seven months, was training at the Pleasanton Fairgrounds (home base), and might not have been aimed dead-eye at today's open stakes. I habitually plot to defeat impressive graded stakes types 4UP following long layoffs when entered at levels below their customary class. Provided, of course, I have formed an opinion worth pursuing.

When the wagering in southern California on Casual Lies proved excessively light (9–2), I buttressed a key bet to win with exacta boxes coupling the class of the field and my Horse To Watch. Not for the first time in 1993, the protection returned my investment.

Desert Sun ran his best, but settled for second. He was well beaten by Casual Lies. A companion straightened me up on the outcome by observing, "class tells." No apologies. I'll take the bet repeatedly. The percentages and probabilities will sustain me in the end.

That night, not to my surprise, a handicapping friend of northern California called to advise me he had had the foresight to back Casual Lies, not in northern California, where he went favored at 2–1, but in southern California, where he was a "remarkable overlay" at 9–2. Good play!

If June was slipping away, I was glad to give the month a shove. Between the Belmont Stakes on the first Saturday and the Golden Gate stakes on the last, June became my month of mishaps. The stakes ledger revealed a glaring loss.

Nonetheless, I found myself eager for an all-out assault on the Fourth of July weekend, one of the busiest added-money agendas on the national calendar.

SUMMER

JULY

No less than eighteen stakes pull the country's racetracks into the heat of summer. Seven are either Grade 1 or Grade 2. I liked two of the most traditional as key bets, the Hollywood Gold Cup (Gr. 1) at Hollywood Park and the Dwyer (Gr. 2) at Belmont Park.

Both were scheduled as legs of an innovation called the Summer Stakes Festival, a July 3rd triple-header at three tracks that also included the Molly Pitcher (Gr. 2) at Monmouth Park. Central to a ninety-minute ESPN telecast of the triple-header would be a national Pick-3 pool. I anticipated the wager, my favorite, avidly, but, alas, it was rescinded within forty-eight hours of show time when, officials claimed, state-by-state regulations could not be reconciled.

In the ten-furlong Hollywood Gold Cup, Hollywood Park's signature race, Best Pal won, and Bertrando finished second.

The less related about my key bet, Latin American, the better.

At his favorite distance, Best Pal finally delivered. The speed figure was legitimate at 117. Do not be fooled. The jaded champions and post division leaders do explode, but once in a while only. I immediately relegated Best Pal to the Horses To Beat category.

A more intriguing aspect of the Gold Cup was Bertrando's second. Bertrando set fast fractions (surprise, surprise!), dug in tenaciously when Best Pal came alongside, was beaten a mere length, and finished seven lengths in front of the third horse.

Precedents abound. Four-year-olds (and 3YOs) that cannot manage a mile and one-quarter at first try often can do it later. Maturity and seasoning at the distance play complementary roles. A few seasons ago, the good import In Excess spit it out badly at ten furlongs twice during winter at Santa Anita. That fall he slaughtered the Suburban and Woodward Stakes (Gr. 1s) at Belmont Park and promptly was nominated as a Horse of the Year candidate.

The unanimous juvenile champion Chief's Crown labored noticeably in the stretch at Churchill Downs while barely holding the show in the Kentucky Derby. Later he won the Travers Stakes nicely.

So handicappers must stay on alert when good horses act as if they might continue the pattern, as with Bertrando in the second half of 1993. There is a catch: inauthentic at the distance, they get the mile and one-quarter, but in a labored, unconvincing style. A comparably talented and authentic distance runner can pass them easily.

In the Dwyer at Belmont Park, at last I found the appropriate spot for the improving 3YO Cherokee Run, a Horse To Watch. He led a dubious five-horse field, with only Miner's Mark deserving a long look.

Which 3YO do handicappers prefer?

Miner's Mark went favored in this spot. If both colts retain fine form, Cherokee Run warrants the play. If his efforts in the Preakness and Belmont Stakes did not dull his edge, Cherokee Run should outrun Miner's Mark, maybe handily, and he did.

The margin was six lengths. Not many handicappers were napping here. Cherokee Run paid $5.40.

In the Molly Pitcher, to complete the fictional triple, three fillies and mares proved inseparable, on figures, class, form, and the rest. I gave the edge to the 4YO You'd Be Surprised. The odds near post looked like this:

Quilma	6–5
You'd Be Surprised	5–2
Wilderness Song	5–1

In contentious stakes, the textbook says to take the overlay. I did. Wilderness Song came shining through, winning off.

She got an assist. You'd Be Surprised stumbled badly at the start, and was running rank into the clubhouse turn and into the backstretch. She then launched a sweeping move while five wide around the far turn, before tiring. She finished fifth of seven. I excused the race and placed You'd Be Surprised on the Horses To Watch list, a trip playback.

I had set my sights on five additional stakes during the Fourth of July weekend. Four of the bets were sent to Las Vegas, with instructions to parlay the profits from any of three earlier winners to Toussad in the American Handicap (Gr. 2) at Hollywood Park. The Suburban Handicap at Belmont Park was simulcast extensively, and a key bet on Devil His Due was sent to Philadelphia Park.

I set a 5–2 line on each horse. All five horses won. On all fronts I experienced the modern handicapper's predicament. None of the winners paid 5–2. To wit:

Suburban Handicap (Gr. 1)	Devil His Due	$5.60
Arlington Classic (Gr. 2)	Boundlessly	3.60
American Handicap (Gr. 2)	Toussad	4.60
Prioress Stakes (Gr. 2)	Classy Mirage	3.80
Firecracker (Open)	Cleone	3.80

The long weekend concluded with a five-and-a-half-furlong dash on the Hollywood Park grass, and a fair bet. Examine the 1–2 favorite, and the mare I much preferred:

Hollywood Park

8 *5½ Furlongs.* (Turf). (1:01) 10th Running of THE VALKYR HANDICAP. Purse $100,000 Added. Fillies and Mares 3-year-olds and upward. By subscription of $100 each which shall accompany the nomination, $1,000 additional to start with $100,000 added, of which $20,000 to second, $15,000 to third, $7,500 to fourth and $2,500 to fifth. Weights Wednesday, June 30. Starters to be named through the entry box by closing...

Knight Prospector
Own: Gaswirth & Mirage Stable
DESORMEAUX K J (263 66 63 32 .25)
B. f. 4
Sire: Native Prospector (Mr. Prospector)
Dam: Knights Crozier (Knights Choice)
Br: Marikian Charles (Cal)
Tr: Lewis Craig A (70 14 10 9 .20)
L 121
Lifetime Record: 12 7
1993 3 3 0 0 $77,850 Turf
1992 7 4 0 1 $70,750 Wet
Hol Ⓣ 1 0 0 0 Dist

11Jun93-7Hol fst 5½f :214 :441 :56 1:021 3↑ Porterhouse 55k 113 5 1 11½ 11½ 11½ 13½ Desormeaux K J LB 114 *.90 101-09 Knight Prospector1143½ Anjiz1161½ Cardmania1
15May93-7Hol fst 6f :212 :434 :554 1:082 ⒻAlw 45000N3X 107 2 1 12 13 13 13½ Desormeaux K J LB 117 *.30 98-09 Knight Prospector1173½ Garden Gal1161 Forest
28Apr93-7Hol fst 6f :213 :44 :56 1:083 3↑ ⒻAlw 39000N2X 104 1 1 13½ 16 15 14 Pincay L Jr LB 117 *1.20 97-09 Knight Prospector1174 Priceless Picture1162¾
5Aug92-8Dmr fst 7f :214 :442 1:092 1:221 ⒻⓈFleet Trt 62k 75 5 1 1½ 12 21½ 39 Pedroza M A LB 114 *1.00 80-10 BlondeFever1162 ForstHvn1167 KnightProspct
1Jly92-8Hol fst 6½f :212 :433 1:083 1:151 3↑ ⒻAlw 32000 97 3 1 11 12½ 14 13½ Pedroza M A LB 113 *.50 96-09 Knight Prospector1133½ Second Stop1167 Gold
17Jun92-5Hol fst 6f :212 :44 :554 1:082 ⒻClm 50000 102 2 3 1½ 13 15 14½ Pedroza M A LB 119 *1.10e 98-08 KnightProspector1194½ AngelOfVengeance116
25May92-2Hol fst 6f :22 :443 :564 1:093 ⒻClm 50000 90 4 1 12 15 13 14½ Desormeaux K J LB 116 *1.50 92-09 Knight Prospector1164½ Sharply1165½ Sand Dar
Lugged out early, drifted out 1/4, handily
15May92-5Hol fm 1 1/16 Ⓣ :224 :47 1:11 1:412 ⒻAlw 34000 67 8 3 31½ 3½ 76 89¼ Pedroza M A LB 115 17.10 79-08 Red Bandana119no Terre Haute117¾ Onesta119
22Mar92-4SA my 6½f :213 :443 1:093 1:161 ⒻⓈBoo La Boo 51k 76 3 3 11½ 1hd 33 511 Pedroza M A LB 115 3.60e 78-16 Wicked Wit122½ Mother Bear1157 Galore's Mag
11Mar92-6SA fst 6½f :214 :444 1:094 1:164 ⒻⓈMd 32000 75 10 1 13 16 110 16 Pedroza M A LB 117 6.60 86-16 KnightProspector1176 FriendlyHelen1173 Truly
WORKOUTS: ●Jun 29 SA 4f fst :47 H 1/32 Jun 22 SA 4f fst :481 H 16/45 ●Jun 19 SA 3f fst :35 H 1/23 ●Jun 7 SA 4f sl :481 H 1/39 Jun 1 SA 4f fst :48 H 3/30 May 23 SA 4f fst :483 H 13

Bel's Starlet
Own: Golden Eagle Farm
STEVENS G L (154 35 23 18 .23)
Ro. m. 6
Sire: Bel Bolide (Bold Bidder)
Dam: Vigor's Star (Vigors)
Br: Mabee Mr-Mrs John C (Cal)
Tr: Mandella Richard (82 14 16 14 .17)
L 122
Lifetime Record: 27 10
1993 6 1 3 1 $92,580 Turf
1992 8 4 1 0 $214,825 Wet
Hol Ⓣ 11 3 3 1 $187,887 Dist

30May93-8Hol fm 1⅛ Ⓣ :463 1:094 1:33 1:45 3↑ ⒻGamely H-G1 103 6 1 11½ 1½ 11½ 32 Stevens G L LB 116 5.50 97-02 Toussaud1161 Gold Fleece1141 Bel's Starlet116
9May93-4Hol fm 1 1/16 Ⓣ :232 :464 1:094 1:391 ⒻAlw 55000N$mY 105 1 1 1½ 1½ 12 12 Stevens G L LB 114 *1.40e 100-04 Bel's Starlet1142 Heart Of Joy1143 Terre Haute
23Apr93-3Hol fm 1 Ⓣ :241 :48 1:114 1:342 ⒻAlw 55000N$mY 99 4 2 21 2½ 2½ 2no Stevens G L LB 116 2.20 93-06 Sacque116no Bel's Starlet1162½ Elegance116¾
21Mar93-5SA fm *6½f Ⓣ :214 :442 1:072 1:133 ⒻⓈShywing H 50k 94 2 8 43½ 21½ 2½ 2¾ Desormeaux K J LB 124 *.80 88-10 Bold Windy1152¾ Bel's Starlet1243 Charm A Gee
7Mar93-7SA fm *6½f Ⓣ :212 :434 1:063 1:123 ⒻB Thtful 50k 87 6 10 109¾ 85¾ 55 47¼ Delahoussaye E LB 124 *.70e 88-08 HertOfJoy1212 WorldlyPossession1161¾ Certm
3Feb93-8SA fm *6½f Ⓣ :212 :432 1:063 1:124 ⒻMonrovia H-G3 101 6 6 76½ 54 21½ 21 Delahoussaye E LB 122 *.60 93-06 Glen Kate1181 Bel's Starlet1222¾ Heart Of Joy11
27Nov92-8Hol fm 5½f Ⓣ :214 :442 :554 1:02 3↑ Hol Tf Ex H 200k 88 11 3 106 106½ 97½ 95½ alvarado F T LB 119 10.40 90-05 Answer Do121no Repriced118no Gundaghia1171
7Nov92-4SA fm *6½f Ⓣ :212 :434 1:071 1:132 3↑ ⒻⓈCa Cp Dstf 100k 100 11 1 73¾ 62¾ 2hd 13½ Desormeaux K J LB 124 *.60 92-08 Bel's Starlet1243½ Another Natalie116 Forest H
Clipped heels 1/4, steadied 3/16
7Oct92-8SA fm *6½f Ⓣ :212 :423 1:052 1:113 ⒻAutmn Dys H 83k 100 8 1 42 23 1hd 1nk Desormeaux K J LB 120 *1.80 101 — Bel's Starlet120nk Glen Kate-Ir1171½ Brisa De
6Aug92-8Dmr fst 7f :22 :45 1:092 1:214 3↑ ⒻFantstic G H 62k 90 8 1 73½ 51¼ 3½ 53 Desormeaux K J LB 119 *1.50e 88-12 Bountiful Native116hd Mama Simba1171¼ Nicee
Steadied, boxed in 1/4
WORKOUTS: Jun 28 Hol 4f fst :48 H 10/35 ●Jun 20 Hol 3f fst :341 H 1/28 May 24 Hol 4f fst :49 H 26/51 May 7 Hol 3f fst :39 H 22/22 May 2 Hol 3f fst :394 B 28/28 ●Apr 16 SA 6f fst 1:11

So often a false dichotomy, here, at a glance, Knight Prospector is the speed and Bel's Starlet is the class. The last lines of each qualify as polar extremes, Knight Prospector earning a Beyer Speed Figure of 113 in an overnight sprint handicap, Bel's Starlet finishing close in a Grade 1 grass route. How to reconcile?

In open stakes, as in the Valkyr, either advantage can tell. Price can make the difference, and so can a bit more handicapping. I preferred Bel's Starlet strongly. Not only has Knight Prospector run poorly on grass, but she might be pressed early by other fillies. If Knight Prospector weakens, she becomes an easy target for Bel's Starlet.

The clincher is Bel Starlet's pace figure in the Grade 1 stakes. It is high enough to defeat Knight Prospector in a sprint on the square. Bel's Starlet relishes short races on the grass and she approaches this dash in peaking form. As a nonfavorite, she's irresistible.

Knight Prospector ran poorly here, never getting the front and bearing out badly on the far turn. She apparently does not feel secure on the lawn, a possibility the bettors who took 1–2 did not entertain very seriously.

Bel's Starlet lagged for the first quarter-mile, but quickly caught the jet stream on the far turn, burst through in between horses into the upper stretch, and sailed home uncontested. The payoff was a mere 2–1, but a fair line in a small field really reduced to a two-horse race. In two-horse toss-ups handicappers should take the higher odds—always.

Flat bets of $200 on four stakes over the weekend resulted in three winners and a net profit of $1580. I regretted missing the five underlays that won. I regretted missing the national Pick-3. It might have been a sensational July Fourth.

A July weekend in Phoenix and Prescott, Arizona, might have remained unremarkable, except for the simulcasting opportunity that came to pass.

I had arrived with Lawrence Lopes, marketing director for *Today's Racing Digest,* the impressive high-quality daily publication of handicapping data in southern California for two decades. The *Digest* had begun branching out to simulcast markets taking southern California races and Lopes had recruited me to assist in the effort.

Turf Paradise, in Phoenix, and Prescott Downs, in Prescott, were taking partial cards from Hollywood Park, eight races on weekdays and four races on weekends. What I did not know was the Phoenix tracks did not commingle, but depended upon local pools. On Saturday, at Prescott Downs, the pools proved to be inescapably small. Local favorites became odds-on favorites. And so it was with the Hollywood Park simulcasts. Favorites and low-priced contenders at Hollywood Park would be seriously overbet in Arizona. Kent Desormeaux's mounts were knocked down for the count automatically.

At Prescott Downs and Turf Paradise, the track monitors alternated displaying the odds at Hollywood Park and the odds at the local track. Phoenix and Prescott handicappers knew exactly how southern California bettors were betting. In consequence, the respective pools looked remarkably similar.

The best chance, the only chance, would be a false favorite at Hollywood Park that would be excessively overbet in Phoenix. The imbalance would create a corresponding overlay in Phoenix.

Nothing exciting happened on Saturday.

On Sunday, the feature at Hollywood Park was the Grade 1 Hollywood Oaks, limited to 3YO fillies. Champion Eliza had been sidelined. The second-ranking 3YO filly of southern California was Likeable Style, a member of my Horses To Beat list. A Grade 1 winner and multiple graded-stakes winner not nearly as talented as Eliza, Likeable Style showed par speed figures and below-par pace figures.

On first click at Turf Paradise, Likeable Style was 1–9. Anything else handicappers preferred was a giant overlay.

By happy coincidence, the Hollywood Oaks qualified as a fascinating handicapping puzzle. Speed handicappers and pace analysts would be parting company. Three fillies were exiting the Grade 2 Princess Stakes at Hollywood Park where Eliza had faltered badly, running out, and the three had finished a neck apart. Unknown to many speed handicappers, one of the three actually stood out in comparison with the other two.

Examine the past performances for the three contenders, paying closest attention to the last running line of each:

Fit To Lead
Own: Colbert & Hubbard & Sczesny
MCCARRON C J (194 29 39 34 .15)

Dk. b or br f. 3 (May)
Sire: Fit to Fight (Chieftain)
Dam: Islands (Forli)
Br: Laura Leigh Stable (Ky)
Tr: Mandella Richard (88 17 16 15 .19)

L 121

Lifetime Record:					
1993	5	2	2	1	$169,790
1992	7	2	2	0	$65,625
Hol	5	2	2	0	$110,350

19Jun93- 8Hol fst 1 1/16 :223 :452 1:092 1:422 ⒻPrincess-G2 92 3 2 21¼ 22 11 1hd Delahoussaye E LB 117 4.20 89-11 Fit To Lead117hd Swazi's Moment115hd F
29May93- 8Hol fst 7f :214 :442 1:091 1:222 ⒻRailbird-G2 93 1 5 21 31 21 2hd Nakatani C S LB 121 6.90 92-12 Afto114hd Fit To Lead121hd Nijivision113
Brushed late, gamely
4Apr93- 8Kee fst 7f :222 :444 1:101 1:262 ⒻBeaumont-G2 85 1 10 22 31 33 36 Day P L 122 3.80 71-11 RoaminRchel1223 AddedAsset1143 FitT
31Jan93- 8SA fst 7f :222 :444 1:092 1:222 ⒻSanta Ynez-G2 93 4 5 3½ 2hd 11½ 15½ Nakatani C S LB 116 8.60 91-12 Fit To Lead1165½ Nijivision114nk Booklo
22Jan93- 8SA gd 1 1/16 :234 :474 1:13 1:443 ⒻS Ysabela 75k 88 3 1 11½ 11 2hd 22 Nakatani C S LB 117 8.00 79-19 Likeable Style1152 Fit To Lead1176 Ama
19Dec92- 7Hol fst 1 1/16 :24 :481 1:123 1:433 ⒻHol Starlet-G1 63 3 4 41¼ 42½ 45 711¾ Black C A LB 120 49.20 71-17 CreakingBoard1208 PssingVice120hd M
11Nov92- 8Hol fst 7f :22 :444 1:094 1:224 ⒻMoccsn B C 102k 70 3 4 2½ 2hd 1hd 2nk Valenzuela P A LB 118 9.80 90-09 Blue Moonlight121nk Fit To Lead118hd
30Sep92-11Fpx fst 1 1/16 :223 :463 1:122 1:444 ⒻBlk Swan 35k 69 8 3 41½ 53¼ 66¾ 69¾ Sorenson D LB 116 3.70 74-19 Madame l'Enjoleur113¾ Baja Belle1136
23Sep92-12Fpx fst 6½f :212 :452 1:111 1:181 ⒻⓇBarrts Deb 110k 64 8 7 3½ 2½ 22½ 21½ Nakatani C S LB 115 3.10 83-14 Blue Moonlight1151½ Fit To Lead115 T
28Aug92- 8Dmr fst 7f :221 :452 1:101 1:223 Balboa-G3 47 6 2 11 2½ 56½ 617¾ Nakatani C S B 119 23.10 69-13 Devil Diamond1175 Wheeler Oil1191¼ C
WORKOUTS: Jly 5 Hol 3f fst :36 B 6/33 ●Jun 13 Hol 6f fst 1:113 H 1/17 May 26 Hol 4f fst :482 H 16/42 ●May 19 Hol 7f fst 1:253 H 1/7 May 13 Hol 5f fst :592 H 2/36 May 6 Hol 4f

Passing Vice
Own: Iron County Farms Inc
DESORMEAUX K J (295 76 65 34 .26)

B. f. 3 (Mar)
Sire: Vice Regent (Northern Dancer)
Dam: Passing Look (Buckpasser)
Br: North Ridge Farm (Ky)
Tr: Lewis Craig A (78 15 10 9 .19)

L 121

Lifetime Record:					
1993	6	1	0	1	$75,000
1992	9	2	3	0	$107,350
Hol	8	1	2	1	$103,650

19Jun93- 8Hol fst 1 1/16 :223 :452 1:092 1:422 ⒻPrincess-G2 92 4 5 515 512 44½ 3nk Desormeaux K J LB 119 15.30 89-11 Fit To Lead117hd Swazi's Moment115hd P
5Jun93- 8Hol my 1 1/16 ⊗ :243 :491 1:141 1:461 ⒻHoneymoon H-G3 84 5 4 42½ 31 43½ 56½ Flores D R LB 116 9.20 63-32 Likeable Style1221¼ Adorydar1141¾ Vinist
Wide, brushed 1/2, brushed late
15May93- 8Hol fm 1 Ⓣ :233 :463 1:101 1:342 ⒻSenorita B CG3 89 5 7 77¼ 76¾ 76¼ 54¼ Flores D R LB 121 65.20 89-09 Likeable Style1211 Adorydar113½ Icy War
7Mar93- 8SA fst 1 1/16 :23 :471 1:11 1:424 ⒻS A Oaks-G1 77 2 4 42 46½ 812 712½ Pedroza M A LB 117 108.30 77-14 Eliza1172¼ Stalcreek1171 Dance For Vann
13Feb93- 8SA fst 1 :224 :463 1:104 1:363 ⒻLs Virgenes-G1 68 4 4 42¾ 55¼ 67¾ 612¾ Flores D R LB 119 13.90 74-15 Likeable Style1173 Incindress1171½ Blue
16Jan93- 8BM sly 1 1/16 :224 :462 1:112 1:441 ⒻB Mdws Oaks-G3 80 1 1 1½ 11½ 11½ 14 Flores D R LB 116 2.90 82-19 PssingVice1164 MdmeL'enjoleur1165 Enc
19Dec92- 7Hol fst 1 1/16 :24 :481 1:123 1:433 ⒻHol Starlet-G1 69 1 6 74¼ 75¼ 55¼ 28 Stevens G L LB 120 7.20 75-17 CreakingBoard1208 PssingVice120hd Mdn
29Nov92- 5Hol fst 1 1/16 :23 :462 1:113 1:44 ⒻAlw 33000N1X 79 6 6 68 54¼ 2hd 17 Delahoussaye E LB 119 *1.70 81-17 Passing Vice1197 Silky Sand Sammy116nc
11Nov92- 8Hol fst 7f :22 :444 1:094 1:224 ⒻMoccsn B C 102k 67 5 7 65¾ 64¾ 53¼ 41¾ Flores D R LB 113 3.60 88-09 Blue Moonlight121nk Fit To Lead118hd Ni
17Oct92- 3SA fst 1 :22 :453 1:111 1:371 ⒻMd Sp Wt 74 6 7 66½ 31½ 2½ 12 Flores D R LB 116 5.70 81-12 Passing Vice1162 Anzali11610 Minidar116
WORKOUTS: Jly 7 SA 5f fst 1:024 H 25/40 Jun 30 SA 4f fst :491 H 26/39 Jun 13 SA 4f fst :484 H 15/40 May 31 SA 5f fst 1:003 H 4/38 May 25 SA 5f fst 1:01 H 13/45 ●May 8 SA 7f fst

The Beyer Speed Figures of June 19 for the three are the same, a 92. So which stands out?

It's Fit To Lead, and the situation is crucial to grasp. Notice the beaten-lengths at the pace call (circled) for each. Notice the fractional times. Now which filly looks best?

Swazi's Moment and Passing Vice lagged behind the blistering pace that Fit To Lead stalked. The trio finished a neck apart, with Fit To Lead winning. Fit To Lead had run a marvelous race. The others had picked up a collapsing pace. A juxtaposition of the speed and pace figures crystallizes the situation:

	BEYER SPEED	QUIRIN SPEED AND PACE	
Swazi's Moment	92	110	105
Fit To Lead	92	116	105
Passing Vice	92	106	105

A pace analysis favors Fit To Lead unmistakably, and handicappers are urged to agree. Any horse that has pressed or stalked a sprinter's pace at a middle distance and has finished well deserves more credit than do closers that have simply picked up the same rapid pace. When 3YOs perform the feat, double the extra credit. Go to the pressers and stalkers, not the closers.

As for Likeable Style, odds-on throughout the wagering at Turf Paradise, she deserved to be favored perhaps, but not by a landslide. The record tells a complicated tale:

Likeable Style had won every race she contested, except one, where she started poorly, but without once exceeding par for the class. Her pace figures tended to be ordinary and the last, in the mud, was desperately slow:

	PACE	SPEED
Par 105	92	105

A "double-fig" on Beyer Speed, with a two-length advantage at best, Likeable Style might have been favored here justifiably, but odds-on? Nearing post, at Turf Paradise, Fit To Lead was 13–1 against Likeable Style and the others. With gusto, I took a key bet to win and boxed Fit To Lead in exactas with the closers exiting the Grade 2 Princess Stakes. The exacta payoffs were projected as huge, upwards of 150-1.

Events proceeded as if they were scripted. Fit To Lead grabbed a lonesome lead and rated smoothly. The fractions were a full second slower than those on the day Fit To Lead chased Eliza. When Likeable Style failed to threaten around the far turn, Fit To Lead appeared to be home free. From the pilot's position, jockey Chris McCarron was glancing back confidently. I began to estimate the profits.

But Fit To Lead did not make it safely. She was beaten in a long hard stretch drive by the outsider that had stalked her all the way, a shipper recently sent to Neil Drysdale from Florida named Hollywood Wildcat. The outcome annoyed me terrifically at the time and my irritation deepened the day after.

First, check out Hollywood Wildcat's past performances:

A Grade 3 and four-time winner (five starts) as a juvenile, as a 3YO Hollywood Wildcat had blanked in four attempts. Her Beyer Speed Figures were not competitive. She had not worked out in more than three weeks. Drysdale, a formidable horseman, had had the filly for less than two weeks and was quoted as aiming Hollywood Wildcat at the Del Mar grass stakes. She was 16–1 at Hollywood Park. Here is the result chart:

EIGHTH RACE
Hollywood
JULY 11, 1993

1⅛ MILES. (1.46⁴) 48th Running of THE HOLLYWOOD OAKS. Grade I. Purse $200,000 Added. Fillies 3-year-olds. By subscription of $200 each which shall accompany the nomination, $2,000 additional to start, with $200,000 added, of which $40,000 to second, $30,000 to third, $15,000 to fourth and $5,000 to fifth. Weight,121 lbs. Starters to be named through the entry box by closing time of entries. Hollywood Park reserves the right not to divide this race. Should this race not be divided and the number of entries exceed the starting gate capacity, preference will be given to those horses with the highest total earnings in 1993 and an also eligible list will be drawn. Failure to draw into this race at scratch time cancels all fees. A trophy will be presented to the winning Owner, Trainer and Jockey. Closed Wednesday, June 30 with 12 nominations.

Value of Race: $220,400 Winner $130,400; second $40,000; third $30,000; fourth $15,000; fifth $5,000. Mutuel Pool $347,249.00 Exacta Pool $308,725.00 Trifecta Pool $228,186.00

Last Raced	Horse	M/Eqt. A.Wt	PP	St	¼	½	¾	Str	Fin	Jockey	Odds $1
19Jun93 9Crc3	Hollywood Wildcat	LB	3 121	4	4	2^1	2^1	2^2	1^{hd}	$11\frac{3}{4}$	Delahoussaye E	16.60
19Jun93 8Hol1	Fit To Lead	LB	3 121	3	1	1^1	1^1	$1\frac{1}{2}$	2^5	$26\frac{1}{2}$	McCarron C J	8.30
5Jun93 8Hol2	Adorydar	B	3 121	9	2	$5\frac{1}{2}$	4^1	$3\frac{1}{2}$	$31\frac{1}{2}$	3no	Almeida G F	5.80
19Jun93 8Hol3	Passing Vice	LB	3 121	8	5	9	$7\frac{1}{2}$	5^1	4^{hd}	$4\frac{1}{2}$	Desormeaux K J	6.90
5Jun93 8Hol1	Likeable Style	LB	3 121	2	7	$62\frac{1}{2}$	5^{hd}	7^3	5^{hd}	$52\frac{1}{4}$	Stevens G L	0.70
20Jun93 9CD2	Added Asset		3 121	6	3	$32\frac{1}{4}$	3^2	$41\frac{1}{2}$	6^2	$61\frac{3}{4}$	Valenzuela P A	28.40
19Jun93 8Hol2	Swazi's Moment	B	3 121	1	8	4^{hd}	6^1	6^{hd}	7^5	$75\frac{1}{2}$	Nakatani C S	7.50
5Jun93 8Hol4	Nortena	LBb	3 121	7	6	$71\frac{1}{2}$	9	9	$83\frac{1}{2}$	8^{13}	Flores D R	66.40
1Jly93 1Hol3	Fondly Remembered	LBb	3 121	5	9	8^1	8^{hd}	8^{hd}	9	9	Pincay L Jr	63.60

OFF AT 5:22 Start Good. Won driving. Time, :22⁴, :46², 1:10³, 1:35³, 1:48² Track fast.

$2 Mutuel Prices:
4–HOLLYWOOD WILDCAT	35.20	12.40	6.40
3–FIT TO LEAD		8.60	4.80
9–ADORYDAR			4.40

$2 EXACTA 4–3 PAID $305.20 $2 TRIFECTA 4–3–9 PAID $2,171.00

Dk. b. or br. f, (Feb), by Kris S–Miss Wildcatter, by Mr Prospector. Trainer Drysdale Neil. Bred by Cowan Irving & Marjorie (Fla).

HOLLYWOOD WILDCAT, away in good fashion, sat just off FIT TO LEAD through the early stages while that opoonent established the pace, engaged for the lead approaching the quarter pole, was not asked in earnest until inside the final furlong and drew clear in the last sixteenth under right handed pressure. FIT TO LEAD went to the front at once, established the pace through the early stages while going easily, resisted stubbornly after being taken on by HOLLYWOOD WILDCAT approaching the quarter pole to battle for command with that rival to the sixteenth marker, could not match that rival's response in the final sixteenth but was well in front of the others at the end. ADORYDAR, in contention early, got closer nearing the three-eighths pole, did not have the needed punch in the drive but eked out the show. PASSING VICE, last early, made a steady move down the backstretch while wide, entered the stretch five wide and lacked the necessary response in the drive. LIKEABLE STYLE, patiently handled while being outrun early but not far back, failed to accelerate on the far turn when put to a drive and did not threaten in the stretch. ADDED ASSET, close up early, faltered. SWAZI'S MOMENT, also outrun early but not far back, did not have the needed response in the final quarter. NORTENA was four wide into the stretch. FONDLY REMEMBERED had no apparent mishap.

THE DETESTABLE POSTSCRIPT "I hadn't intended to enter the filly," Drysdale told the *Los Angeles Times* after the race. "But that sharp six-furlong workout last week changed my mind."

What "sharp" six-furlong workout?

A Grade 1 filly in a leading stable is a new face training for a Grade 1 race, and an impressive workout *at six furlongs* is missed by all concerned. As Hollywood Wildcat's past performances reveal, the *Daily Racing Form* did not publish the workout. Private clockers missed it too.

I favor Drysdale in stakes races, especially in Grade 1 circumstances, and definitely would have protected a key bet to win on Fit To Lead with Hollywood Wildcat in exacta combinations if her "sharp" six-furlong workout had been recorded and published. The odds would not have been 16–1, but they would have been generous. As it were, with Fit To Lead on the underside, the $2 exacta at Hollywood Park paid $305.20. I put this Grade 1 on the Races To Hate list.

Days later, southern California steward Pete Pederson apologized in the *Los Angeles Times* to the betting public for the omission. Pederson observed that racing's information systems "are not perfect." Thank you very much.

Literally, for months (six) I had been wanting to wager against the champion mare Paseana, a 6YO of 1993, especially since she had ruined my best bet of Breeders' Cup Day in 1992.

My biggest swing that day had been on Versailles Treaty in the Distaff. Paseana had dropped two in a row before the Distaff and had looked hapless chasing the unexceptional Fowda in the Spinster (Gr. 1) at Keeneland. Her numbers had declined in 1992, and they had continued to decline in 1993.

Unsentimental handicappers must be prepared at all times to take a stand against past champions that have passed a peak. As long as handicappers remain careful, not reckless, substantial money can be won. Best opportunities find the stars dimming at the same time a member of the deserving opposition is reaching a top. The class and form interplay favors the underdog. It's convenient too when circumstances conspire against the former champs.

A perfect illustration was the Vanity Handicap (Gr. 1) at Hollywood Park in 1993, in which Paseana would be 4–5 on the morning line and 3–5 at post time. Examine the records of the champ and her 7–2 opponent:

Re Toss (Arg)
Own: Risdon Arthur G & Larry G
DELAHOUSSAYE E (330 58 52 54 .18)

B. m. 6
Sire: Egg Toss (Buckpasser)
Dam: Rezagante (Practicante)
Br: Haras Don Jacinto (Arg)
Tr: Moreno Henry (25 2 2 3 .08)

L 114

Lifetime Record: 33
1993 5 1 0 1 $72,1
1992 12 1 3 4 $236,800
Hol 6 0 2 3 $140,000

12Jun93-8Hol fst 1 1/16 :23 :46 1:094 1:413 3+ (F)Milady H-G1 105 6 7 710 75¼ 33 31 Delahoussaye E LB 116 8.80 92-13 Paseana125½ Bold Windy114½ Re Toss1165
Wide trip, drifted out late
23May93-8Hol fst 1 1/16 :222 :45 1:091 1:41 3+ (F)Hawthorne H-G2 97 7 10 1013 65½ 34½ 47¼ Lopez A D LB 115 7.90 89-08 Freedom Cry1176½ Vieille Vigne114nk Miss
6Feb93-8SA fst 1 1/16 :232 :472 1:104 1:411 (F)Snta Maria HG1 93 5 6 64½ 53 56 510½ Lopez A D LB 115 9.80 87-12 RaceTheWildWind1172¼ Psen1261¼ South
17Jan93-8SA sly 1⅛ ⊗ :481 1:124 1:381 1:511 (F)Sn Grgrno H-G2 87 4 4 32½ 42 55½ 510½ Lopez A D LB 116 *1.40 63-24 Southern Truce1146 Laura Ly1143 Lite Lig
1Jan93-5SA fst 1 :222 :46 1:094 1:35 (F)Run Roses 62k 98 5 7 75 41½ 3½ 11½ Lopez A D LB 114 6.30 95-10 Re Toss1141½ Exchange117¾ Lite Light1155
29Nov92-7Hol fm 1⅛ (T) :471 1:104 1:34 1:46 3+ (F)Matriarch-G1 100 5 9 97½ 74¼ 90 73 Lopez A D LB 123 47.90 89-07 Flawlessly1231 Super Staff1232 Kostromaa
15Nov92-8Hol fst 1 1/16 :222 :454 1:101 1:423 3+ (F)Slvr Blls H-G2 97 2 7 78 63¾ 32 2hd Lopez A D LB 115 6.20 88-17 Brought To Mind120hd Re Toss115 Interac
Slow early, wide stretch
18Oct92-8SA fm 1⅛ (T) :481 1:114 1:35 1:464 3+ (F)Ls Palmas H-G2 98 5 2 23 21½ 33 34¾ Nakatani C S LB 115 15.10 80-22 Super Staff116¾ Flawlessly1244 Re Toss-A
6Sep92-8Dmr fst 1 1/16 :231 :463 1:103 1:42 3+ (F)Chla Vsta H-G2 91 4 7 74¼ 72¾ 64½ 64½ Solis A LB 116 7.00 87-14 Exchange120¾ Fowda120nk Brought To M
15Aug92-8Dmr fm 1⅛ (T) :513 1:153 1:384 1:50 3+ (F)Ramona H-G1 90 6 3 2½ 2½ 22 23 Solis A LB 115 15.70 83-11 Flawlessly1233 Re Toss115 Polemic116
WORKOUTS: Jly 12 SA 7f fst 1:262 H 1/3 Jly 7 SA 5f fst :594 H 2/40 Jly 1 SA 6f fst 1:13 H 6/10 Jun 25 SA 5f fst 1:001 H 5/29 Jun 19 SA 4f fst :494 H 24/36 Jun 11 Hol 3f fst :364 B 11/1

Paseana (Arg)
Own: Craig Sidney H
MCCARRON C J (213 33 42 36 .15)

B. m. 6
Sire: Ahmad (Good Manners)
Dam: Pasiflin (Flintham)
Br: Haras Vacacion (Arg)
Tr: McAnally Ronald (136 18 24 21 .13)

L 126

Lifetime Record: 22
1993 4 2 2 0 $484,500
1992 9 7 1 0 $1,518,290
Hol 4 4 0 0 $416,400

12Jun93-8Hol fst 1 1/16 :23 :46 1:094 1:413 3+ (F)Milady H-G1 107 1 5 42 31 1hd 1½ McCarron C J LB 125 *.40 93-13 Paseana125½ Bold Windy114½ Re Toss1165
16Apr93-9OP fst 1 1/16 :23 :461 1:103 1:414 (F)Apple Blsm HG1 107 1 4 43 4¾ 12½ 13½ McCarron C J L 124 *.40 92-13 Paseana1243½ Looie Capote1154½ Luv Me
28Feb93-8SA fst 1⅛ :481 1:121 1:364 1:492 (F)S Margrta H-G1 100 2 2 3½ 1½ 1hd 2hd McCarron C J LB 125 *.40 83-17 Southern Truce115hd Paseana1251¾ Guiza
Rider dropped right rein briefly 1/8
6Feb93-8SA fst 1 1/16 :232 :472 1:104 1:411 (F)Snta Maria HG1 108 3 3 31½ 32 21 22¼ McCarron C J LB 126 *.70 96-12 RaceTheWildWind1172¼ Pasen1261¼ Sout
31Oct92-6GP fst 1⅛ :47 1:104 1:353 1:48 3+ (F)Br Cp Dstff-G1 105 14 4 3½ 1hd 13 14 McCarron C J L 123 2.70e 97-03 Paseana-Ar1234 VersaillesTrety123½ Mgi
11Oct92-8Kee fst 1⅛ :48 1:123 1:371 1:494 3+ (F)Spinster-G1 102 4 5 63 52 22 22¼ McCarron C J LB 123 *.30 84-25 Fowda1232¼ Paseana-Ar1236 Meadow Sta
30Aug92-4Dmr fst 1¼ :461 1:102 1:35 2:004 3+ Pac Cls 1000k 101 2 2 2½ 3½ 31½ 56¼ McCarron C J LB 119 *1.70 89-11 Missionary Ridge-GB1243½ Defensive Pla
19Jly92-8Hol fst 1⅛ :47 1:103 1:351 1:48 3+ (F)Vanity H-G1 98 2 2 2hd 1hd 11½ 12 McCarron C J LB 127 *.30 94-12 Paseana-Ar1272 Fowda1181¼ Re Toss-Ar
13Jun92-8Hol fst 1 1/16 :223 :454 1:10 1:412 3+ (F)Milady H-G1 102 7 6 53 4¾ 11½ 12¾ McCarron C J LB 125 *.40 94-12 Paseana-Ar1252¾ Re Toss-Ar115¾ Fowda
17Apr92-9OP fst 1 1/16 :233 :464 1:11 1:42 (F)A Blossom H-G1 114 1 4 33 2hd 13 14¼ McCarron C J L 124 *.40 91-23 Paseana-Ar1244¼ Fit for a Queen1213½ Sli
WORKOUTS: Jly 16 Hol 4f fst :474 H 5/32 Jly 9 Hol 1 fst 1:402 H 1/3 ● Jly 3 Hol 6f fst 1:12 H 1/16 Jun 27 Hol 5f fst 1:013 H 24/54 Jun 21 Hol 4f fst :512 H 48/49 Jun 5 Hol 1 fst 1:391

On Beyer Speed, from the middle of her 5YO season until now, Paseana repeatedly had declined by three to six lengths, or from 114–115 to 107–108. To put it differently, Paseana now typically was running par for established Grade 1 females, not four and five lengths faster than par.

Early in 1993 at Santa Anita, on February 28, Paseana had lost in a drive to Southern Truce, a rehabilitated claimer. Last out, at 2–5, she had survived another long hard drive, now against Bold Windy, a sprinter stretching out. The first lady was eminently beatable in the Vanity. I had the horse, and I waited patiently to make the wager.

Re Toss made my day. She was making her third start following a four-month layoff and her form cycle practically announced out loud that today would be a best effort. Handicappers should pause to appreciate that.

I had taken Re Toss at the odds against Paseana in the Milady (Gr. 1) on June 12. She was 8–1 there, too much of a tilt against Paseana's 2–5. Re Toss was not quite revved up that afternoon, but had lost only by a slow-gaining length. Now, in the Vanity, Re Toss would benefit from a longer distance and a pace equally as rapid as last time. Eddie Delahoussaye was back aboard. Re Toss had worked out five times since the Milady. She was set.

Extended to withstand Bold Windy in the Milady, Paseana cannot be expected to improve today, and she might decline. A best scenario found Paseana staying close to a sprinter's pace (Bold Windy was back), and unable to turn back Re Toss in the final furlong.

When the gate sprang, a speed horse named Saros On The Town stumbled so badly she tossed jockey David Flores. The early pace became 23⅘, 47⅖, and 110⅖, dulling my aspirations. Paseana moved up prematurely along the inside between calls, advancing from fifth after a half mile to first after six furlongs. She completed that quarter mile in 22⅗. Re Toss sat chilly, eight lengths behind after six furlongs.

After that, events turned. Saving lots of ground on the inside, Delahoussaye erupted in a memorable run into the upper stretch, gaining quickly on Paseana. Just as I dared to relax, assuming I had backed the eventual winner, Re Toss was forced to alter course at the eighth pole, losing time and stride. But the maneuver was executed superbly by Delahoussaye, and Re Toss soon overtook Paseana and edged clear. She won by a length and a quarter.

Seeing Paseana at a glorious 3–5, I had doubled down on Re Toss, my only win-bet of the day. She paid $9.20. The outcome felt especially sweet, like poetic justice.

An interesting aspect of the Vanity was the reappearance of Bold Windy, the erstwhile sprinter who had extended Paseana to a half length after scorching a sprinter's pace in the Grade 1 Milady. Bold Windy might be tossed here unceremoniously. Examine her form cycle. What conclusion is inescapable?

Bold Windy									B. f. 4											Lifetime Record:		
Own: Dilbeck Ray									Sire: Bold Tropic (Plum Bold)											1993 5 2 2 0 $139,175		
									Dam: Windy P J (Nevada P J)											1992 8 3 3 0 $71,850		
									Br: Raymond T. Dilbeck (Cal)									L 114		Hol 4 3 1 0 $132,550		
BLACK C A (307 33 31 43 .11)									Tr: Jones Gary (63 10 15 8 .16)													
12Jun93-8Hol	fst	1 1/16		:23	:46	1:094	1:413	3↑	Ⓕ Milady H-G1	106	3	2	2hd	2hd	2hd	2½	Desormeaux K J	LB 114	8.30	92-13	Paseana125½ Bold Windy114½ Re Toss11	
8May93-8Hol	fst	7f		:214	:44	1:082	1:213	3↑	Ⓕ A Gleam H-G2	98	9	1	1hd	2½	2hd	1hd	Stevens G L	LB 115	5.30	90-09	Bold Windy115hd La Spia115½ Bountiful	
18Apr93-3SA	fst	6½f		:213	:442	1:091	1:154		Ⓕ Strt Dncr 50k	86	3	3	2½	2½	32½	43½	McCarron C J	LB 116	*1.10	88-09	Another Natalie1161¾ Interactive1171¼ F	
21Mar93-5SA	fm	*6½f	Ⓣ	:214	:442	1:072	1:133		Ⓕ S Shywing H 50k	100	1	4	11	11½	1½	12¼	McCarron C J	LB 115	7.40	90-10	Bold Windy1152¼ Bel's Starlet1243 Char	
15Feb93-7SA	gd	7f		:224	:461	1:11	1:234		Ⓕ I O'Brn H 55k	95	3	3	2hd	1hd	1½	2hd	Desormeaux K J	LB 114	5.60	84-19	Freedom Cry119hd Bold Windy1142½ Rej	
7Nov92-4SA	fm	*6½f	Ⓣ	:212	:434	1:071	1:132	3↑	Ⓕ S Ca Cp Dstf 100k	80	9	4	2hd	2hd	3½	118¼	Stevens G L	LB 114	14.50	84-08	Bel's Starlet1243½ Another Natalie116 F	
9Oct92-8SA	fst	6½f		:212	:441	1:092	1:154	3↑	Ⓕ Alw 38000	84	8	5	73¼	62¾	63½	54¼	Alvarado F T	LB 115	*2.10	87-14	Damewood1161½ Cadillac Women114 Ar	
Disqualified, placed sixth, wide early bumped, impeded foe late Disqualified and placed 6th																						
17Aug92-7Dmr	fst	6½f		:214	:443	1:091	1:154	3↑	Ⓕ Alw 42000	88	1	5	31	3nk	1hd	2½	Alvarado F T	LB 114	9.40	93-10	Interactive117½ Bold Windy114 Cadillac	
24Jun92-3Hol	fst	6½f		:212	:441	1:094	1:162	3↑	Ⓕ Alw 35000	87	4	2	31	21	11	1¾	Alvarado F T	LB 116	3.60	90-12	Bold Windy116¾ Interactive113 Manipu	
25May92-5Hol	fst	6f		:221	:452	:573	1:094	3↑	Ⓕ S Alw 32000	87	7	1	11	11½	12	16	Alvarado F T	LB 115	7.00	91-09	Bold Windy1156 Sal's My Gal115 Imprin	
WORKOUTS: ● Jly 14 Hol 4f fst :461 H 1/48 Jly 9 Hol 7f fst 1:253 H 1/1 ● Jly 4 Hol 6f fst 1:121 H 1/17 Jun 29 Hol 5f fst 1:011 H 6/15 Jun 24 Hol 4f fst :481 H 13/42 Jun 7 Hol 5f fst																						

Remember this. A dyed-in-the-wool sprinter that stretches out against classier competition and runs its lungs out while trying to win can rarely repeat the performance. Handicappers can anticipate a monumental flop, or "bounce."

In the Vanity, after setting slow fractions for four furlongs, Bold Windy retreated badly. She finished fifth of eighth, beaten eight lengths, as an underlay. Do not be fooled. Throw them out.

I had planned an excursion to Las Vegas for simulcasting bets on the weekend of July 24. I canceled. First, the second national Pick-3 scheduled as an integral component of the Summer Stakes II again had been decimated. Untidy state regulations were blamed.

Second, more important, the weekend's stakes schedule shaped up as another procession of underlays. Besides, the local simulcast of Belmont Park's Ballerina Stakes might offer a low-priced overlay on my Horse To Watch from Monmouth Park, the filly You'd Be Surprised, the trip playback. In a six-horse field, I wanted 5–2.

You'd Be Surprised did win Belmont's Ballerina, a 2–1 shot at Belmont Park. She paid $7.40 in the southern California simulcast. Not much, but enough.

The handicapping angle that set the wager regards the Ballerina's heavy favorite, a situation that presents itself at major tracks frequently enough to warrant commentary here.

Owned by the family of Phipps, trained by the remarkable

Shug McGaughey, arguably the nation's best horseman, and featured in several newspaper articles leading up to the weekend stakes, the filly Deputation almost assuredly would be overbet. A winner of one allowance race in ordinary time and manner, Deputation was unclassified, and probably severely outclassed. She had a marvelous chance to disappoint.

Too easily seduced by leading connections, handicappers waste amazing amounts of money on false favorites competing in the leading stables' colors. On the West Coast for decades the same phenomenon was part and parcel of the favorites trained by Charles Whittingham. Many were bogus. Putting icing on a fruit cake, public selectors never fail to indicate the horses come from leading connections and should be taken seriously.

So what? The horses still figure to lose.

New York's McGaughey has inherited the burden. The handicapper's chore consists of distinguishing the favorites having high potential from the ordinary others. Deputation did not make the board in the Ballerina Stakes, and never looked like a threat. Well-versed handicappers might have predicted that beforehand.

Late in July, I departed Los Angeles for the summer season at Del Mar, in northern San Diego, where I had not played day-by-day since 1980. With its short stretch, sharp unbanked turns, and horses-for-courses reputation, well-deserved, Del Mar had never constituted my dream vacation. It's an inappropriate place for class evaluation. The peculiar course has been more hospitable to handicappers emphasizing trips and biases.

Sunny Del Mar has changed dramatically in recent years, including a longer stretch and a predisposition to the only kind of track bias that actually can favor class horses. A condo on the ocean near the racetrack suddenly symbolized the very joys of summer.

In the afternoons, trips and biases held sway, but with a twist nicely suited to my purposes. Inside speed at Del Mar now tires, and often collapses. Outside speed gets more than a fair share.

But the greatest advantage has shifted to outside closers, or at least to off-pace types that rally wide on the far turn.

Biases that favor off-pace horses on the outside are atypical in American racing, and a salient aspect of the phenomenon is rarely remarked upon. Outside biases that favor off-pace runners and latecomers also favor class. The most likely winner is the best horse coming from behind the pace, either stalkers or deep closers capable of overpowering a weakening pace.

That kind of class play will arise most frequently in nonclaiming races, especially the stakes. My formula for success at the new Del Mar would be simple: prefer the best horses on the outside and behind the pace, including stalkers, mid-pack runners and closers that should be propelled by the bias.

I would not have long to wait for the dividends.

Opening day at Del Mar favored speed, but the remainder of the week unwrapped an increasingly intense bias favoring closers on the outside. The bias provided class analysts with a pair of mutuels otherwise prohibitive, and both are well worth a recap.

On the third afternoon, Friday, July 30, perhaps the most severely biased off-pace surface of the meeting, the seventh was an overnight handicap for fillies and mares, 3UP. The field contained the fastest female sprinter in southern California. It also contained five additional speed horses and a classy 4YO returning from a six-and-one-half-month layoff, a closer.

The past performances for the speed demon and the class prospect are presented nearby. Examine them. Provided also are the speed and pace figures for six of the horses, along with the odds to win on each.

Which horse deserves a bet?

P 107 / 44.7 109'

6 Furlongs. (1:07³) THE FANTASTIC GIRL HANDICAP. Purse $55,000 – Added. Fillies and mares, 3-year-olds and upward. By subscription of $50 each, which shall accompany the nomination, $150 to pass the entry box, with $55,000 added, of which $11,000 to second, $8,250 to third, $4,125 to fourth and $1,375 to fifth. Weights: Sunday, July 25. High weights preferred. Starters to be named through the entry box Wednesday, July 28, by the closing time of entries. Closed Friday, July 23, with 13 nominations.

6 FURLONGS

Knight Prospector
Own: Gaswirth & Mirage Stable
†DESORMEAUX K J (—)

B. f. 4
Sire: Native Prospector (Mr. Prospector)
Dam: Knights Crozier (Knights Choice)
Br: Marklan Charles (Cal)
Tr: Lewis Craig A (—)

L 120

Lifetime Record: 13 7 0
1993 4 3 0 0 $80,350 Turf
1992 7 4 0 1 $70,750 Wet
Dmr   3 0 0 1 $9,000 Dist

109 / 111 109 AA P.22

Magical Maiden
Own: Hirsch C L
†STEVENS G L (—)

Dk. b or br f. 4
Sire: Lord Avie (Lord Gaylord)
Dam: Gils Magic (Magesterial)
Br: Wynne H S (Ky)
Tr: Stute Warren (—)

L 120

Lifetime Record: 15 5 4
1993 1 0 0 1 $15,000 Turf
1992 10 3 3 2 $415,775 Wet
Dmr   0 0 0 0   Dist

	PACE	SPEED	ODDS
Bountiful Native	105	106	1.9
La Spia	101	107	5.6
Knight Prospector	114	108	1.1
Magical Maiden	107	107	6.8
Walk Of Fame	106	105	19.7
Nanetta	107	106	16.9

Magical Maiden, and five dead front-runners. The lone closer was also the class of the field. I loved Magical Maiden in this spot. With its stratospheric pace figure, what should happen to Knight's Prospector on a track surface inhospitable to early speed?

On the Beyer scale, the brilliant Knight Prospector qualified as a "triple-fig," its latest three speed figures on the main track superior to any figure of the other contenders. I loved it. Her pace figures assured Knight Prospector a three-length edge at the quarter pole. I loved it.

Magical Maiden had finished third as a 3YO versus older horses in the 1992 Breeders' Cup Distaff, behind Paseana and Versailles Treaty, the top two females in the nation. Magical Maiden had been a Grade 1 winner at three and with a single exception had not faced ungraded stakes conditions in two seasons. She had won that allowance event (October 9), beating solid older fillies and mares in a breeze.

Knight Prospector depended upon blazing speed absolutely, and she might be outgunned under normal circumstances in a graded sprint. At six furlongs, alternatively, Knight Prospector might run away from an overnight handicap.

Could Magical Maiden overtake the speed at six furlongs? Assisted by a strong closer's bias, why not? If the distance had been six and a half furlongs, instead of six, I would have considered Magical Maiden a standout. In any case, I placed a key bet on Magical Maiden and coupled her in multiple exactas with the classy Bountiful Native.

The horses broke and Knight Prospector as usual shot to the lead. Forced to run twenty-one flat for the first quarter by Nanetta on the outside, Knight Prospector arrived at the quarter pole in 44⅕ seconds. Magical Maiden was behind by eight and one-half lengths. Knight Prospector was not slowing down as she raced through the upper stretch. Bountiful Native was chasing, but not gaining. Nearing mid-stretch, the race looked like a romp.

Finally, Magical Maiden began to rally. And Knight Prospector began to weary. The result chart captures the furious finish:

SEVENTH RACE	6 FURLONGS. (1.07³) THE FANTASTIC GIRL HANDICAP. Purse $55,000 – Added. Fillies and mares,

Del Mar

JULY 30, 1993

6 FURLONGS. (1.07³) THE FANTASTIC GIRL HANDICAP. Purse $55,000 – Added. Fillies and mares, 3–year–olds and upward. By subscription of $50 each, which shall accompany the nomination, $150 to pass the entry box, with $55,000 added, of which $11,000 to second, $8,250 to third, $4,125 to fourth and $1,375 to fifth. Weights: Sunday, July 25. High weights preferred. Starters to be named through the entry box Wednesday, July 28, by the closing time of entries. Closed Friday, July 23, with 13 nominations.

Value of Race: $56,700 Winner $31,950; second $11,000; third $8,250; fourth $4,125; fifth $1,375. Mutuel Pool $325,151.00 Exacta Pool $332,625.00

Last Raced	Horse	M/Eqt.	A.	Wt	PP	St	¼	½	Str	Fin	Jockey	Odds $1
10Jan93 8SA3	Magical Maiden	LB	4	120	4	4	5hd	52½	41½	1hd	Stevens G L	6.80
5Jly93 8Hol5	Knight Prospector	LB	4	120	3	3	11	12	12	21	Desormeaux K J	1.10
5Jly93 8Hol2	Bountiful Native	LB	5	121	1	5	42½	3½	21½	33½	Valenzuela P A	1.90
24Jun93 8Hol5	Nannetta	LBb	4	115	6	2	23½	22½	3hd	42	McCarron C J	16.90
25Jun93 8Hol3	Walk Of Fame	LBb	4	113	5	1	3hd	43½	52½	5hd	Flores D R	19.70
7Jly93 8Hol1	La Spia	LBb	4	116	2	6	6	6	6	6	Delahoussaye E	5.60

OFF AT 5:11 Start Good. Won driving. Time, :21, :44¹, :56³, 1:09³ Track fast.

$2 Mutuel Prices:

4–MAGICAL MAIDEN	15.60	5.20	3.20
3–KNIGHT PROSPECTOR		3.00	2.40
1–BOUNTIFUL NATIVE			2.40

$2 EXACTA 4–3 PAID $52.00

Dk. b. or br. f, by Lord Avie–Gils Magic, by Magesterial. Trainer Stute Warren. Bred by Wynne H S (Ky).

MAGICAL MAIDEN, allowed to settle into stride early after being brushed in the initial strides, unleashed a strong kick in the final quarter and just got up. KNIGHT PROSPECTOR, brushed in the opening strides, outsprinted opponents while setting a fast early pace and was not quite able to hold on. BOUNTIFUL NATIVE, within easy striking distance early, came on readily to loom menacingly at the top of the stretch, threatened through the final furlong but did not have the needed punch in deep stretch. NANNETTA, an early pace factor, ran a bit erratically approaching the far turn and weakened in the drive. WALK OF FAME, wide down the backstretch, was four wide into the stretch. LA SPIA, outrun early, failed to threaten and was five wide into the stretch.

Owners— 1, Hirsch C L; 2, Gaswirth & Mirage Stable; 3, Wygod Mr & Mrs Martin J; 4, Esprits De Corps & Millard & Rsmssn; 5, Sido Stable; 6, Broccoli Mr & Mrs Albert

Trainers— 1, Stute Warren; 2, Lewis Craig A; 3, Hendricks Dan L; 4, Sadler John W; 5, Vienna Darrell; 6, Winick Randy

Scratched— Bonne Nuite (9Jly93 9PLN2)

POSTSCRIPT Barely up in the final stride, without the bias, Magical Maiden would have been trounced. Knight Prospector delivered her finest performance ever, almost overcoming a twenty-one flat opening quarter in the teeth of a disastrous speed bias.

It's prudent therefore not to overstate the case. Yet the bottom line is well taken. An outside closer's bias always favors the class horses rallying from behind. If the horses will be exiting routes for sprints, and enjoy a decisive class edge, à la Magical Maiden, the odds will be wonderful. Once the class horses begin to roll, they gather a fantastic momentum and will literally fly past any one-dimensional sprinters that have been tiring. Because she appeared to the crowd as if she could not sprint, Magical Maiden paid $15.60 on a track surface she relished.

Twenty-four hours following the Magical Maiden finish, the closer's bias still in force, the nine-furlong San Diego Handicap (Gr. 3) extended to class handicappers another shot at a rallying upset.

In a short field of five, a pair of Grade 2 winners were guaranteed to contest an early fiery pace. Two other stakes winners would be stalkers. The last would be a deep closer coming on strongly.

So which horse do handicappers prefer?

Continued

The closer, obviously, is Fanatic Boy. He is just as obviously the least talented animal in the field. But Fanatic Boy is no bum. He'a a Grade 3 type that last out split the field in the Grade 1 Suburban Handicap in New York. Fanatic Boy gets Chris Mc-Carron today, a hot pace to tag, and a closer's bias to exploit.

At 7–1, Fanatic Boy looked wonderful on the racetrack, just as inviting as he looked on the tote board.

To deal swiftly with Sir Beaufort, the Whittingham-trained 6YO had been just awful since he had won March 6 at a mile and one-quarter in the Santa Anita Handicap. A superb long sprinter and miler, Sir Beaufort had to be seriously overextended in winning the Santa Anita Handicap. The exalted triumph had robbed Sir Beaufort of his peaked form, a condition handicappers should not forget.

On his best afternoon, unaided by a bias, Fanatic Boy cannot get within six lengths of Memo or Missionary Ridge, but on this day he won going away, and the result chart tells all:

EIGHTH RACE

Del Mar
JULY 31, 1993

1⅛ MILES. (1.46) 52nd Running of THE SAN DIEGO HANDICAP. Purse $125,000 Added. Grade III. 3-year-olds and upward. By subscription of $100 each, which shall accompany the nominations with $1,000 additional to start, with $125,000 added, which $25,000 to second, $18,750 to third, $9,375 to fourth and $3,125 to fifth. Weights, Monday, July 26. Starters to be named through the entry box Thursday, July 29, by the closing time of entries. A trophy will be presented to the owner of the winner. Closed Wednesday, July 21, with 7 nominations. (Winners Preferred).

Value of Race: $130,700 Winner $74,450; second $25,000; third $18,750; fourth $9,375; fifth $3,125. Mutuel Pool $458,191.00 Exacta Pool $376,420.00

Last Raced	Horse	M/Eqt.	A.Wt	PP	St	¼	½	¾	Str	Fin	Jockey	Odds $1
4Jly93 9Bel4	Fanatic Boy-Ar	LB	6 114	3	5	5	5	5	3½	12½	McCarron C J	7.40
17Jly93 8Hol2	Memo-CH	LB	6 116	5	1	2½	1hd	1hd	11	2¾	Atkinson P	1.60
3Jly93 3Hol5	Missionary Ridge-GB	B	6 116	4	2	1hd	22½	22½	21½	3nk	Desormeaux K J	3.10
21Jly93 3Hol1	L'Express-Ch	LB	4 116	1	4	47	47	43½	41	49	Delahoussaye E	5.20
6Jun93 8Hol5	Sir Beaufort	LB	6 119	2	3	3hd	31½	31½	5	5	Valenzuela P A	2.50

OFF AT 5:59 Start Good. Won driving. Time, :223, :453, 1:093, 1:352, 1:482 Track fast.

$2 Mutuel Prices:

3-FANATIC BOY-AR	16.80	6.20	3.00
5-MEMO-CH		3.40	2.40
4-MISSIONARY RIDGE-GB			2.80

$2 EXACTA 3-5 PAID $46.60

B. h, by Mat Boy-Ar-Frau Paula, by Frari. Trainer McAnally Ronald. Bred by Haras La Biznaga (Arg).

FANATIC BOY lagged far back early, commenced rallying after a half, look dangerous nearing the stretch, came into the stretch four wide, was under a steady drive in the stretch run, tried to drift in leaving the sixteenth marker, gained the lead in the final sixteenth and was going away at the end. MEMO vied for the early lead outside MISSIONARY RIDGE, had the advantage with a furlong to go, was overtaken by FANATIC BOY in the last sixteenth but held on for the place. MISSIONARY RIDGE vied for the early lead inside MEMO, was under some right handed pressure before reaching the clubhouse turn and weakened a bit in the last furlong. L'EXPRESS, in contention early and wide down the backstretch, lacked the necessary response in the final quarter and was five wide into the stretch. SIR BEAUFORT delayed the start when unwilling to be loaded into the gate, raced close up early and faltered in the last quarter. LATIN AMERICAN (6) WAS WITHDRAWN. ALL WAGERS ON HIM IN THE REGULAR, LATE DOUBLE AND EXACTA POOLS WERE ORDERED REFUNDED AND ALL OF HIS TRIPLE SELECTIONS WERE SWITCHED TO THE FAVORITE, MEMO (5).

Owners— 1, Cella Charles; 2, Panter Stud; 3, Wall Peter; 4, Hirsch & Mathewson; 5, Calantoni Victoria

Trainers—1, McAnally Ronald; 2, Mandella Richard; 3, Frankel Robert; 4, Stute Warren; 5, Whittingham Charles

Scratched— Latin American (17Jly93 8HOL5)

POSTSCRIPT Which horse ran the best race? Memo ran a superlative race, maybe the best of his career. He simply met the same fate as had Knight Prospector. When I noticed the fractional times as the race was under way, I whispered to colleagues I would like to double the wager. At 8–5, Memo became a deadly underlay on this track surface, but he took them as far as he could.

I was tempted to put Memo on the Horses To Watch list, but resisted. The 6YO probably did too much in a vain attempt to outrun the bias. The overexertion against a vicious bias extracts too much energy. Memo might veer off form for a time. I would wait to see.

Shortly after Fanatic Boy had overhauled the San Diego Handicap horses, Trevor Denman announced that Miner's Mark had won the Jim Dandy Stakes (Gr. 2) at Saratoga. I had sent a bet to Las Vegas. I had backed Miner's Mark against a lineup of 3YOs that included Kentucky Derby hero Sea Hero and Belmont Stakes hero Colonial Affair.

Frankly, I had not bothered to evaluate the past performances. Along with Diazo and Cherokee Run, Miner's Mark qualified as a third post-classics 3YO to catch my eye. The Derby and Belmont winners were prepping in the Jim Dandy for the Travers Stakes, not to mention the potential compromise in form each colt might have suffered after battling in the classics. It's convenient each season to identify a few powerful 3YOs that did not dispute the Kentucky Derby, The Preakness, and the Belmont Stakes. Those 3YOs will be relatively fresh, and improving.

I wanted 5–2 on Miner's Mark in the Jim Dandy, but the Saratoga bettors handed me 2–1. I might have got a better price in the Del Mar simulcast, but the track did not take the signal.

Prior to Del Mar's opening, the grapevine intimated handicappers at the seaside resort track might be treated to each day's feature race from Saratoga. I looked forward to the simulcasts avidly. They never came. Too bad. Saratoga offers racegoers the finest racing in the United States, and by a clear-cut margin. Del Mar handicappers could be expected to misjudge the relative abilities of several Saratoga stakes prospects. I had planned to play the unfamiliar overlays that figured best, the essential strategy for simulcast handicappers with access to cross-track betting. Maybe next year?

AUGUST

On the second Wednesday of Del Mar, August 11, an abrupt change enveloped the proceedings. The track surface became hard-rock fast. The afternoon featured the strongest speed bias of the season. Every winner led at the pace call, and seven of eight dirt winners led at the first call. Sprint winners, with no exceptions, had the top pace figures in the fields.

I felt as if I had been alerted to the form reversal. The reality was mundane, however, a matter of keeping records and doing homework. When the winner of the first race, on August 11, a mile, won by six, in par time, I was thinking how the flat-mile times had been slow until now. When the winner of the second went wire to wire, winning off at 21–1, in time five lengths faster than par, I decided the track must have changed. The winner was an obscure first starter out of a low-percentage stable. Handicappers who calculate daily track variants and construct track profiles (the running styles and beaten-lengths of winners at crucial points of call) supply themselves with a precious edge that might be cashed in repeatedly at several racetracks. The tactics will be mandatory at places like Del Mar, horses-for-courses racetracks, if handicappers want to win. A severe track bias can overwhelm an edge in class, even in a graded stakes. On the second Friday of the meeting, Magical Maiden would have had no hope of getting there. On the second Saturday, Fanatic Boy would have been whipped by open lengths. Class handicappers need to understand that.

The first simulcast at Del Mar did not arrive until the Travers Stakes, four weeks along. My playing partner at Del Mar was Bill Robertson, a complete handicapper, aggressive bettor, and a devotee of track profiles. I liked The Travers, but Bill relished the race. He liked, believe it or not, Sea Hero, citing his demonstrated advantage at a mile and a quarter (velocity ratings) and a form cycle bringing the Derby winner back to a peak.

For the same reasons, I liked Sea Hero, but I liked Miner's Mark just as much. One of my three much-prized, post-Derby 3YOs, Miner's Mark had been escorted carefully to the telltale race of his young career by the partnership of Phipps and McGaughey. Miner's Mark had not attempted ten furlongs, but had just handled Sea Hero by four lengths in Saratoga's nine-furlong Jim Dandy Stakes. That was a tune-up for Sea Hero, no doubt. Maybe Sea Hero, like Best Pal in 1991, was a 3YO at his best beyond middle distances.

Sea Hero had recorded a Beyer Speed Figure of 105 at ten furlongs. Miner's Mark had recorded a Beyer Speed Figure of 105 at nine furlongs. Miner's Mark's dosage index was 3.76, an acceptable blend of speed and stamina. My line was 4–1, a 20 percent chance, on each. The longer I pondered the pair, the more I leaned toward Miner Mark's potential for improvement and away from Sea Hero's inconsistency.

Simulcast bettors at Del Mar picked Kissin Kris as their Travers choice. A deep closer I have never admired, Kissin Kris was fresh from a two-length victory in Monmouth Park's Haskell Stakes (Gr. 1), limited to 3YOs, at nine furlongs. Kissin Kris got a 107 Beyer that day. At ten furlongs, Kissin Kris had earned a dismal 95 Beyer; at twelve furlongs he showed a 101 Beyer. In stakes I had watched, Kissin Kris had closed steadily, not strongly. I didn't want Kissin Kris in a Grade 1 classic.

Halfway through the wagering at Del Mar, Miner's Mark was

8–1, and Sea Hero was 10–1. In the end, I favored Miner's Mark, and hedged the bet incorrectly. Instead of betting both colts to win (two overlays), and coupling them in exactas, I bet Miner's Mark to win and covered with exactas using Sea Hero.

As convincingly as he had the Kentucky Derby, Sea Hero trounced The Travers, circling the leaders on the far turn, and drawing away unchallenged. A two-time winner only, Sea Hero endures as the most distinguished 3YO of 1993. And the next time Sea Hero goes to the gate at a mile and a quarter, I hope the race will be simulcast and the horse will be an overlay.

Miner's Mark, no threat to win, got first run at second. At the sixteenth pole, I thought he had secured the place and I was poised to convert a handsome exacta. Miner's Mark could not hold. He was no ten-furlong specialist. Kissin Kris nailed him nearing the wire for the place.

I congratulated Bill Robertson, who was smiling broadly while totaling the handsome profits from a $20 winner and three-digit exacta. I got nothing.

On the same afternoon, Del Mar presented the million-dollar Pacific Classic (Gr. 1), also at a mile and one-quarter. Once again Best Pal and Bertrando were getting the headlines and would be taking the lion's share of the wagering. A horse-for-course dynamo at Del Mar and a ten-furlong specialist anywhere, who had just exhibited his top form in the Hollywood Gold Cup, Best Pal was an odds-on favorite I longed to bet against. At 3–1, I did not want Bertrando either. I passed.

Bertrando's victory did not surprise me entirely. As mentioned earlier, young horses, threes and fours, that cannot negotiate a mile and a quarter when initially tested, in spring, often do win at the classic distance later. Assign it to the interplay among talent, maturity, and competitive seasoning. I do.

Bertrando's Beyer Speed Figure zoomed to 117. The post-race commentary indicated the presence of a speed bias. I double-checked my records. The five sprints at less than seven furlongs had been won on the front (four wire to wire). The sprint variant was Fast 3. The Pacific Classic was the only dirt route. Bertrando had gone Fast 6.

If I had recognized a speed bias, I would have supported Bertrando with both hands. Speed biases help front-runners at a mile and a quarter as much or more than at any other distance, probably because the early pace tends towards slow. Without a bias, Bertrando had been completing the classic distance with greater verve. With a bias, he would be virtually uncatchable. In that context, the 3–1 I did not approve looked like a racetrack gift.

Late in August, Arlington Park presents a two-day stakes extravaganza billed in grandiose terms as Arlington's International Stakes Festival. The idea is to attract a barnful of foreign stakes stars and match them against America's best. The centerpiece is the Arlington Million (Gr. 1), an event among my favorites. The support stakes are likewise an imposing pair, the Grade 1, $500,000-added Beverly D., for older fillies and mares, and the Grade 2, $250,000-added Secretariat Stakes, for 3YOs. The three stakes are conducted on grass, the direct link to European imports.

Because the Arlington races attract so many unfamiliar stakes horses, foreign and American, the simulcast opportunities can be tantalizing, but simulcast handicappers were forced to wait until 1994. An equine virus at Arlington Park repelled European and American horsemen alike, decimating the fields.

On top of that, a hard rain pounding Chicago resulted in late scratches, producing short fields, underlays, and unpredictable outcomes.

With Arlington a lost cause, the weekend might have been lost, until on examining the Del Mar entries I came upon the opportunity I had been awaiting for months. The talented 3YO Diazo was entered. Most admired of my post-Derby 3YOs, Diazo was running on the grass in an overnight called the Relaunch Handicap, purse of $50,000-added, limited to 3YOs which were non-winners of $35,000 (first money) at a mile or over in 1993.

On sheer ability, Diazo towered above the sophomores he would encounter on the Del Mar grass. His record now looked like this:

Aggressively placed above his conditions, Diazo's run in the Kentucky Derby had been remarkable. Examine the internal move, carried almost to the eighth pole. While far wide in a bulky field, Diazo had erased seven and one-half lengths between the six-furlong call and the mile. After a powerful gain, in twenty-four seconds, and grossly inadequate stakes seasoning, Diazo managed to finish fifth of nineteen, beaten by six lengths for the roses. He had completed the flashiest mid-race move in the race.

I had judged Diazo nothing less than the nation's most talented 3YO. Facing a 120-day layoff, and a first attempt on turf, handicappers at Del Mar might not share my abundant enthusiasm. I might get a fair price, maybe a good price.

On the night before Diazo's Del Mar comeback, I routinely consulted the workout report provided by professional clocker Bruno De Julio in *Today's Racing Digest*. I was startled at the descriptions of Diazo's workouts:

Diazo	8/6	Dmr\Fast 6f	113.4h

Finished in company and outworked a Maiden-Claimer, while looking all out down the lane. Follow other drills closely.

	8/16	Dmr\Fast 7f	128.1h

Didn't care for this work. Highly touted 3-year-old stopped late. Fin: 1/4 in 26.1 after weak splits of 11.4 and 50 flat. Was being aske: late. Maybe the track had something to do with it, but the guess is he isn't doing well.

De Julio's comments bothered me so much I checked with two additional clockers. Both confirmed De Julio. Diazo had been looking disturbingly poor in the mornings. So poor, according to clockers, he might not be right. Good horses, notably younger horses, usually work well.

An hour before Diazo's race on Saturday, I was visited at the box by Bob McNamara, a good friend and racing insider I had notified of my intention to make a serious wager. McNamara told me he had consulted Paddy Gallagher, assistant trainer to Bill Shoemaker, about Diazo's workouts.

"Paddy says Diazo has always worked poorly. He's a poor workout horse. He's sound. It's a go. Just ignore the clockers."

Conflicting information is standard fare at the racetrack. It's resolved best by assigning priority to the cold dope, the data. The clocker information remained too disconcerting for a large bet.

The decision-making became a moot point regardless. In a good field, Diazo would be overbet by the crowd, notwithstanding the layoff and switch to grass. The colt was as low as 9–5 near post time. No bet.

Under Laffit Pincay, Jr., Diazo found traffic and trouble in the running. Regardless, Diazo won. He went 134⅘, and finished with total authority. It was a melancholy climax to my four-month surveillance. Following Cherokee Run and Miner's Mark, now all three of my post-Derby 3YOs had won. I was still waiting for a generous reward. I put Diazo on the Horses To Watch list.

All was not lost. The most impressive performer at Del Mar during August was the 3YO filly Hollywood Wildcat. As he had intended since acquiring the horse, trainer Neil Drysdale had prepared the filly for a pair of Del Mar grass stakes. Hollywood Wildcat blew them down once, and she blew them down again. Whatever key Drysdale had turned, Hollywood Wildcat by now resembled nothing less than the outstanding distaffer in the nation, dirt and grass.

I was arguing that case one day in the box, when Andrew

Beyer announced he had taken 30–1 on Hollywood Wildcat in The Mirage Future Book. Beyer happened to be in Las Vegas for book promotions (*Beyer On Speed*) on the Saturday morning The Mirage opened its Breeders' Cup Future Book. Hollywood Wildcat was listed at 30–1 in the Distaff. Beyer took $300 worth.

A few days later I followed that lead. Hollywood Wildcat was no longer 30–1. At The Mirage, she was 15–1. I took $200 worth.

In the Classic, Diazo was offered at 30–1. I was looking for 50–1.

September

Super Saturday! It must be coming to a racetrack near you as part of the Fall Festivals of Thoroughbred Racing.

September arrives fresh with hope, for owners, breeders, trainers, and even handicappers. The advertising pages of *Daily Racing Form* are brimming with the advanced notices of Super Saturday (Belmont Park), the Molson Million (Woodbine), the Super Derby Stakes Festival (Louisiana Downs), California Cup Day (Oak tree at Santa Anita), Breeders' Cup Preview Day (Belmont Park), the Festival of the Sun (Calder), the Hollywood Park International Turf Festival (Hollywood Park), and the fountainhead of all stakes festivals, Breeders' Cup Championship Day.

I do admit, I love them all. Not only might class handicappers find unsurpassed action in the panoply of stakes festivals each fall, in 1993 I had identified five horses that qualified for unqualified support in their next starts, wherever they went: Diazo, Bien Bien, The Wicked North (sprinter-miler), Hollywood Wildcat, and Megan's Interco, a filly who had looked sensational on the grass during August at Del Mar.

The first good bet of September came unexpectedly, at Del Mar, six days into September. The night before the Del Mar Derby, run on grass, the probable winner jumped at me as I perused the past performances. At nine furlongs on the turf, the Del Mar Derby demands a distinct style of handicapping, at least in comparison with other derbies, the ones on dirt.

A full field of twelve was entered, in itself a delightful change of pace. Among public selectors, and the bettors, the race was considered extraordinarily contentious. The betting favorite would be a healthy 9–2. To me, however, one horse stood out. Examine the past performances for three crucial contenders:

By conventional handicapping, the 1993 Del Mar Derby would be rated a toss-up. The speed and pace figures of five contenders looked highly competitive. Horses rated slightly below the leading contenders were exiting troubled trips. A pair of contenders from top barns were recent imports, without showing as much as a workout in this country.

First, consider the speed and pace figures of the three contenders shown (Par is 109):

	Pace	Speed	Beyer Speed
Zignew	120	108	94
Dare To Duel	118	111	95
Guide	100	105	86

Dare To Duel looks best, Zignew a strong contender, and Guide an outsider.

Handicappers might have noticed too that Dare To Duel and Guide have exited split divisions of Del Mar's opening-day Oceanside Stakes, restricted to 3YOs who are non-winners of $35,000 first money. Each colt had won, but Dare To Duel's division had completed the mile a full second faster. Much of the pre-Derby discussion fastened on the distinction.

But the Del Mar Derby, and the Oceanside Stakes, are conducted on grass, and turf races are vastly dissimilar from their counterparts on dirt. Suppose the key data for the three contenders were presented as follows:

	FINAL FRACTION	TURF FIGURE
Zignew	31⅕	96
Dare To Duel	23⅘	105
Guide	23	111

Now which contender do handicappers prefer? I prefer Guide, who had in the Oceanside finished fastest by four lengths in comparison to Dare To Duel.

To dispense with Zignew, his races have been remarkably similar (note Beyer Speed Figures), including closing times that cannot withstand the furious finish that is commonplace in top-grade grass stakes. Zignew's pace figures are consistently superior to his speed figures, a configuration that does not work often when 3YOs run on the grass. Tired, or tiring, horses never figure to prevail on the grass.

Dare To Duel has run faster at a mile than Guide, but Guide has finished faster than Dare To Duel. The faster finish deserves the nod on grass. To pursue the reasoning, consider again the six-furlong fractional times of the split divisions of the Oceanside Stakes.

Dare To Duel goes 111⅖ seconds. Guide remains a length and three-quarters behind at 1:13 flat. If the four-furlong fractions are considered, Dare To Duel (47⅗) has outrun Guide early (49⅘) by more than two seconds. Aren't the fractional times clearly in support of Dare To Duel's chances against Guide?

They are not.

Both fractional times are relatively slow. The fractional par at a mile on grass for stakes horses at Del Mar is 1:10 2-5. Although Dare To Duel may be traveling faster than Guide early, *both* colts are traveling relatively slowly. That's the critical consideration.

Turf races are persistently characterized by relatively slow fractional times. Whenever the six-furlong pace is slower than par by a second or greater, the horses, certainly stakes horses, will have plenty left. Those horses separate themselves in the run from the prestretch call to the wire, and not before that.

As far as handicappers could determine, Guide would outkick Dare To Duel. In fact, in a stakes derby judged extremely close on conventional dope, Guide's turf figure was two lengths superior to his closest rival. It was four lengths superior to any of the other contenders. On turf figures, by Quinn at least, Guide stood apart.

The result chart describes a drawing away outcome that was no fluke. I hope handicappers can appreciate that.

EIGHTH RACE

Del Mar

SEPTEMBER 6, 1993

1⅛ MILES. (Turf)(1.46³) 49th Running of THE DEL MAR DERBY. GRADE II. Invitational. Purse $300,000. 3–year–olds. By invitation, with no nomination or starting fees. The winner to receive $165,000 with $60,000 to second, $45,000 to third, $22,500 to fourth and $7,500 to fifth. Weight, 122 lbs. The Del Mar Thoroughbred Club will invite a representative field of horses to compete. The field will be drawn by the closing time of entries, Saturday, Sept. 4. A trophy will be presented to the owner of the winner. 15 invitations, Monday, August 30, 1993.

Value of Race: $300,000 Winner $165,000; second $60,000; third $45,000; fourth $22,500; fifth $7,500. Mutuel Pool $575,013.00 Exacta Pool $561,639.00

Last Raced	Horse	M/Eqt.	A.Wt	PP	St	¼	½	¾	Str	Fin	Jockey	Odds $1
28Jly93 5Dmr1	Guide-FR	LB	3 122	5	6	6hd	9½	8½	51	11½	Desormeaux K J	5.50
15Aug93 8Dmr6	Future Storm	B	3 122	12	8	112½	101	71	8½	2hd	Valenzuela P A	8.60
15Aug93 8Dmr5	The Real Vaslav	B	3 122	8	7	9½	8hd	9hd	7hd	3no	Nakatani C S	10.50
28Jly93 5Dmr5	Ⓓ Nonproductiveasset	LB	3 122	10	4	51	4hd	3½	1hd	4½	Atkinson P	28.70
14Jly93 STC4	Fatherland-IR	Bb	3 122	11	12	12	12	12	11½	5hd	Delahoussaye E	4.80
17Aug93 Yor6	Blues Traveller-IR	B	3 122	7	9	10½	112½	10½	10½	6no	Gryder A T	7.30
15Aug93 8Dmr3	Hawk Spell	Bb	3 122	1	1	1hd	1½	1hd	31	71½	Day P	7.90
15Aug93 8Dmr4	Zignew	LBb	3 122	3	10	3hd	6hd	5hd	4hd	8nk	Flores D R	10.30
5Aug93 7Dmr2	Art of Living	LBb	3 122	6	5	7hd	71½	6½	6½	9½	Black C A	27.20
15Aug93 8Dmr1	Manny's Prospect	LB	3 122	2	2	21	2½	11½	91	10hd	McCarron C J	14.20
28Jly93 8Dmr1	Dare To Duel	B	3 122	4	3	4½	3½	2½	2hd114		Stevens G L	9.70
21Aug93 7Sar5	Devoted Brass	LBbf	3 122	9	11	81	51	4½	12	12	Pincay L Jr	7.50

Ⓓ–Nonproductiveasset disqualified and placed 11th.

OFF AT 5:59 Start Good. Won driving. Time, :23³, :48², 1:124, 1:37³, 1:49³ Course firm.

$2 Mutuel Prices:	5–GUIDE-FR	13.00	6.80	4.40
	12–FUTURE STORM		9.60	6.00
	8–THE REAL VASLAV			7.00

$2 EXACTA 5–12 PAID $177.20

Dk. b. or br. c, (Feb), by Local Suitor–Norfolk Lily, by Blakeney. Trainer Hess R B Jr. Bred by McAlpine Sir Robin (Fr).

GUIDE, outrun early, saved ground around the far turn while boxed in, continued boxed in until angling to the outside early in the stretch run, accelerated after passing the furlong marker under right handed pressure, took the lead in the final sixteenth and drew clear. FUTURE STORM, devoid of early speed, came into the stretch seven wide, bumped with THE REAL VASLAV leaving the furlong marker, closed with a rush and got up for the place. A claim of foul against GUIDE by the rider of FUTURE

Earlier on Del Mar Derby Day, a familiar handicapper asked me whether I preferred the import from Great Britain named Blues Traveller. He noted the colt had finished third in the Epsom Derby, a European classic, purse of $1.2 million. The colt subsequently had delivered an excellent showing against older handicap horses in a $400,000-added Group 1 stakes at St. Cloud, in France.

I did not like Blues Traveller. The colt's record is instructive. Take a long look:

146

SUMMER

As a maiden winner in September of 1992, Blues Traveller had been thrust into the Group 1 Dewhurst Stakes at Newmarket prematurely. He was 66–1 that day!

In the Epsom Derby eight months later, Blues Traveller was 150–1! He finished third, outperforming his odds by a wide margin. The colt has talent.

But Blues Traveller is the embodiment of a badly managed young thoroughbred. Not only was the colt misplaced in the Epsom Derby, but also afterward he was pushed headlong into the Group 1 Grand Prix Saint-Cloud, in France, against older stakes stars. The winner that day was User Friendly, among the top handicap horses on the continent.

Again, Blues Traveller distinguished himself, finishing fourth, beaten by a mere three lengths.

Not yet satisfied, the colt's managers next entered the Group 1 Juddmonte International Stakes, back in England, again against the best older horses in training. Finally, Blues Traveller cracked. He did not belong in hard battles against older stakes winners and the efforts undoubtedly extracted a tremendous toll.

The August 17 race occurred three weeks prior to the Del Mar Derby, too-fast a turnaround for an immature colt that had been so overextended throughout the summer. I would have been amazed if Blues Traveller had prevailed at Del Mar. He did not get a serious call.

Too much too soon amounts to severe overextension among

147

3YOs, and a regression is part and parcel of the pattern. Handicappers should not expect too soon a resurgence.

As happened throughout the winter at Santa Anita, again on Florida Derby day, again on Arlington Million day, and again and again in 1993, in the days preceding Super Saturday the skies parted and the rain came cascading down. On Friday in New York, it poured so relentlessly hard, the races at Belmont Park were canceled. On hearing the news, I christened the 1993 racing season The Year of the Downpour.

Super Saturday consisted of four Grade 1s, a Grade 2, and an ungraded support stakes. I abandoned the handicapping effort, but not the program. Bertrando was now a near cinch in the nine-furlong Woodward Stakes (Gr. 1), a perfect distance around one turn. Wet-fast is Bertrando-fast.

As a colleague casually remarked, "If you could bet the limit on Bertrando in the Metropolitan Mile, you certainly can bet the limit under these conditions; the race is ideal." It was true. So I sent a $1,000 win-bet to New York via Las Vegas, but attached minimum odds of 3–2.

Bertrando pranced to victory in the goo by 13 lengths in blazing time. Bertrando's Beyer Speed Figure was a whopping 125. He paid $3.80 at Belmont Park, sixty cents more than he paid in southern California.

Prior to the rains, I had been keenly attracted to the Man-of-War Stakes (Gr. 1), at 1⅜ miles on the turf, where Star Of Cozzene would be heavily favored and Bien Bien would be my alternative. By now I realized I had underestimated Star Of Cozzene, a genuinely top grass runner who had beaten Lure, not once, but twice. A soft-course monster, Star Of Cozzene had annihilated the opposition in the Arlington Million on a yielding course softened by rain. On a firm grass at Belmont Park, Star Of Cozzene would be severely overbet. Bien Bien relished firm turf.

But now the Belmont grass would be soft and yielding, made

to order for Star Of Cozzene. In a repeat of his strong performance at Arlington Park, Star Of Cozzene won the Man-of-War by
five and one-half lengths. Bien Bien ran, but showed nothing. I
could only plan ahead. Once again, I put Star Of Cozzene on the
Horses To Beat list. I kept Bien Bien on the Horses To Watch
list.

On Super Saturday, as so often in the slop, several winners
ran off and hid. Bertrando's Beyer Speed Figure might be an
awesome 125, but 'twas not to be confused with his two-turn
speed figures at a mile and one-quarter.

In the Belmont Futurity (Gr. 1), the unbeaten juvenile Dehere lost by a half-length to the front-runner Holy Bull. Maybe
the odds on Dehere would be higher next time. Maybe Dehere
was not the superstar his legions of admirers had avowed. New
Yorkers suffer a deep instinct to transform any authentically talented colt into Super Horse, a predisposition destined to end in
sorrow, regret, and penance. No one could fail to admire Dehere's
multiple stakes wins at Saratoga, but none of his speed figures
were superlative; just good. The colt possessed a high dosage
index. How would he handle two turns? On Dehere, the verdict
remained out.

If surrendering Super Saturday to the storms was frustrat-
ing, the next afternoon would prove agonizing. On Sunday, Belmont's track surface was labeled "muddy" for the Ruffian
Handicap (Gr. 1), a $200,000-added prize for fillies and mares,
3UP. New Yorkers and southern California bettors, respectively,
could be expected to favor either Paseana (6–5) or Turnback The
Alarm (5–2). I liked neither.

After consulting the past performances at length, I found no
alternative to the favorites. I should have guessed it. The longest
shot in the five-horse field (13–1) led all the way. A curt reminder
to all: unless the horses improve in mud and slop, handicappers
cannot afford to accept 5–2 or lower, no matter how appealing
the horses look on paper.

On that same Sunday, Canada offered the nine-furlong

Molson Export Million, a million-dollar purse for 3YOs. Entered from the states were Sea Hero (Kentucky Derby, The Travers), Colonial Affair (Belmont Stakes), and Kissin Kris (Haskell Stakes). The race was billed as one of Canada's biggest spectacles ever.

Entered on the behalf of Canada was the 1993 Canadian Triple Crown winner. A glimpse at this colt's brilliance and it became difficult to imagine the U.S. classic winners even getting close. It looked like this:

Over a relaxed Sunday breakfast miles away, I wondered whether it would be a waste of time to drive to Fairplex Park (the nearest simulcast site) to inspect the odds on the Molson Million. The case for Peteski was almost impenetrable.

The U.S. shippers were deep closers whose best efforts began at a mile and a quarter, a furlong beyond today's middle distance. In twenty-three starts among the trio in 1993, they had won seven races, not exactly models of consistency. Peteski might be a lone frontrunner and in any event would dominate the early pace. Maybe the American bettors would allow 2–1?

I could not resist. I drove to Fairplex early, bet the contents of my wallet on Peteski, and left. Not until the next morning did I learn Peteski had waltzed to victory by four and one-half lengths. Even so, I took the worst of it. Peteski paid $5.30 at Woodbine, but $4.20 at Fairplex Park. The difference in profit exceeds 50 percent.

Of the U.S. stalwarts, only Sea Hero hit the board.

Before leaving September, a few timely comments on the pari-mutuels. In the stakes ranks, the fall begins a harvest of what I like to call low-priced overlays. The stakes horses have been sorting themselves into class levels for months, and handicappers have become well informed. Overlays can never be ignored. In the straight pools, however, it's convenient to remember the rate of profit is most tightly tied to the win percentage. Low-priced overlays can be excellent bets too, and will be regularly in the stakes races of fall. Surprisingly good money can be accumulated. The next example should testify persuasively on the issue.

My final key bet of September set up wonderfully well at first, but had to be altered in the end. The Pegasus Stakes is a Grade 1 event at The Meadowlands, extending $250,000-added to 3YOs going nine furlongs. Trainer Bill Shoemaker picked this spot for his stable leader Diazo and I picked it for a maximum wager. With no simulcast to southern California, I would depend upon local odds. My line was 5–2.

The opposition included the overrated eastern colts Storm Tower, Press Card, and Schossberg. The latter had just won New York's Grade 1 Jerome Handicap, and leading jockey Jerry Bailey was traveling to The Meadowlands for the ride. Either Storm Tower (Wood Memorial) or Schossberg should be favored.

On race day, *Daily Racing Form*'s lead handicapper for New Jersey, John Piesen, did not include Diazo among his top three picks. He listed Diazo at something like 8–1. Unknown to Piesen, none of the eastern 3YOs stood much of a chance against Diazo, a circumstance the eastern handicappers apparently did not yet appreciate. The Beyer Speed Figures for the three eastern contenders looked competitive and Diazo was coming off a grass race. The odds might be surprisingly high. I allowed myself to imagine this might be one of the sweetest bets of 1993.

Late in the game, sure enough, Storm Tower was scratched. Diazo might not be a terrific price, after all.

The actual handicapping of The Pegasus illustrates a contemporary twist of class evaluation this book has intended to emphasize. Review the past performances for the three contenders:

Press Card
Own: Mohammed Al Maktoum
SMITH M E (2 0 1 0 .00)
B. c. 3 (Apr)
Sire: Fappiano (Mr. Prospector)
Dam: Courtly Dee (Never Bend)
Br: Alexander & Aykroyd & Groves (Ky)
Tr: Schulhofer Flint S (1 0 1 0 .00)
116
Lifetime Record: 6 3 1 1 $152,68
1993 4 2 1 0 $77,080 | Turf 0 0 0 0
1992 2 1 0 1 $75,600 | Wet 0 0 0 0
Med 0 0 0 0 | Dist 2 1 1 0

6Sep93-10Pha fst 1⅛ :47 1:11 1:363 1:491 Pa Derby-G2 100 3 5 57 56½ 4½ 2nk Velasquez J 117 6.20 92-08 Wallenda114nk Press Card1172½ Saintly Prospector1223½
5Aug93-7Sar fst 1⅛ :473 1:113 1:362 1:492 3↑ Alw 30500N2X 94 5 2 21 2½ 1½ 11½ Krone J A 112 *1.60e 89-11 Press Card1121½ Very Personal112no Compadre112¾
17Jly93-6Bel fst 7f :224 :454 1:092 1:22 Screen King 45k 87 1 4 34½ 42½ 44½ 45 Krone J A 117 1.90 88-14 Evil Bear117hd Punch Line122¾ Digging In1194 La
24May93-8Bel fst 7f :223 :454 1:104 1:231 Alw 26500N1X 98 6 1 34 22½ 12½ 14 Krone J A 117 *.60 87-22 Press Card1174 Shu Fellow1171½ Takin' Names1176
10Oct92-7Bel gd 1 :22 :443 1:09 1:344 Champagne-G1 77 7 10 76 76½ 37½ 311½ Krone J A 122 2.90e 84-04 Sea Hero1225¾ Secret Odds1225¾ Press Card122
21Sep92-4Bel fst 1 :223 :451 1:102 1:37 Md Sp Wt 77 6 4 33½ 21 1½ 19 Krone J A 118 *1.50 85-10 Press Card1189 Glenbarra118hd Gravel Ridge118
WORKOUTS: ●Sep 21 Med 4f sly :462 H 1/17 Sep 14 Bel 4f fst :502 B 22/29 Sep 3 Bel 4f fst :474 H 3/46 Aug 29 Sar 5f fst :594 H 2/15 Aug 24 Sar 4f fst :493 B 15/21 Aug 19 Sar 4f fst :484 B 8/21

Schossberg
Own: Stavro Steven A
BAILEY J D (—)
Dk. b or br c. 3 (Apr)
Sire: Broad Brush (Ack Ack)
Dam: Bye the Bye (Balzac)
Br: Knob Hill Stables (Ont-C)
Tr: England Phillip (—)
116
Lifetime Record: 5 4 0 1 $175,416
1993 4 3 0 1 $161,136 | Turf 0 0 0 0
1992 1 1 0 0 $14,280 | Wet 0 0 0 0
Med 0 0 0 0 | Dist 0 0 0 0

6Sep93-8Bel fst 1 :232 :461 1:102 1:352 Jerome H-G1 103 5 2 21 21 2hd 1hd Bailey J D 113 f 2.40 91-12 Schossberg113hd Williamstown118½ Mi Cielo116½
21Aug93-9Sar fst 7f :214 :442 1:091 1:213 KingsBshp-G2 100 10 1 32½ 51½ 41½ 33 Kabel T K 115 f 6.70 94-12 Mi Cielo1152½ Williamstown122½ Schossberg1152¼
28Jly93-8WO fst 7f :23 :454 1:102 1:23 3↑ Alw 22600N2X 96 4 2 1nk 2nk 11½ 14¾ Kabel T K 117 *.45 96-14 Schossberg1174¾ Greatsilverfleet1201¼ Mrchprospect1241 Some
11Jly93-3WO fst 6½f :22 :442 1:092 1:154 Alw 21200N2L 92 8 3 42¼ 1nk 12½ 11½ Kabel T K 119 *.75 96-06 Schossberg1191½ Donedeed1195 Collosseum Cat116hd I
26Jly92-6WO fst 6f :222 :454 1:103 Ⓢ Md Sp Wt 89 7 4 53½ 31½ 12 16¾ Kabel T K 118 b 13.90 92-13 Schossberg1186¾ All An Angel115nk Explosive Red118
WORKOUTS: Sep 19 WO 5f fst 1:002 B 2/21 Sep 16 WO 3f fst :373 B 10/16 Sep 1 WO 5f fst 1:022 B 9/22 Aug 29 WO 3f fst :38 B 10/14 Aug 17 WO tr.t 4f sly :50 B 4/8 Aug 10 WO 4f fst :49 B 2/8

Diazo
Own: Paulson Allen E
PINCAY L JR (—)
Ch. c. 3 (Mar)
Sire: Jade Hunter (Mr. Prospector)
Dam: Cruella (Tyrant)
Br: Paulson Allen E (Ky)
Tr: Shoemaker Bill (—)
117
Lifetime Record: 7 3 1 0 $91,70
1993 5 3 0 0 $85,400 | Turf 1 1 0 0
1992 2 M 1 0 $6,300 | Wet 0 0 0 0
Med 0 0 0 0 | Dist 1 0 0 0

29Aug93-5Dmr fm 1 Ⓣ :222 :46 1:102 1:344 Ⓡ Relaunch H 50k 100 5 7 65 63½ 62¾ 11¼ Pincay L Jr B 117 b *1.80 97-09 Diazo1171¼ Moscow Changes1171¼ D'hallevant1161
Off slowly, boxed in far turn, 5 wide stretch
1May93-8CD fst 1¼ :463 1:111 1:364 2:022 Ky Derby-G1 96 18 11 119 41½ 43 56 Desormeaux K J L 126 b 17.40e 92-07 Sea Hero1262½ Prairie Bayou126hd Wild Gale126nk
Bid 4 wide far turn, wknd
17Apr93-9OP fst 1⅛ :454 1:094 1:352 1:48 Ark Derby-G2 100 10 4 43 41½ 31½ 51¾ Desormeaux K J 118 b 4.20 94-15 Rockamundo1181½ Kissin Kris122no Foxtrail122hd
21Mar93-7SA fst 1 1/16 :224 :463 1:11 1:421 Alw 36000N1X 105 5 5 31½ 32 1½ 13½ Desormeaux K J B 117 b *1.50 93-11 Diazo1173½ Star Of The Eagle1202½ Dinand1203½
27Feb93-3SA fst 7f :222 :451 1:092 1:22 Md Sp Wt 94 5 3 21½ 2½ 1½ 13½ Valenzuela P A B 118 b 8.80 93-11 Diazo1183½ Lucky Navajo1184 Torole118¾ Gre
6Dec92-6Hol fst 6f :213 :443 :572 1:103 Md Sp Wt 64 4 9 75½ 78¼ 51½ 57 Almeida G F B 118 5.10 80-11 D'hallevant1183 Real Hit118hd Whosthepurplecomet1182 Lu
6Sep92-6Dmr fst 6f :214 :444 :572 1:102 Md Sp Wt 74 6 7 76¾ 77½ 35½ 23 Pincay L Jr B 117 3.70e 84-11 Mr. Expo1173 Diazo1173½ Bagdad Road117 Str
WORKOUTS: Sep 17 Dmr 6f fst 1:143 H 8/12 Sep 11 Dmr Ⓣ 1 fm 1:334 H 1/1 Sep 5 Dmr 3f fst :364 H 12/27 Aug 22 Dmr 6f fst 1:134 H 3/20 Aug 16 Dmr 7f fst 1:281 H 6/8 Aug 6 Dmr 6f fst 1:134 H 3/10

By conventional standards, class handicappers probably would prefer Schossberg. After all, Schossberg is the Grade 1 winner. Arguably, Diazo looks like the least accomplished of the three. Schossberg also flashes the strongest Beyer Speed Figure last out, in the Jerome. Press Card qualifies as a close runner-up in a Grade 2 stakes (Pennsylvania Derby) and Diazo has been a minor stakes winner who has run well in Grade 1 derbies. All three colts can be accepted as legitimate contenders in a Grade 1 stakes having no certifiable Grade 1 horses.

That's the twist. As put forth here, the definition of a Grade 1 horse is a two-time winner of Grade 1 titles. Schossberg does not fit that definition. His Grade 1 win can be accepted as less than definitive. Fully extended to prevail in the Jerome and wearing front tendon wraps lately, Schossberg had accomplished nothing special. On speed figures, the three colts cannot be distinguished clearly. If Schossberg improved and can handle the extra distance, he might be difficult to beat in the Pegasus, but I knew it would take a special 3YO to match Diazo.

I knew something too about Press Card. I had backed the Fappiano colt in the Pennsylvania Derby, where he almost tallied at 6–1. Press Card had led late in the race, but was overtaken by Wallenda, a deep closer making a steady gain. Press Card had trained sharply in the slop at The Meadowlands, but if Press Card could not outrun Wallenda, he could not outrun Diazo.

When the wagering began, Diazo was immediately backed. The betting continued to be strong. Diazo would not be the 5–2 shot I had ordered as a minimum. No matter. Below 5–2, I had ordered exactas with Diazo keyed equally atop Schossberg and Press Card. Diazo left the gate an 8–5 favorite, a tribute to Jersey handicappers. The underlay left me needing a one-two finish to collect.

From approximately three lengths behind Schossberg's early pace, Diazo accelerated like the superb horse he is and moved quickly into a 110⅕ pace on the far turn. Then he just exploded through the stretch. The Pegasus was over within seconds. But who got second?

Press Card finished a dull second. The $2 exacta paid $18, or 3.5–1 for a $4 investment (two horses). My profit was $700, and I was stirred to imagine Diazo may soon be destined to become my personal horse-of-the-year. The Beyer Speed Figure was 109, second highest of the year among 3YOs to Peteski's Molson Million (111). This was one devastating performance and I was looking forward to Diazo's next, which no doubt would place him against older stakes stars.

With September closing on a positive beat, officially ending summer racing, the Breeders' Cup races were six weeks removed. Already I had decided about two of the championship races. Getting down advantageously on those ahead of time can be a handicapper's first official act of fall.

FALL

OCTOBER

The race books of Mexico, officially L. F. Caliente, are located conveniently approximately 250 meters beyond the Mexican border. Customers can park on the U.S. side and walk across. There they will find parlors that are modern, comfortable, and colorful, analogous in furnishing and decor to the race books of Las Vegas or the sports bars and grills in the States. Service is fast and courteous.

Disconnected from the pari-mutuel pools of U.S. racetracks, the Mexican books post no limits on wagers on horses at the three major southern California tracks. Outside of southern California, limits are posted. Pick-6 winnings are paid in full, minus the customary 1 percent tax. Bettors are served a buffet of racetracks from New York to Florida to Chicago to Los Angeles, and points in between.

Among the advantages extended by the Mexican books is a

future-book odds line significantly more realistic than bettors can find in Las Vegas. Simply put, higher odds. The Caliente race book remains legendary for the future-book line posted on Winning Colors' chances of winning the 1987 Kentucky Derby, a fabulous 50–1. That line was thirty points higher than the corresponding line in Las Vegas. When the gray filly toppled the colts, the Mexican book was rocked for an alleged million dollars. They paid without a whimper.

I was introduced to L. F. Caliente during Del Mar by Andy Cylke, an excellent professional handicapper who resides in San Diego and crosses the border routinely to pursue Pick-6 carryovers. On October 1, I received a wake-up call from Cylke, who advised me the new edition of the Mexican future-book was out and Hollywood Wildcat was 15–1 still. I inquired about Diazo; 30–1. In Vegas, Hollywood Wildcat had tumbled to 5–1; Diazo was 10–1.

On October 2, I drove to L. F. Caliente with Cylke, who immediately went to the window carrying $400 for me, only to return with the cash in hand. Hollywood Wildcat was no longer 15–1; she was 10–1. Diazo was not 30–1; he was 20–1. Later I checked another two windows, but the information was the same.

This is a pet peeve. The race books publish future-book betting lines that do not exist. The actual odds inevitably will be lower at the windows. Book managers, of course, insist the lines were moved by betting action. Fair enough. That's the idea, but my experience at L. F. Caliente begs the question. We had arrived twenty-four hours after the new edition had been published, on a Friday, following no stakes racing, and presumably little betting action.

The next morning, Saturday, a coincidence let the future-book cat out of the bag. On trainer Roger Stein's morning radio talk show in southern California, a Mr. Paul Mendez, general manager of L. F. Caliente, advised the racing audience that the new edition of his Future Book on the Breeders' Cup prospects was out. Mendez specifically quoted the new lines on Hollywood Wildcat and Diazo. He listed Hollywood Wildcat at 15–1 and Diazo at 30–1, referring to the published material. And that's the way that game is played, I suppose.

At L. F. Caliente on Friday, I also asked for a line on a foreign horse named Wolfhound in the Breeders' Cup Sprint, a John Gosden-trained longshot that did not appear in the book's second edition. A mutuel clerk checked behind the scenes. He returned, and advised me to return tomorrow (Saturday). On Saturday, I asked the same clerk for the line on Wolfhound. He checked behind the scenes. He returned, and told me to return the next weekend.

I assured the fellow I would not be back, but I did take $50 to win on Hollywood Wildcat in the Distaff and $50 to win on Diazo in the Classic. If Hollywood Wildcat won, my combined take from Caliente and Las Vegas would be $2,000.00. A Diazo upset would give me $1,000. Cylke had expressed interest in Hollywood Wildcat, but at 10–1 abstained, probably the smart decision.

Later on Saturday, I experienced some unexpected consolation. I planned a key bet on the Super Derby, a national simulcast from Louisiana Downs. My pick was a southern California shipper named Future Storm, who had finished second in the Del Mar Derby (on grass) following a wide and troubled trip. L. F. Caliente did not take the Louisiana signal, but I intended to shop for the best odds from the half-dozen tracks that did. I got 18–1 in Chicago, or so I thought.

"They don't take bets on simulcasts to other tracks," Cylke explained, "unless they take the signal from the host track directly as well." This I did not realize. When Future Storm finished a close fifth in the Super Derby, I took consolation.

By October handicappers know almost everything there is to know about the stakes horses on the national scene. The knowledge can be converted in multiple ways. With every important horse in the nation warming up for the Breeders' Cup, key bets can be found at home or at simulcast sites on every weekend.

Other talented horses, especially horses not eligible to the Breeders' Cup, may be shipping to golden opportunities elsewhere. In 1993, I was planning a major wager on The Wicked North, who on October 23, would be starting in the Washington, D.C. International mile, at Laurel. The Wicked North, a sprinter-miler type, really belonged in the Breeders' Cup Sprint, but he was not eligible, and the connections passed on paying the $120,000 penalty to supplement.

Knowing the stakes horses well also facilitates exotic wagering, the trifectas, the Pick-3's, the Pick-6's, and even the national Pick-7 scheduled every Breeders' Cup championship day. As will be seen, I was looking forward with unprecedented enthusiasm to Santa Anita's Pick-3 wagering format on Breeders' Cup day.

My first fall dividend occurred on October 9, at Belmont Park, when Star Of Cozzene was entered (new owners) in that track's Grade 1, $500,000-added Turf Classic Invitational, at a mile and one-half. At last, my chance. Although I had underestimated Star Of Cozzene, I had kept the grass star on my Horses To Beat list. A guaranteed underlay, Star Of Cozzene had finished first or second in all 10 of its 1993 races, astonishing consistency, with its latest two efforts over soft grass being best. Now *the course was firm*.

I was uncertain whether Star Of Cozzene's form would suffer a reversal, but I didn't care. A French import had caught my eye, and I thought the 4YO simply was better. I knew its odds would be better. Examine the past performances for the pair:

Star Of Cozzene
Own: Tomaeata Farm
SANTOS J A (109 22 24 12 .20)

Dk. b or br h. 5
Sire: Cozzene (Caro–Ire)
Dam: Star Gem (Pia Star)
Br: Double J Farm (Ky)
Tr: Hennig Mark (18 3 6 3 .17)

126

Lifetime Record:	32	14	8	3	$2,060,343					
1993	10	6	4	0	$1,635,744	Turf	23	11	5	2
1992	8	2	1	1	$107,859	Wet	2	1	1	0
Bel Ⓣ	4	4	0	0	$432,420	Dist Ⓣ	0	0	0	0

18Sep93–7Bel	sf	1⅜	T	:503	1:183	1:441	2:23	3↑	Man O'War-G1	117	4	5	53½	43	2½	15½	Santos J A		126	*.80	36–64	Star Of Cozzene1265½ Serrant126nk Dr. Kiernan126nk	Wid
29Aug93–10AP	sf	1¼	Ⓣ	:502	1:154	1:423	2:072	3↑	Arl Million-G1	115	4	5	44½	41½	32	13¼	Santos J A	L	126	*.80	60–40	Star Of Cozzene1263¼ Evanescent1262½ Johann Quatz1262½	Blo
11Aug93–9Sar	fm	1⅛	Ⓣ	:464	1:094	1:331	1:452	3↑	B Baruch H-G2	106	1	5	53½	42	41¼	21	Santos J A		123	*1.00	101–07	Furiously1191 StrOfCozzen123no RoylMountinInn1143	Boxed i
27Jun93–5Atl	fm	1³⁄₁₆	Ⓣ	:47	1:104	1:35	1:531	3↑	Csrs Intl H-G2	117	6	5	54	32	22	11	Santos J A	L	120	2.50	94–08	Star Of Cozzene1201 Lure1233¼ Finder's Choice1142½	
6Jun93–8Bel	gd	1¼	T	:481	1:12	1:353	1:584	3↑	ET ManhattanG2	116	7	5	52	31	31	1¾	Santos J A		118	2.70	96–14	Star Of Cozzene118¾ Lure1247 Solar Splendor1122½	
14May93–11Pim	fm	1⅛	Ⓣ	:464	1:104	1:351	1:473	3↑	ET Dixie H-G3	106	3	6	610	66½	33½	21½	Stevens G L	L	119	1.40	95–03	Lure1241½ Star Of Cozzene1192 Binary Light1151¾	W
30Apr93–8CD	fm	1⅛	Ⓣ	:47	1:104	1:342	1:461	3↑	ET Classic HG3	110	3	5	56	54½	43	2¾	Stevens G L	L	118	2.80	100 —	Lure123¾ Star Of Cozzene1182 Cleone116no	
10Apr93–8SA	fm	1	Ⓣ	:232	:474	1:112	1:35		El Rincon H-G2	104	5	5	42	32	3½	22	Stevens G L	LB	122	*.80	88–20	Val DesBois1182 StarOfCozzene1223½ C.SamMaggio113¾	Off
23Jan93–8SA	gd	1¼	Ⓣ	:482	1:131	1:371	2:013		Sn Marcos H-G2	107	3	6	63¾	31½	31½	11	Stevens G L	LB	120	*1.10	79–21	Star Of Cozzene1201 Kotashaan1162 CarnivalBaby1121½	Wid
1Jan93–8SA	gd	1⅛	Ⓣ	:474	1:114	1:361	1:481		Sn Gabrl H-G3	107	3	5	41½	52¾	1hd	13	Stevens G L	L	118	*1.40	78–10	Star Of Cozzene1183 Bistro Garden1143 Leger Cat115¾	

4 Wide stretch, ridden out

WORKOUTS: Oct 5 Bel 4f fst :482 B 12/57 Sep 29 Bel 4f fst :482 B 9/42 Sep 15 Bel 3f fst :363 B 2/13 Sep 8 AP 4f fst :51 B 31/49 ●Aug 24 Sar 5f fst 1:002 B 1/12 Aug 5 Sar 5f fst :593 H 2/21

Apple Tree (Fr)
Own: Sultan Mohammed Al Kabeer
SMITH M E (187 49 29 28 .26)

Ch. c. 4
Sire: Bikala (Kalamoun)
Dam: Pomme Rose (Carvin II)
Br: Paul de Moussac (Fr)
Tr: Fabre Andre (1 0 1 0 .00)

126

Lifetime Record:	15	4	3	3	$494,161					
1993	7	1	3	1	$203,552	Turf	15	4	3	3
1992	5	2	0	2	$281,951	Wet	0	0	0	0
Bel Ⓣ	0	0	0	0		Dist Ⓣ	8	1	3	2

19Sep93♦ Longchamp(Fr)	sf	*1¼ ⓉRH	2:144	3↑	Stk 60500 Prix du Prince d'Orange-G3	12½	Jarnet T	126	*.50	—	—	Apple Tree1262½ Marildo130½ Jackdidi1213	Tracked leader,ridden into lead 1-1/2f out,drew cl
15Aug93♦ Gelsenkrchn(Ger)	sf	*1½ ⓉRH	2:36	3↑	Stk 237000 Aral-Pokal-G1	77½	Jarnet T	132	*1.80	—	—	[D]George Augustus119nk Monsun132hd Shrewd Idea119½	Raced in mid-pack throughout, nev
4Jly93♦ Saint-Cloud(Fr)	gd	*1½ ⓉLH	2:282	3↑	Stk 442000 Grand Prix de Saint-Cloud-G1	21½	Guignard G	132	2.70	—	—	User Friendly1311½ Apple Tree134½ Modhish1341	Reserved in 5th, up for 2nd near line, no chance v
4Jun93♦ Epsom(GB)	gd	1½ ⓉLH	2:351	4↑	Stk 216000 Coronation Cup-G1	2hd	Jarnet T	126	5.50	—	—	Opera House126hd [D]Apple Tree126no Environment Friend1265	Tracked,led 2-1/2f out,drifted left,caught at line. D(
18May93♦ Saint-Cloud(Fr)	gd	*1½ ⓉLH	2:361	4↑	Stk 93000 Prix Jean de Chaudenay-G2	2hd	Jarnet T	134	*1.20	—	—	Modhish132hd [DH]Apple Tree134 [DH]Luazur1281½	6th early, 5th 3f out, bid with winner between horses,
30Apr93♦ Newmarket(GB)	gd	1½ ⓉRH	2:312	4↑	Stk 92800 Jockey Club Stakes-G2	2nk	Jarnet T	126	6.50	—	—	Zinaad121nk Apple Tree1262 Jeune121¾	Raced in 5th,led 3f out,clear 1f out,weakened,heac
4Apr93♦ Longchamp(Fr)	sf	*1¼ ⓉRH	2:073	4↑	Stk 94200 Prix d'Harcourt-G2	41	Jarnet T	130	6.20	—	—	Marildo123hd Dear Doctor130nk Polytain130¾	Unhurried in 6th,rallied fnl frlng,late gain but neve
27Sep92♦ Cologne(Ger)	gd	*1½ ⓉRH	2:313	3↑	Stk 350000 Europa-Preis-G1	11½	Jarnet T	122 b	1.60	—	—	Apple Tree1221½ Platini1221½ Hondo Mondo1321½	Tracked in 3rd, close up 2f out, led final fur
13Sep92♦ Longchamp(Fr)	gd	*1½ ⓉRH	2:324		Stk 138000 Prix Niel-G2	3½	Jarnet T	128	7.50	—	—	Songlines128no Petit Loup128½ Apple Tree1281	Tracked in 3rd, brushed with 2nd 1-1/2f out, fin
7Jun92♦ Chantilly(Fr)	yl	*1½ ⓉRH	2:301		Stk 794000 Prx du Jockey-Club(Frnch Drby)-G1	77½	Jarnet T	128	5.00	—	—	Polytain1281½ Marignan128¾ Contested Bid128¾	Prominent along rail, lacked rally, nev

A few specifics intrigued me. Except on soft grass, Star Of Cozzene had never won a Grade 1 stakes. He was a 5YO. His victories over Kotashaan (2) had occurred when his opponent was clearly below his best form and the turf was "off," officially labeled "good." His victories over Lure (2) occurred when his opponent was stretched to distances he found uncomfortable. Star Of Cozzene was a good one, but he was beatable.

Examine Apple Tree, trained by Europe's best, André Fabre. The 4YO's single Grade 1 was run in Germany, usually a negative, though the purse could not be dismissed. But in June and July of 1993, Apple Tree had finished second to Europe's finest turf horses, Opera House (head) and User Friendly. His "worst" races had occurred on soft ground; firm today. Apple Tree is a classic mile and one-half specialist. His last was easy. And top European grass racing remains pounds superior to the best U.S. grass racing.

Add that mix to Star Of Cozzene at 1–2 and Apple Tree at 9–2, and handicappers have found a solid bet. In a five-horse rendition of the Turf Classic, I gladly took Apple Tree as a key bet, and I also keyed the import atop exactas with the other three runners. Here is the result chart:

TURF CLASSIC

SEVENTH RACE
Belmont
OCTOBER 9, 1993

1½ MILES. (Turf)(2.24^{2}) 17th Running of THE TURF CLASSIC INVITATIONAL. Purse $500,000. (Grade I). 3-year-olds and upward. By subscription of $250 each which should accompany the nomination on Wednesday, December 16, 1992 or $500 on Monday, March 15, 1993 with the following eligibility payments; $650 due on or before Tuesday, June 1; $850 due on or before Sunday, August 15. Supplemental nomination and entry fee of $30,000, subject to invitation, may be made on or before the closing day of entries. The Racing Secretary will name a field of starters with also eligibles in order of preference five days prior to the day of running of the race; $5,000 additional to enter with 60% to the winner, 22% to second, 12% to third and 6% to fourth. Starters to be named at the closing time of entries. Weight for Age. Weights: 3-year-olds, 121 lbs. Older, 126 lbs. Fillies and mares, allowed 3 lbs. Trophies will be presented to the winning owner, trainer and jockey. The New York Racing Association Inc. reserves the right to transfer this race to the Main Track. Nominations closed Monday, March 15 with 36 invitees.

Value of Race: $500,000 Winner $300,000; second $110,000; third $60,000; fourth $30,000. Mutuel Pool $348,615.00 Exacta Pool $554,678.00

Last Raced	Horse	M/Eqt.	A.	Wt	PP	¼	½	1	1¼	Str	Fin	Jockey	Odds $1
19Sep93 Lch^{1}	Apple Tree-FR	• b	4	126	5	$4^{1\frac{1}{2}}$	$4^{\frac{1}{2}}$	$4^{1\frac{1}{2}}$	4^{1}	$2^{1\frac{1}{2}}$	$1^{2\frac{1}{4}}$	Smith M E	4.70
6Sep93 ^{5}Bel^{1}	Solar Splendor		6	126	2	$1^{1\frac{1}{2}}$	$1^{1\frac{1}{2}}$	$1^{1\frac{1}{2}}$	$1^{1\frac{1}{2}}$	1^{1}	$2^{\frac{1}{2}}$	McCauley W H	7.40
5Sep93 BAD^{3}	George Augustus	b	5	126	4	5	5	5	5	$4^{\frac{1}{2}}$	3^{1}	Bailey J D	17.40
18Sep93 ^{7}Bel^{1}	Star Of Cozzene		5	126	1	2^{hd}	2^{hd}	2^{hd}	2^{hd}	3^{hd}	$4^{1\frac{1}{4}}$	Santos J A	0.50
18Apr93 ^{4}SA^{3}	Fraise	b	5	126	3	3^{1}	3^{1}	3^{1}	3^{hd}	5	5	Valenzuela P A	3.30

OFF AT 4:18 Start Good. Won driving. Time, :26, :51^{2}, 1:16^{3}, 1:41, 2:04^{4}, 2:28^{1} Course firm.

$2 Mutuel Prices:

5-(E)-APPLE TREE-FR	11.40	7.40	11.60
2-(B)-SOLAR SPLENDOR		13.00	18.80
4-(D)-GEORGE AUGUSTUS			12.60

$2 EXACTA 5-2 PAID $97.40

Ch. c, by Bikala–Pomme Rose, by Carvin II. Trainer Fabre Andre. Bred by Paul de Moussac (Fr).

APPLE TREE settled just behind the leaders while three wide to the far turn, circled four wide entering the stretch, charged to the front inside the furlong marker then drew away under a vigorous hand ride. SOLAR SPLENDOR sprinted clear in the early stages, raced uncontested on the lead while setting moderate fractions for a mile, maintained a clear advantage into midstretch but couldn't withstand the winner's late charge. GEORGE AUGUSTUS trailed to the turn while saving ground, angled out approaching the stretch then rallied mildly to gain a share. STAR OF COZZENE under a snug hold early while saving ground, raced just behind the pacesetter while trapped along the inside leaving the backstretch, remained a factor to the top of the stretch then lacked a strong closing bid. FRAISE under a snug hold while a bit rank in the early stags, raced just outside STAR OF COZZENE to the quarter pole then lacked a further response.

POSTSCRIPT This was no contest. Apple Tree devoured the final quarter-mile of the twelve furlongs in 23⅕ seconds, leaving no doubt of his superiority.

The exacta paid a healthy $97.40. Normal-sized wagers against the odds-on favorite, win plus exacta, returned almost $2,000. Handicappers cannot fail to attack odds-on favorites that reveal any cracks.

Handicappers should appreciate too that bets like the one on Apple Tree cannot be placed with confidence, except as Star Of Cozzene's season has been observed intimately. The pattern of stakes races is far more meaningful than any race studied independently, or even a few races in combination. Star Of Cozzene is a very good horse, but he's especially vulnerable here and now.

And if Star Of Cozzene had spoiled the script, by winning again, no one could express surprise, including me.

On the same afternoon that Apple Tree defeated Star Of Cozzene, another future-book bet popped up unexpectedly. The brilliant California juvenile filly Sardula lost at 1–5 at Oak Tree in the Grade 1 Oak Leaf Stakes. The winner was Phone Chatter, the distant second choice, trained by the excellent Dick Mandella. The finish was fast and furious, the speed and pace figures of both fillies solid.

Almost instantly, I decided I would back Sardula next time, which meant the Breeders' Cup Juvenile Fillies, either in the Future Book, if the odds crept up, or on race day at a simulcast site, probably Philadelphia Park.

The Oak Leaf was Sardula's first route. She was pressed relentlessly on the front for six furlongs, then challenged severely in the upper stretch by Phone Chatter. Obviously tired, Sardula dug in, struggling until the end. She lost by a long neck. My reaction was that Sardula would turn the tables on Phone Chatter next time, perhaps by several lengths.

For this position, I can cite ample precedent. As a young 3YO, unseasoned at the route, Winning Colors lost a close call to Charlie Whittingham's Goodbye Halo on their first engagement. On the second, three weeks later, Winning Colors won by ten. Goodbye Halo never came close to Winning Colors again.

A few seasons ago at Del Mar the champion juvenile filly Lite Light trounced a Jack Van Berg filly named Beyond Perfection at seven furlongs. Weeks later, in the first route for each, Beyond Perfection upset Lite Light wire to wire by two lengths. Beyond Perfection never finished within Lite Light's shadow again.

In the seven-furlong sprint prior to the 1993 Oak Leaf, Sardula had bludgeoned Phone Chatter by seven lengths. Phone Chatter won by a neck at a mile and one-sixteenth. Why? In my opinion, because Sardula lacked experience and seasoning at the route, not to mention the hard-pressed pace she had battled. Sardula tired, and was beaten. It happens.

When it does, handicappers might expect the authentically outstanding horses to rebound feverishly. Sardula represented that kind of filly.

The question was whether the future-book odds on Sardula would be raised. From a 2–1 floor, I wanted 5–1. After her loss, surprise surprise, Sardula stayed stuck at 2–1. My line was 2–1 too, but the bet would be sent on race day to Philadelphia Park.

The weekend of stakes-festival weekends began with a bang on Friday night, October 15, at The Meadowlands, with the Grade 1, $500,000-added Meadowlands Cup. The moment Bill Shoemaker announced Diazo would start instead in the next day's Jockey Club Gold Cup, in New York, Bobby Frankel's southern California shipper Marquetry became a standout. The eastern handicappers did not altogether agree.

The connections of the journeyman handicap horse Valley Crossing had completed the week's pre-race maneuvers by switching their five-year-old from the Jockey Club Gold Cup, purse of $850,000-added, to the Meadowlands Cup. Valley Crossing had been participating in a series of graded stakes for older handicap horses, winning once, and the bettors accepted him as a main contender at the Meadowlands. He went to the post a 3–1 shot.

I gave Valley Crossing scarcely a look.

The three-year-old Press Card was also 3–1. I gave Press Card scarcely a shot.

Marquetry was so much the best, how could he possibly be 5–2? He promptly sailed around the course unchallenged and paid $7. The margin of victory was eight lengths and it could have been twice as great. In retrospect, The Meadowlands Cup strikes me as the year's best bet.

I did not see the race until afterwards. The outcome frustrates an out-of-town handicapper because he realizes he might have risked more money. Expecting Marquetry to go as a heavy favorite, I had included the Frankel shipper in a package of weekend wagers I judged appropriate to the occasion.

The weekend of October 15–17 preceded the Breeders' Cup by three weeks. The nation's major tracks literally would be staging grounds for the preliminary stakes to the championships. The tracks trotted out an avalanche of big-ticket stakes. I counted fifteen graded stakes on Saturday, another twelve on Sunday.

That menu did not encompass a program of nine stakes races at Oak Tree, all limited to Cal-breds, on the annual California Cup card.

On an afternoon billed as Breeders' Cup Preview Day, Belmont Park scheduled four Grade 1s and two Grade 3s, including the Jockey Club Gold Cup, The Beldame, The Champagne, and The Frizette Stakes, traditional mainstays all.

The weekend inventory totaled thirty-six stakes, none of them carrying a purse value below $50,000. The overkill might have been too much, except for a strategy I have learned to rely upon on this special weekend. Favor the favorites, and the well-bet co-favorites.

The logic is oversimplified deliberately, and the strategy strictly empirical. In prepping for the Breeders' Cup, the horses will be sharp as knives, and with so many spots to choose from, horsemen can find easy pickings. As a result, most of the events qualify as carefully chosen warm-ups for the main event. It's poor form to lose the stepping-stone stakes. No wonder the data show Breeders' Cup winners have tended to win their preceding race.

Why fight it? My strategy was to spread a number of $200 win wagers in Las Vegas on selected good things, setting betting lines as low as 2–1 and 3–2. By winning half the bets I would double my money. Here is the 1993 scorecard:

Of fourteen stakes, nine selections won. Only five races proved bettable, three winners, two losers. Much ado about noth-

STAKES	TRACK	HORSE	LINE	ODDS	FIN	NET
FRIDAY						
Meadowlands Cup (Gr. 1)	Med	Marquetry	2	5–2	1	$500
SATURDAY						
Jockey Club Gold Cup (Gr. 1)	Bel	Diazo	2	2	Out	200
The Champagne (Gr. 1)	Bel	Dehere	3–2	1–5	1	No Play
The Frizette (Gr. 1)	Bel	Heavenly Prize	1	2	1	$480
Beldame Stakes (Gr. 1)	Bel	Dispute	2	7–5	1	No Play
Kelso Handicap (Gr. 3)	Bel	Lure	3–2	3–5	1	No Play
Laurel Futurity (Gr. 3)	Lrl	Dove Hunt	2	1–2	1	No Play
Selima Stakes (Gr. 3)	Lrl	Irish Forever	2	2	1	$400
Keeneland BC (Gr. 3)	Kee	Adam Smith	2	6–5	Out	No Play
SUNDAY						
Spinster Stakes (Gr. 1)	Kee	Paseana	3–2	6–5	1	No Play
Rothman's Int'l (Gr. 1)	WO	Modhish	2	8–5	Out	No Play
E.P. Taylor Stakes (Gr. 2)	WO	Hero's Love	2	1–1	1	No Play
Goodwood Handicap (Gr. 2)	SA	Region	5–2	7–2	2	(200)
Colonel Koester (Gr. 2)	SA	Leger Cat	2	1–1	Lost	No Play

ing? Not exactly. The profit was $980. It's fun, and it works. The ROI was 1.98, exceedingly high. If favorites should be bet at all, this is the ripest moment.

The weekend's stakes menagerie also should supply valuable insights into the coming Breeders' Cup competition. The Jockey Club Gold Cup became a stinging disappointment. Diazo fell onto the lead in milkwagon fractions of 25⅕, 49⅗, 114⅕, and 138⅗ to the mile, but collapsed when challenged. Coming off Belmont's far turn, Diazo's action was strange, his head cocked sideways right, his stride and extension short. The entire field blew by him in a rush. He summoned no response. Not even Diazo's most fanatical supporter (me) could imagine him bouncing back to win the Breeders' Cup Classic in three weeks. Diazo probably would not even start. My future-book wager was dead on arrival.

Another aspect of the Jockey Club Gold Cup warrants commentary. Prior to the race, the outcome appeared to many observers wide open. *Daily Racing Form* executive columnist Joe Hirsch viewed the race as an open affair. That being so, Hirsch suggested handicappers best prefer the older horses, notably Devil His Due and the vastly improved 4YO Brunswick.

That tradition has long since been unmasked. The trio of 3YOs in the gate, Diazo, Miner's Mark, and Colonial Affair, not only fit the class of the race snugly, in 1993 they figured to finish one, two, three. Whenever the older handicap division has been thin and weak, the ranking 3YOs definitely belong. Authentically talented 3YOs can win powerfully.

If the older handicap division has been stocked with excellence, that's different. Now the 3YOs must be genuinely supreme to prevail. Most leading 3YOs will be outclassed. In recent seasons, however, the graded stakes of fall open to 3UP have been consistently hospitable to the 3YOs.

Miner's Mark nipped Colonial Affair by a lip in the Jockey Club Gold Cup. The older handicap horses did not get a smell.

When the big race was over, another subtlety of handicapping went unremarked. When fractional times creep along as slowly as they did in the 1993 Jockey Club Gold Cup, the furious driving finishes can be entirely misleading. Miner's Mark completed the final quarter-mile of the twelve furlongs in 23⅘ seconds. Colonial Affair roared home in 23⅗ seconds.

More often than not, the powerful finishes will not be repeated when fractional times return to normal. After merely galloping, stakes horses *should* roar home. The circumstance is run-of-the-mill in grass racing, notably in Europe. Forced to trail a normal pace, and gain on the pace between calls, the same closers do not roar home.

Turf writers who accepted the energetic late flourishes of Miner's Mark and Colonial Affair as evidence the 3YOs were primed to shine in the Breeders' Cup Classic did not know what they were talking about. The 3YOs of 1993 were an undistinguished crop from January to June to November. Both of these unremarkable 3YOs would be outsiders in the world's championship race.

A preview stakes that hit the bull's-eye dead center was the Frizette for juvenile fillies. The colt Dehere may have looked like a division leader at 1–5 in The Champagne, but Heavenly Prize had delivered the faster performance from start to finish. Review the comparative times:

The Champagne	Dehere	23⅕,	46⅗,	112	135⅘	by four
The Frizette	Heavenly Prize	22⅘,	45⅕,	110	135⅖	by seven

Suddenly, southern California's Sardula and Phone Chatter faced a worthy opponent. Trained by Shug McGaughey, who won an astonishing five stakes on the Belmont Preview program, Heavenly Prize tickled my fancy for the Breeders' Cup Juvenile Fillies.

At Santa Anita, the eastern filly probably would be underbet. Before I could cancel my advanced play on Sardula, the Beyer

Speed Figures for The Frizette came to life. Speed figures apply forcibly to 2YOs. Consider the east and west comparison:

Heavenly Prize
Own: Phipps Ogden
B. f. 2 (Feb)
Sire: Seeking the Gold (Mr. Prospector)
Dam: Oh What a Dance (Nijinsky II)
Br: Ogden Phipps (Ky)
Tr: McGaughey Claude III (—)
119

Lifetime Record :	2 2 0 0	$165,000		
1993	2 2 0 0	$165,000	Turf	0 0 0 0
1992	0 M 0 0		Wet	0 0 0 0
SA	0 0 0 0		Dist	0 0 0 0

16Oct93-4Bel fst 1 :224 :451 1:10 1:352 ⒻFrizette-G1 94 5 6 62½ 2hd 12½ 17 Smith M E 119 2.40 91-12 Heavenly Prize1197 Facts Of Love1194¾ Footing1192½ Wi
15Sep93-5Bel fst 6f :224 :462 :583 1:104 ⒻMd Sp Wt 88 4 4 52¾ 2hd 12½ 19 Smith M E 117 *1.40 86-19 Heavenly Prize1179 Amy Be Happy1171¾ Vibelle117nk
WORKOUTS: ●Oct 14 Bel 3f fst :352 H 1/12 Oct 9 Bel 5f fst 1:00 H 2/25 Oct 4 Bel 4f fst :494 B 19/29 Sep 26 Bel 3f sly :372 B 3/4 ●Sep 12 Bel 4f fst :464 Hg 1/66 Sep 6 Bel 4f fst :491 B 12/29

Sardula
Own: Moss Mr & Mrs J S
B. f. 2 (May)
Sire: Storm Cat (Storm Bird)
Dam: Honor an Offer (Hoist the Flag)
Br: M & M Stables & Overbrook Farm (Ky)
Tr: Mayberry Brian A (13 1 6 1 .08)
119

Lifetime Record :	3 2 1 0	$193,450		
1993	3 2 1 0	$193,450	Turf	0 0 0 0
1992	0 M 0 0		Wet	0 0 0 0
SA	1 0 1 0	$40,000	Dist	1 0 1 0

9Oct93-8SA fst 1 1/16 :222 :462 1:104 1:413 ⒻOak Leaf-G1 97 2 1 1½ 1½ 2hd 2½ Delahoussaye E LB 116 *.20e 95-06 Phone Chatter117½ Sardula1167½ Tricky Code1153 G
4Sep93-8Dmr fst 7f :214 :443 1:091 1:213 ⒻDmr DebutantG2 100 3 2 11 1½ 13½ 17½ Delahoussaye E LB 116 *.70 92-10 Sardula1167½ Phone Chatter119nk Ballerina Gal1142½
A bit greenly, ridden out
7Aug93-6Dmr fst 5½f :213 :443 :561 1:03 ⒻMd Sp Wt 96 5 1 11 2hd 11½ 110 Delahoussaye E LB 117 *.80 96-09 Sardula11710 My Fling1171½ Princess Leia M D1176½
WORKOUTS: Oct 21 SA 4f fst :48 H 11/42 ●Oct 2 SA 5f fst :581 H 1/49 Sep 26 SA 5f fst 1:031 H 44/50 Sep 19 SA 4f fst :483 B 13/50 Aug 28 Dmr 4f fst :474 H 7/48 Aug 21 Dmr 4f fst :473 H 6/41

The big wins notwithstanding, Heavenly Prize might not be Sardula's equal, after all. The speed figures favored Sardula convincingly. All three of Sardula's figures exceeded Heavenly Prize's best. Sardula had run faster around two turns than had Heavenly Prize around one turn.

If handicappers imagine Heavenly Prize might have run faster, if pressed, consider two points. One, 2YOs tend to run as fast as they can for as long as they can, even when clear. Two, the first time good horses encounter a prolonged, exhaustive stretch battle against a comparable foe, they tend to lose.

No one can deny absolutely that Heavenly Prize might continue to improve, but so might Sardula. I kept the southern California filly at the head of the juvenile filly class.

Meanwhile, back in southern California, and the nine-stakes California Cup program, I was destined to enjoy a taste of the good life at the racetrack. I owe a grateful nod to colleagues Tom Brohamer and Frank Romano. The three of us were engaged in an on-site educational program in handicapping, a five-week training program we conducted on weekends called "Playing the Races," sponsored by the Oak Tree Racing Association. The sessions included the application of ideas and methods during the afternoon's races. Oak Tree was offering bettors the rollover triples, an overlapping series of Pick-3's, beginning at the second race. In effect, there are six three-race parlays, and on this day I would be pleased to watch all six parlays click.

Strategy is crucial. By combining key horses and *all* contenders on multiple tickets, bettors provide themselves with an excellent chance to cover any particular leg, and a reasonably good chance to cover the three legs. Costs, at three dollars a parlay, can be controlled. Payoffs are generally generous, and frequently tremendous, though not always. Suffice to say the Pick-3 can be an outstanding betting proposition, and the rollover Pick-3 can become exciting.

To illustrate, below are the win mutuels and Pick-3 payoffs and costs for the half dozen parlays of California Cup day. Key horses, or "singles," are indicated by the race number where they won.

RACES 2,3,4
2nd $24.40
3rd   10.60
4th   8.80 (KEY)
COST: $18.00
PAYOFF: $569.10

RACES 3,4,5
3rd $10.60
4th   8.80 (KEY)
5th   24.80
COST: $45.00
PAYOFF: $1,120.50

RACES 4,5,6
4th $8.80 (KEY)
5th   24.80
6th   4.20 (KEY)
COST: $15.00
PAYOFF: $426.90

RACES 5,6,7
5th $24.80
6th   4.20 (KEY)
7th   8.40 (KEY)
COST: $15.00
PAYOFF: $305.10

RACES 6,7,8
6th $4.20 (KEY)
7th   8.40
8th   2.60
COST: $6.00
PAYOFF: $24.60

RACES 7,8,9
7th $8.40 (KEY)
8th   2.60
9th   6.20
COST: $6.00
PAYOFF: $49.20

TOTAL COST: $105.00   TOTAL PAYOFF: $2,495.40

A multifaceted wager, the rollover Pick-3 is clobbered best when multiple key horses, not necessarily "singles," come through. One key horse can be a favorite, but not an odds-on favorite. Odds-on favorites might be used as contenders, as in Race 8, but not as keys.

The take would have been $569.10 less if Tom Brohamer had not prompted me to use the eventual winner of Race 2. Tom called the horse as a second choice to an odds-on favorite. In addition, I made a fortunate call in Race 5. Surprisingly, all three handicappers at the training session called the same horse as first choice. The race was a contentious sprint and I had marked six contenders. Of the other five, I put the eventual winner on the main ticket. When that horse won, it linked Race 5 to all the horses in the other legs.

In Race 8, the odds-on winner was our friend Best Pal, a Cal-bred who was too much racehorse against other state-breds. I used a second horse in Race 8. The horse placed. If that non-favorite had won, the final two parlays would have paid much more generously.

Unlike state-bred cards and state-bred stakes races else-where, the California Cup program qualifies as a truly classy card. The California breeding program not only reaches deep into the stallion farms of Kentucky and Florida, but also the home front's sires and mares have played an increasingly salient part. In 1993, when Best Pal cruised at 1–5 in the $300,000-added Cal Cup Classic, the nation's top handicap horse, Bertrando, was eligible for the same race. Cal Cup stakes winners as a group have been winners as well of numerous open, listed, and graded stakes. Slow horses need not apply.

Simulcast handicappers should realize too that Cal-breds as a rule do so well in open company, figure handicappers of southern California do not bother to adjust par times for races limited to Cal-breds. No doubt certain nonwinners allowances and Cal-bred stakes will be one, two, three, or several lengths slower than comparable open races, but Cal-breds routinely shape up as competitive with Kentucky-breds and Florida-breds. Out-of-town simulcast handicappers should not be mistaken. Cal-breds deserve the bettor's respect.

On Cal Cup Day, finally, the most provocative handicapping involved one of my Horses To Watch, in the 7th, a grass mile named the Brown Forman California Cup Mile Handicap, $150,000-guaranteed, 3UP. The best bet of the day was 9–2 on the morning line. It's practically imperative to understand why.

Below are the past performances for the favorite and the easiest of winners by three-and-a-half lengths.

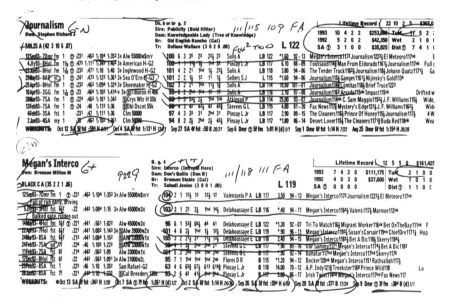

The gelding Megan's Interco had beaten Journalism a month ago by two indisputable lengths. In that encounter, Journalism not only never threatened, but also he appeared to be laboring late.

On Beyer Speed, Megan's Interco was a "double-fig," each of

its last two speed figures superior to any other speed figure in the field. Using speed and pace figures, Journalism showed a combination of 115–109, but Megan's Interco showed a 118–111.

On trip handicapping, in the early phase of the September 12 grass mile at Del Mar, Megan's Interco had been rank. Jockey Pat Valenzuela had attempted to rate the lightly raced 4YO, but to no avail, and rounding the clubhouse turn, he let Megan's Interco go. In grass racing, such an incident typically means the horse will expire in the stretch.

Megan's Interco bounded home handily.

So why was Journalism 5–2 on the morning line and Megan's Interco 9–2? Since class evaluation in stakes is this book's main territory, maybe the answer lies there. Journalism had been a multiple graded-stakes winner of 1993. Megan's Interco had never won a stakes.

How to reconcile?

A few fine points of class evaluation carry the cause well here, with the relevant clues evident in the recent records.

First, of Journalism, here was a high-priced claiming horse who changed hands privately earlier in 1993 and suddenly jumped up seriously in class. Notoriously a rugged miler, with back class, Journalism was fully capable of defeating undistinguished stakes line-ups on his best days. He did exactly that.

When this type of hardhitting veteran gets awfully good, handicappers must string along until the peaked form slackens. Once form dulls, handicappers should back off just as quickly. The horses have begun to regress. They rarely return to top form soon, and maybe never. Journalism's loudest shots had been fired from March to July, a rejuvenated form cycle experienced handicappers will have witnessed repeatedly. At lower stakes levels, Journalism has been not unlike another born-again stakes winner of 1993, and of this manuscript, Jovial.

Megan's Interco had not yet won a stakes, but he represents one of the surest class bargains in racing: the talented, lightly raced, 4YO now putting it all together and improving impressively while moving ahead in class. Megan's Interco had finished third or worse twice in twelve starts, winning five races, *with his best efforts the last two against the most advanced conditions the gelding has faced.*

It helps that Megan's Interco's sire is Interco, a successful turf sire. Trainer Jenine Sahadi, a new face of 1993, had displayed a deft hand from the outset, winning above the 20 percent threshold on dirt and grass, short and long.

Finally, the Cal Cup Mile is not a Grade 1 or Grade 2 event. It's a stakes limited to Cal-breds. Of the eleven horses competing, six were obviously outgunned.

Megan's Interco dominated the race as if he were an odds-on favorite. He split horses with rapid acceleration entering the far turn, sped to the front, and drew off. Getting not enough respect on the tote, Megan's Interco paid $8.40, a definite overlay. Review the result chart.

SEVENTH RACE
Santa Anita
OCTOBER 16, 1993

1 MILE. (Turf)(1.32^3) 4th Running of THE BROWN FORMAN CALIFORNIA CUP MILE HANDICAP. $150,000 Guaranteed. 3-year-olds and upward, bred in California. By subscription of $50 each (Early Bird Nomination) if made on or before Friday, August 6, 1993, or $300 each (Regular Nomination) if made on or before Thursday, Ocrober 7, 1993, fee to accomapny the nomination. There will be no Supplementary Nominations. All horses shall pay $500 to pass the entry box and $1,000 additional to start, with $82,500 guaranteed to the winner, $30,000 to second, $22,500 to third, $11,500 to fourth and $3,750 to fifth. Weights Monday, October 11. High weights preferred, adjusted for scale and sex allowance. Starters to be named through the entry box by Thursday, October 14, 1993. Trophies will be presented to the winning owner, breeder, trainer and jockey. Closed Thursday, October 7, 1993, with 52 Early Bird and 1 Regular Nominations.

Value of Race: $150,000 Winner $82,500; second $30,000; third $22,500; fourth $11,250; fifth $3,750. Mutuel Pool $509,536.00 Exacta Pool $520,343.00 Quinella Pool $76,023.00

Last Raced	Horse	M/Eqt.	A.	Wt	PP	St	¼	½	¾	Str	Fin	Jockey	Odds $1
12Sep93 7Dmr1	Megan's Interco	LB	4	119	9	7	41½	31	21½	11½	13½	Black C A	3.20
25Sep93 5BM6	Moscow Changes	LB	3	114	4	1	5hd	6hd	41½	32½	24	Atkinson P	7.20
12Sep93 7Dmr2	Journalism	LB	5	122	2	4	1hd	11	1hd	2½	31¾	Solis A	2.00
8Oct93 8SA3	Hill Pass	LBb	4	116	7	9	7hd	5hd	51	54	42¾	Delahoussaye E	4.40
25Sep93 5BM10	Der Rosenkavalier	Lb	3	113	5	3	21½	2½	31½	4hd	51½	Flores D R	a-14.90
25Sep93 5BM5	El Atroz	LB	3	115	10	11	9hd	94	71	62	61¼	Baze R A	a-14.90
10Oct92 2SA2	Breakfast Table	LBf	9	115	3	8	11	10½	108	81	7nk	Stevens G L	10.00
2Oct93 9Fpx6	Town Caper	B	3	111	8	6	62	7hd	8½	71½	86½	Gonzalez S Jr	91.50
15Sep93 7Dmr6	Never Round	LB	4	116	11	10	102	8½	91½	92	95½	Hernandez R A	117.40
28Sep93 12Fpx6	What A Spell	LBbf	5	115	6	5	3hd	42½	6½	1020	10	Desormeaux K J	13.00
26Sep93 11Fpx5	Fax News	LB	4	114	1	2	81½	11	11	11	—	Nakatani C S	13.30

Fax News: Eased
a-Coupled: Der Rosenkavalier and El Atroz.

OFF AT 3:47 Start Good. Won driving. Time, :22^4, :46, 1:09^4, 1:21^4, 1:34 Course firm.

$2 Mutuel Prices:				
	9–MEGAN'S INTERCO	8.40	5.00	3.00
	5–MOSCOW CHANGES		7.60	3.80
	3–JOURNALISM			2.60

$2 EXACTA 9–5 PAID $60.20 $2 QUINELLA 5–9 PAID $34.80

B. g, by Interco–Don's Quillo, by Don B. Trainer Sahadi Jenine. Bred by Bronson Stable (Cal).

MEGAN'S INTERCO, angled in on the first turn to be close up inside down the backstretch, squeezed through between rivals leaving the backstretch to challenge alongside JOURNALISM on the second turn, gained the lead into the stretch and drew clear under steady handling. MOSCOW CHANGES saved ground early, advanced inside on the second turn, angled out for the drive and was best of the rest. JOURNALISM held a short lead inside to the stretch and weakened. HILL PASS, bumped and steadied shaprly early, was bumped between rivals on the backstretch, found the rail on the second turn but lacked the needed rally. DER ROSENKAVALIER, bumped at the start, dueled outside JOURNALISM to the second turn and weakened. EL ATROZ, bumped on the backstretch and checked briefly, also lacked a rally. BREAKFAST TABLE, outrun to the stretch, angled wide and passed tiring rivals. TOWN CAPER raced wide throughout and very wide into the stretch. NEVER ROUND, four wide through the first turn, was bumped on the backstretch. WHAT A SPELL, bumped early, raced wide. FAX NEWS dropped far back and was eased.

POSTSCRIPT The extensive treatment of Megan's Interco makes sense. The illustration is not isolated. Every season at every major track, a few lightly raced 4YOs reach full athletic maturity and begin to soar. As they move ahead in the stakes division, they can overpower much of the competition below Grade 2. As the horses advance, look for improved speed and pace figures in combination.

Do not believe for a moment these talented 4YOs will be outgunned when they advance in the stakes division. They are not.

A week after the Big Preview and two weeks prior to the Breeders' Cup, handicappers will hardly be starved for stakes activity. Keeneland fall continues with its crowded schedule of outstanding stakes, on this weekend featuring the Breeders' Futurity for juvenile colts and the companion Alcibiades Stakes for juvenile fillies. I might have won the 1993 Alcibiades, to be explained shortly.

On the festival circuit, handicappers get the second weekend of Laurel's International Stakes Festival plus a tasty innovation dubbed the Festival of the Sun, at Calder. I wanted a piece of the Festival of the Sun from the moment I became aware of the occasion, but I had no access to the past performances and did not spot a suitable shipper in the entries. Besides, none of the races were simulcast to southern California. Maybe next year?

Keeneland, Calder, and other tracks aside, I was preoccupied this weekend with a major play at Laurel. After waiting for the race for seven weeks, I got down in Las Vegas for $500 on the Washington D.C. International Mile, a simulcast event dripping in international tradition, but in recent seasons reduced from twelve furlongs to ten and again now from ten furlongs to a mile.

I had approached the fall weekend as usual, searching for outstanding horses not eligible to the Breeders' Cup. It's a clever strategy, and I recommend it unhesitatingly. My best bet this year was the southern California shipper The Wicked North, simply the best horse in the race. He had won his last two, a sprint at Del Mar, defeating Thirty Slews, and a grass mile at Bay Meadows, where he cakewalked after pressing a blistering pace. Unless the D.C. Mile would be stocked with outstanding European grass milers, the kind that should be sent to the Breeders' Cup Mile instead, it was not easy (for me) to see The Wicked North as a loser. The colt was another of those rampantly improving 4YOs coming to the pitch of performance.

The days preceding the D.C. Mile were filled with good news and bad news. Although no Breeders' Cup candidates were scheduled to go, several Grade 3 winners from France and England were being pointed toward the $600,000 stakes. The good news was a cargo strike in Paris. The French milers would never leave the ground.

The bad news was all too familiar in 1993; rain. It poured in Maryland throughout the week. Laurel's turf course would be soaked; officially yielding. Having no idea whether The Wicked North would handle soft grass, I canceled the bet.

Then, the day before the D.C. Mile, trainer David Bernstein was quoted, "The Wicked North had a fantastic work on soft grass at Del Mar. We know he can handle the course. We think he's gonna be an important Grade 1 horse in 1994 and we expect him to win this race. If he does, we're thinking about the Breeders' Cup Sprint."

I swallowed Bernstein's line. I reinstated the bet. In a small field, my line was 5–2, which The Wicked North exceeded at 7–2.

Without a Grade 1 or Grade 2 horse behind him, The Wicked North fell onto a relaxed solo lead in dawdling fractions of 24, 48, and 112⅘ after six furlongs. Watching the Santa Anita simulcast I announced smugly The Wicked North would win by open lengths in a breeze. Seconds later, The Wicked North caved in. He almost quit running, and was passed in a hurry. The scene was eerily similar to Diazo's surrender in the slow-paced Jockey Club Gold Cup. The Wicked North straggled in last.

To rub it in, with the turf course still yielding, I skipped the next day's All Along Stakes at Laurel. In a two-horse Grade 2 stakes for older fillies and mares, I had preferred Lady Blessington, who not only won, but won at 4–1.

On Saturday, at Keeneland, I might have backed Wayne Lukas's juvenile filly Stellar Cat in the Alcibiades Stakes (Gr. 2). Steller Cat laughed at the local fillies by six lengths, and paid 3–1.

The results charts for the pair of Grade 2s contain an angle of immense interest to handicappers, an angle that shoots to the surface more than ever in the numerous stakes characterized by small fields. The angle regards betting strategy. Can handicappers recognize it?

ALL ALONG

TENTH RACE	
Laurel	
OCTOBER 23, 1993	

1⅛ MILES. (Turf)(1.46) 6th Running of THE ALL ALONG STAKES. $250,000 Guaranteed (Grade II) Fillies and mares, 3–year–olds and upward. By subscription of $250 each on or before Friday, June 25, 1993 which should accompany the nomination. A sustaining payment of $500 each is due on or before Friday, August 20, 1993. Late nominations may be made on or before Friday October 8, 1993 by payment of $12,500 each, which is inclusive of all fees and should accompany the nomination, of which $11,750 is refundable if the nominee is excluded. A fee of $2,000 should be paid at the time of pre–entry by 3:00 P.M, Wednesday, October 13, 1993. $2,000 to enter with $250,000 Guaranteed to be divided 60% to first, 20% to second, 10% to third, 6% to fourth and 4% to fifth. This race will be limited to a maximum of fourteen (14) starters. A selection committee will name the starters and also eligibles in order of preference on or before 12 noon Thursday, October 14, 1993. Weights: 3–year–olds, 119 lbs. Older, 123 lbs. Non–winners of a G1 race on the turf in 1993 allowed, 3 lbs. G2 race on the turf in 1993, 5 lbs. A G3 race on the turf in 1993, 7 lbs. High weights on the scale preferred. Starters to be named through the entry box on Thursday, October 21, 1993 by 10:00 A.M. In the event that more than fourteen (14) horses pass through then entry box, all the also eligibles will be refunded their pre–entry and entry fee if they fail to draw into the body of the race. Trophies will be presented to the winning owner, trainer and jockey. Closed Friday, October 8, 1993 with 103 nominations.

Value of Race: $250,000 Winner $150,000; second $50,000; third $25,000; fourth $15,000; fifth $10,000. Mutuel Pool $59,180.00 Exacta Pool $93,323.00

Last Raced	Horse	M/Eqt.	A.Wt	PP	St	¼	½	¾	Str	Fin	Jockey	Odds $1
11Sep93 8Bel3	Lady Blessington-FR	L	5 116	4	2	5	5	5	44	1no	Black C A	4.10
28Aug93 9AP3	Via Borghese	L	4 118	2	4	42½	42½	41	3hd	2hd	Velasquez J	0.70
26Sep93 9Pim1	Logan's Mist	Lb	4 116	3	3	2½½	2½	1½	1½	31¾	Prado E S	9.30
9Oct93 10Lrl1	Mz. Zill Bear	L	4 116	1	1	32	33	22	21	45½	Bailey J D	3.50
11Oct93 5Bel5	Grab the Green	L	5 116	5	5	1½	12	33	5	5	Santos J A	6.30

OFF AT 5:24 Start Good. Won driving. Time, :234, :482, 1:132, 1:383, 1:512 Course yielding.

$2 Mutuel Prices:	4–LADY BLESSINGTON–FR	10.20	3.40	2.40
	2–VIA BORGHESE		2.60	2.10
	3–LOGAN'S MIST			2.40
	$2 EXACTA 4–2 PAID $21.20			

Ch. m, by Baillamont–Lady Sharp, by Sharpman. Trainer Hennig Mark. Bred by Horse Breeding Corp (Fr).

ALCIBIADES

EIGHTH RACE
Keeneland
OCTOBER 23, 1993

1¹⁄₁₆ MILES. (1.40⁴) 42nd Running of the ALCIBIADES (GRADE II). Purse $200,000 Guaranteed. Fillies, 2-year-olds. By subscription of $50 each which should accompany the nomination if made on or before April 1, 1992 or $100 each on or before December 1, 1992. To remain eligible a payment of $1,000 each must be made by August 2, 1993; with $1,000 to pass the entry box and an additional $1,000 to start. The added monies and all fees less the awards to the nominators to be divided 65% to the owner of the winner, 20% to second, 10% to third, 5% to fourth. The original nominator of the winner to receive $6,000, $4,000 to second and $2,000 to third. Weight, 118 lbs. The maximum number of starters for the Alcibiades will be limited to fourteen. In the event more than fourteen entries pass the entry box the fourteen starters will be determined at that time with preference to those that have accumulated the highest earnings. Same owner entry cannot start to the exclusion of a single entry. Supplementary nominations may be made at entry time by payments of $5,000 each with $5,000 additional to start. Starters to be named through the entry box by the usual time of closing. A Gold Julep Cup will be presented to the owner of the winner. (The first four finishers in the Alcibiades are automatically made eligible for the Ashland stakes of 1994 as to nominating fee.) Closed with 151 original nominations, 95 second payment nominations, 35 final nominations, 3 supplemental nominations.

Value of Race: $188,000 Winner $122,200; second $37,600; third $18,800; fourth $9,400. Mutuel Pool $258,108.00 Exacta Pool $150,531.00 Quinella Pool $31,896.00

Last Raced	Horse	M/Eqt. A.Wt	PP	St	¼	½	¾	Str	Fin	Jockey	Odds $1
9Oct93 4Kee¹	Stellar Cat (S)	Lb 2 118	1	4	1¹	1¹	1¹½	1⁴	1⁶	Sellers S J	3.40
9Oct93 3Kee¹	Slew Kitty Slew	L 2 118	6	6	6	6	5³	4¹	2¹½	Barton D M	13.40
2Oct93 10WO⁶	Beau Blush (S)	2 118	5	2	3¹½	3¹	3½	2¹	3³	Maple S	18.90
30Oct93 10TP¹	My Sea Castles (S)	2 118	3	1	2½	2ʰᵈ	2ʰᵈ	5	4½	Arguello F A Jr	0.80
28Sep93 7Due¹	Tipper Too	Lbf 2 118	2	5	5¹½	5ʰᵈ	4²½	3ʰᵈ	5	Martinez W	11.90
18Sep93 9AP¹	Mariah's Storm	2 118	4	3	4¹½	4½	6	—	—	Lester R N	3.10

Mariah's Storm:Eased

OFF AT 4:41 Start Good. Won driving. Time, :23, :46², 1:10⁴, 1:37³, 1:44³ Track fast.

(S)—Supplemental Nomination

$2 Mutuel Prices:

1–STELLAR CAT	8.80	5.00	3.20
6–SLEW KITTY SLEW		7.00	3.40
5–BEAU BLUSH			5.00

$2 EXACTA 1–6 PAID $78.00 $2 QUINELLA 1–6 PAID $35.00 CARRY–OVER $32,973.00

Dk. b. or br. f, (Apr), by Storm Cat–Sweet Valentine, by Honey Jay. Trainer Lukas D Wayne. Bred by Richard S. Kaster & Overbrook Farm (Ky).

In each race, an odds-on favorite was beaten. In each race, I had isolated two contenders. Whenever handicappers have identified two contenders in small fields, take the higher-priced horse. It pays, surprisingly well across the long season.

As if to remind a handicapper that overlays can strike when least expected, or that the game is ruled by the percentages and probabilities, a weekend that had transpired in wretched disappointment concluded in serendipity.

Until the betting began, I felt scarcely a twinge of interest in the Las Palmas Handicap (Gr. 2) at Oak Tree, a $100,000-added grass race at nine furlongs for fillies and mares, 3UP. In a six-horse field, leading grass trainer Bobby Frankel would start a three-horse entry, suggesting perhaps the horseman trusted none of them. Frankel's trio was 4–5 on the morning line.

The Frankel entry might disappoint. None of the three had ever won a Grade 2 stakes. The three of them had managed to win just three of twenty-two starts for the ten months of 1993.

As the wagering progressed, my interest was aroused when a last-out Grade 3 winner I preferred was being steadily overlooked. Among four betting interests, the horse became the field's longshot at 9–1. To stress a point too often ignored in Grade 3 and Listed stakes, examine the past performances of Miatuschka and the horse in the Frankel entry that figured best. Take note of the last running line for each.

Each contender exited a Grade 3 stakes at Louisiana Downs, which each had won. The races were carded two days apart. The Beyer Speed Figures are inconclusive. When speed figures are inconclusive, or missing, Grade 3 and listed stakes winners can sometimes be distinguished by purse sizes, the point too much ignored. Trainers are attracted by purse size. In general, bigger purses attract better fields.

Miatuschka won the Golden Harvest Handicap, purse of $200,000-added, a big pot. I was unable to locate the purse value of the River City Budweiser Breeders' Cup Stakes, Skimble's Grade 3 score, but I felt confident the money was less. The $200,000 Golden Harvest purse was double today's Oak Tree money. I leaned toward Miatuschka.

When I rated the closing times of the two horses, my mind was made up:

Miatuschka (June 20)	Finish	23⅘	Figure 111
Skimble (Oct. 7)	Finish	31⅖	Figure 98

The tracks and distances of the rated races were widely dissimilar, but so were the grass figures. I suspected Miatuschka could outfinish Skimble. In grass stakes, I emphasize late speed and relative class.

It was a close call, but Miatuschka did outfinish Skimble. The result chart documents how much an overlay the winner became:

EIGHTH RACE
Santa Anita
OCTOBER 24, 1993

1⅛ MILES. (Turf)(1.43^4) 25th Running of THE LAS PALMAS HANDICAP. Purse $100,000 Added. Grade II. Fillies and mares, 3–year–olds and upward. By subscription of $100 to each, $1,000 additional to start with $100,000 added, of which $20,000 to second, $15,000 to third, $7,500 to fourth and $2,500 to fifth. Weights, Tuesday, October 19. High weights preferred. Starters to be named through the entry box by the closing time of entries. A trophy will be presented to the owner of the winner. Closed Wednesday, October 13, with 16 nominations.

Value of Race: $107,600 Winner $62,600; second $20,000; third $15,000; fourth $7,500; fifth $2,500. Mutuel Pool $249,488.00 Exacta Pool $231,420.00 Quinella Pool $24,355.00

Last Raced	Horse	M/Eqt.	A.	Wt	PP	St	¼	½	¾	Str	Fin	Jockey	Odds $1
3Oct93 ^{8}LaD^1	Miatuschka	LB	5	114	5	2	$3^{1\frac{1}{2}}$	$3^{3\frac{1}{2}}$	$3^{1\frac{1}{2}}$	2^{hd}	1^{hd}	Black C A	9.60
1Oct93 ^{7}LaD^1	Skimble	B	4	115	4	1	1^{1}	$1^{\frac{1}{2}}$	$1^{\frac{1}{2}}$	$1^{\frac{1}{2}}$	2^{hd}	Day P	a-1.00
28Aug93 ^{8}Dmr^1	Potridee-Ar	LB	4	115	2	4	$2^{\frac{1}{2}}$	$2^{1\frac{1}{2}}$	$2^{1\frac{1}{2}}$	3^{2}	$3^{2\frac{3}{4}}$	Solis A	1.90
9Oct93 ^{3}BM^1	Gravieres-Fr	LB	5	116	3	6	6	6	$5^{\frac{1}{2}}$	$4^{\frac{1}{2}}$	4^{4}	Delahoussaye E	a-1.00
6Aug93 ^{8}Dmr^5	Villandry	LB	5	114	1	5	5^{1}	5^{1}	6	$5^{1\frac{1}{2}}$	$5^{\frac{3}{4}}$	McCarron C J	a-1.00
5Sep93 ^{8}Dmr^5	Campagnarde-Ar	LB	6	116	6	3	4^{hd}	4^{1}	4^{hd}	6	6	Desormeaux K J	2.80

a–Coupled: Skimble and Gravieres–Fr and Villandry.

OFF AT 4:41 Start Good. Won driving. Time, :23^4, :48, 1:12, 1:36^1, 1:47^4 Course firm.

$2 Mutuel Prices:			
4–MIATUSCHKA	21.20	3.80	—
1X–SKIMBLE (a–entry)		2.40	—
3–POTRIDEE–AR		—	—

$2 EXACTA 4–1 PAID $50.20 $2 QUINELLA 1–4 PAID $17.20

Gr. m, by General Holme–Melite, by Caro. Trainer Jackson Bruce L. Bred by Comtesse Battyhany (Ky).

MIATUSCHKA close up a bit off the rail to the second turn, angled out three deep leaving the turn and finished gamely outside to get the nod. SKIMBLE sprinted to the front at once, set all the pace to the stretch and responded gamely along the inside through the drive to just miss. POTRIDEE hopped slightly at start, stalked the early pace a bit off the rail, ranged up outside SKIMBLE into the second turn and finished gamely between rivals. GRAVIERES, unhurried to the second turn, swung out to move up outside rivals on that bend but could not match the top three in the drive. VILLANDRY raced a bit off the rail throughout but lacked the needed rally. CAMPAGNARDE, outside VILLANDRY on the first turn, advanced between rivals into the second turn but lacked a further response. FEMININE WILES (2) WAS WITHDRAWN. ALL REGULAR, EXACTA, QUINELLA AND DOUBLE WAGERS ON HER WERE ORDERED REFUNDED AND ALL HER PLACE PICK NINE, PICK SIX AND TRIPLES WERE SWITCHED TO THE FAVORITE, ENTRY OF VILLANDRY (1), GRAVIERES (1A) AND SKIMBLE (1X).

Owners— 1, Bollinger & Ramirez & Varni; 2, Juddmonte Farms; 3, Grimm Leslie R; 4, Frankel & Gann; 5, Wildenstein Stable; 6, Paulson Allen E

POSTSCRIPT The win mutuel was sweet, but not the sweetest part. Miatuschka meant I would be "alive" on a nine-dollar Pick-3 ticket to three horses in the ninth race, and one of them won, at 5–1.

The odds of the three winners were: 7th race, 6–5; 8th race, 9–1; 9th race, 5–1. Guess what the Pick-3 paid? Every dollar of $1,639.80!

November: The Festival of Festivals

"Now *that* was a day at the races. . . ."

—Mike Downey, columnist,
Los Angeles Times,
November 7, 1993

At the moment Breeders' Cup day dawns, the pull has become irresistible. Horse-racing aficionados cannot wait to go to the racetrack. The fastest fabled thoroughbreds in all the world have been primed to run the races of their lives.

The atmosphere is vital, throbbing, glamorous, intoxicating, and as supercharged as Secretariat flying in the stretch. No one who enters these gates—owners, breeders, horsemen, handicappers, bettors, and their special guests—can doubt for a moment that in a mere decade it's this Saturday that reigns the most glorious in racing.

On November 6, 1993, the tenth anniversary year, Santa Anita was bustling by 8:00 A.M. (first post 10:10) and jammed by 9:00. The Great Race Place had not looked much like its moniker in recent times, the quality of racing there in decline and racegoers staying away in inexorably greater numbers. Several track employees remarked that it felt oddly nostalgic to experience this magnificent setting suddenly coming alive again.

Even more. With the southern California sun shining, the air clear as crystal, and the temperature a balmy seventysomething, this championship day will live on as Santa Anita's liveliest in a decade, and maybe its best ever.

Not to be overlooked is the anticipation that sweeps to a crescendo in the week preceding the Breeders' Cup. It's a glamorous time. Everybody is there. As racing's people renew acquaintances in a recreational community, opinions fly as freely and as fiercely as the eagles, and the social atmospherics ignite.

Although the Breeders' Cup is enjoyed by all, a persistent observation finds that none appreciate the tony texture of the championships quite as keenly as do handicappers. Owners, breeders, horsemen, and guests identify inevitably with the horses they represent or favor. They await most eagerly the Distaff, or the Sprint, or the Mile, or the Juvenile, or the race to which so many hopes and dreams have been pinned.

The handicappers savor it all. They experience the full force of the Breeders' Cup, from the preliminary stakes a month away to the relentless prerace discourse to the races themselves. They pick favorites, or overlays, or longshots in each of the magnificent seven. Everything culminates in the mental challenge of handicapping what is by a landslide the most competitive program on the American racing calendar.

As always, too, a not unimportant matter, handicappers, outstandingly more than anyone else, anticipate the fantastic profits to be scooped out of the season's largest pari-mutuel pools, if only they can be right. For handicappers who follow the game closely, this is the dearest betting day of them all. Because overlays abound, profits can soar.

New, innovative developments have intensified that thought. Handicappers having well-heeled opinions now enjoy amazingly diverse channels of expression: the national Pick-7, the national trifecta hinged to the Classic, the future-books, and the latest wrinkle, the rollover Pick-3s, beginning at the Sprint and rolling along to the Classic, and further perhaps to local stakes on the undercard. Toss the toniest horses in training into the mix, and that's a bettor's brew.

On an excellent, entertaining pre–Breeders' Cup television show on a local independent station in southern California, handicappers Jeff Siegel and Andy Beyer were brimming with authentic enthusiasm for the remarkable day to begin. At the show's introduction, Siegel motioned to Beyer, "A handicapper named Mark Cramer wrote recently in *Daily Racing Form* that the national Pick-7 amounts to pie in the sky. What's your reaction?"

In the succinct, witty, and intelligent style that has marked him so indelibly as the bettors' spokesperson, Beyer responded, "What's wrong with pie in the sky? I have some strong opinions about tomorrow's program and if I'm right I intend to win a million dollars." The vintage Beyer goes down with the players like a magical drink.

My enthusiasm had been equally confident, but was directed instead toward those rollover triples. I expected to hit on all seven parlays, with each returning me $1,000 at least. With

Beyer reaching for one million, I would settle for $10,000.

Long before the bets are placed, the handicapping begins. At best advantage will be handicappers who have been paying attention to the stakes throughout the core season. Greater attention can be allocated to betting strategy.

A crucial admonition, certain well-laid handicapping traps must be steadfastly avoided. It requires a degree of will power. The handicapper's approach to the glitzy program might be divided into three parts: the prerace information blitz, the past performances, and the bets. The objective is (a) to pick winners and (b) to identify overlays intelligently.

THE PRERACE INFORMATION BLITZ A year's worth of studying the stakes divisions will be spoiled rotten if handicappers make the mistake of falling into the information traps.

Trap number one regards the avalanche of historical data dished out to handicappers in the guise of pattern recognition. In 1993, handicappers were browbeaten with analyses of the previous nine Breeders' Cup programs, the analysts purporting to isolate positive patterns, everything from preliminary races the winners had exited to the winning post positions. Imports especially are submitted to statistical analyses that defy the imagination, from the number of days the foreigners have been in the country to the number of workouts they show on the all-weather European surfaces.

Until another twenty runnings have elapsed, the historical data is virtually meaningless. Nine repetitions of an event lends itself to no meaningful conclusions. They contribute few reliable trends. If four winners of the Breeders' Cup Juvenile also have won Santa Anita's Norfolk Stakes (34.5 percent), do handicappers imagine this year's Norfolk graduate deserves the edge? I hope not.

Neither do the historical data related to post positions, days away, trainers, jockeys, pedigrees, and the rest mean anything.

Almost ludicrous will be data describing track surfaces, even though the Breeders' Cup last was decided over the local course years ago.

In 1993, pattern studies purported to inform handicappers that Santa Anita is a speed track where horses must be close to the pace at the prestretch call to win. To document the assertion, data from Breeders' Cup 1986 was resurrected. On Breeders' Cup day, 1993, below are the track profiles (beaten lengths of winners at the first and second calls) from six furlongs on dirt to twelve furlongs on grass:

	1ST CALL	2ND CALL
6F	6.7	6.5
7F	7.8	4
8.5F	6	3.9
9F	10.7	6.5
10F	4.5	4
1M(T)	0	0
12F (T)	7	1.5

That an opposite pattern surfaced in 1993 should surprise no one. Handicappers who relied upon the historical data describing Santa Anita's track surface got buried.

Trap number two regards the workouts. In recent seasons, workout information has exploded. Private clockers now roam the morning training sessions in abundance. The reports they issue can be helpful in spots, but the majority qualify as routinely superfluous and absolutely superfluous on Breeders' Cup day.

As a rule, as all know, good horses should be working out sharply, unless they typically work slowly. The same circumstances attach rather obviously to Breeders' Cup preparations.

The routinized commentary from clockers that the nation's leading stakes horses are looking and acting superbly amounts to much ado about nothing. So what?

In this wild arena, it's painstakingly difficult to separate the wheat from the chaff. One of the finest professional clockers is Bruno De Julio, of southern California, who in 1993 began to perform under contract for *Today's Racing Digest*, the high-quality, comprehensive information resource in southern California for more than two decades. De Julio blanketed the 1993 Breeders' Cup workouts for weeks. His reports are highly detailed.

Consider De Julio's commentary for top contenders in two of the seven legs:

Thirty Slews

Been training strongly for Baffert and looks in fantastic shape. He worked a super 59.3h back on 10/7, a 58.3h and out in 100.4 on 10/14 and superb 111h on 10/27. Look for the defending champion to run very well and pay no mind to Delahoussaye choosing Cardmania over the big gray gelding. 'A lot of people have sort of written him off, but he's feeling as good as he has since he went to Florida last year', admitted Baffert.

Brocco

'Bring on Dehere!' Brocco has trained like a high-class colt. His last three works have been outright impressive. Two-year-old colt acts like an older horse. He finishes powerfully through the lane and gallops out full of run. He does get a little warm, but he seems to be a very intense horse. He finished strongly with Gary Stevens on 10/21, and 10/27. His latest work on 11/2 was breath-taking. He broke off quickly from the pole with splits of 11.3, 22.4 through the turn. Monster finish through the lane with the last 1/8 in 11.3 and galloped out 5/8ths in 58.3.

Thirty Slews was outrun without threatening; Cardmania won. Brocco won in style.

Which training comments should handicappers take more seriously?

Thirty Slews was a 5YO that had dispensed a truly discouraging season after winning the Breeders' Cup Sprint of 1992. He was winless in four 1993 efforts and had looked particularly dull in his last start. Sharp workouts do not redeem the declining performances of older stakes stars. Because the 1993 Sprint qualified as a wide-open contest on the fundamentals of handicapping, Thirty Slews warranted inspection from every angle. But handicappers are urged to remember that among established horses workouts remain an indicator of form and not of ability.

Brocco was a 1993 juvenile. He had dispensed only a pair of improving sprints. A series of exciting workouts reinforces a pattern of impressive improvement that should continue and probably escalate. If improved races followed by improved workouts often represents a pattern of peaking form, which they do, Brocco fits the pattern impressively. De Julio's interpretive comments on Brocco, in the context of a rampantly improving, but untested unclassified 2YO, adds luster to the handicapper's evaluation of the past performances.

In general, workout commentary should be significantly more meaningful among the juveniles, imports, and horses returning from layoffs. The latter category does not normally apply, although Precisionist won the 1985 Breeders' Cup Sprint following a many-months layoff and a pattern of sizzling workouts.

In addition, if a talented trusted clocker submits a negative report on an established older horse, 3UP, that should be working well and probably will be overbet, I like that. Otherwise, assign the sharp workouts of older horses the respect they deserve, but nothing more.

Another source of pre–Breeders' Cup information is the right stuff, and is vastly underestimated by handicappers. If a competent handicapper expresses a strong opinion about one of the races, associates should snap to attention. Ask the colleague for an explanation. If the explanation rings true, prepare to use the horse. The analysis may differ markedly from your own, but so what? Where races will be extremely contentious, another opinion can provide an assist. If it's Breeders' Cup week and the horse should be an overlay, another opinion may provide a windfall.

In 1991, I listened while a respected handicapper explained in logical detail why Sheik Albadou should be an attractive overlay in the Sprint. I already had landed on Pleasant Tap, a deep closer. When Sheik Albadou won and Pleasant Tap placed, I collected my windfall.

In 1993, I deliberately conducted a week-long informal survey of opinions from much-respected handicappers on the Sprint, but no one admitted to an opinion worth stating. I knew the Sprint was a baffling opener.

Which brings us to the past performances, and a strategy I heartily recommend.

THE PAST PERFORMANCES Notwithstanding the talented horses, and despite the contentious aspect of the proceedings, maybe the least complicated component of the Breeders' Cup is the actual handicapping. A trick is not to overindulge.

Unless an undeniable champion or division leader stands astride the opposition, another trick is not to attempt to pick the winners. Become contented with identifying the contenders; main contenders and interesting outsiders. To afford themselves an 80 percent chance of covering the winner, handicappers must identify several contenders, at least much of the time.

In 1993, I could not resist the charms of Hollywood Wildcat in the Distaff. She was my choice, as early as August. In the other six events, my contenders ranged from three to eight. Contenders sometimes will be bet to win, but more often will be combined with one another, and with contenders in other legs, in exotic wagers. Those decisions do not arrive until race day.

If handicappers have been taking this book's prescription, concentrating on the various stakes divisions throughout the season, the handicapping will be greatly facilitated. I recommend these procedures.

When pre-entries are taken, ten days beforehand, purchase

the special edition of *Daily Racing Form* having the past performances of the ninety to one hundred horses scheduled to participate. Approach the various races distinctly.

For the Distaff, Mile, Turf, and Classic, identify the horses that have won two or more Grade 1 races. These are the authenticated Grade 1 representatives. Not only does the procedure reduce the fields to their barest elements in a jiffy, I dare say the winners almost inevitably will survive the cut. A second line of defense includes any Grade 1 winner also showing one of the top two Beyer Speed Figures in the field, provided the figure was recorded in a Grade 1 or Grade 2 stakes.

In 1993, the procedure dissected the four events as follows:

DISTAFF	MILE	TURF	CLASSIC
Dispute	Bigstone	Apple Tree	Bertrando
Hollywood Wildcat	Flawlessly	Bien Bien	Best Pal
	Ski Paradise	Fraise	Devil His Due
Jolypha	Wolfhound	Hatoof	
Paseana	Lure	Hernando	
Sky Beauty		Intrepidity	
		Kotashaan	
		Opera House	

In 1993, the procedure nailed three of the four one-two finishes.

A few additional hot tips. If a prospect is a 3YO, the Grade 1 titles should include either one of the classic stakes limited to 3YOs or a Grade 1 stakes of fall open to older horses. If a 3YO has not defeated Grade 1 older horses, but has repeatedly finished close (within a length) to that kind, accept them. Be flexible. Of the two candidates below, I accepted one, but not the other.

Ski Paradise

Own: Estate of Zenya Yoshida

Gr. f. 3 (May)
Sire: Lyphard (Northern Dancer)
Dam: Ski Goggle (Royal Ski)
Br: Fontainebleau Farm Inc (Ky)
Tr: Fabre Andre (—)

10Oct93♦Longchamp(Fr)	sf *7f	ⓉRH 1:26⁴ 2↑ Stk 151000			2nd	Jarnet T
		Prix de la Foret-G1				
5Sep93♦Longchamp(Fr)	gd *1	ⓉRH 1:37³ 3↑ Stk 270000			2nd	Jarnet T
		Prix du Moulin de Longchamp-G1				
15Aug93♦Deauville(Fr)	gd *1	Ⓣ Str 1:39⁴ 3↑ Stk 284000			2nd	Eddery Pat
		Prix Jacques le Marois-G1				
31Jly93♦Deauville(Fr)	sf *1	Ⓣ Str 1:39² 3↑ⒻStk 85200			1½	Guillot S
		Prix d'Astarte-G2				
6Jun93♦Chantilly(Fr)	gd *1	ⓉRH 1:36⁴ ⒻStk 62200			13	Jarnet T
		Prix de Sandringham-G3				
16May93♦Longchamp(Fr)	gd *1	ⓉRH 1:36² ⒻStk 312000			2nd	Boeuf D
		Poule d'Essai des Pouliches-G1				
21Apr93♦Evry(Fr)	gd *1	ⓉLH 1:39² ⒻStk 38800			1¹	Jarnet T
		Prix d'Angerville (Listed)				
3Nov92♦Saint-Cloud(Fr)	hy *6f	ⓉLH 1:20¹ Alw 31500			11½	Jarnet T
		Prix Gardefeu				
9Oct92♦M-Laffitte(Fr)	hy *6f	Ⓣ Str 1:17¹ Alw 33300			21½	Jarnet T
		Prix Gris Perle				
7Sep92♦Longchamp(Fr)	sf *5f	Ⓣ Str :58⁴ Stk 71700			32¼	Jarnet T
		Prix d'Arenberg-G3				
1Sep92♦Evry(Fr)	sf *6f	Ⓣ Str 1:15¹ Alw 29500			21½	Jarnet T
		Prix d'Ommeel				

Barathea (Ire)

Own: Sheikh Mohammed

B. c. 3 (Mar)
Sire: Sadler's Wells (Northern Dancer)
Dam: Brocade (Habitat)
Br: Gerald W Leigh (Ire)
Tr: Cumani Luca M (—)

25Sep93♦Ascot(GB)	yl 1	ⓉRH 1:42⁴ 3↑ Stk 500000			21½	Roberts M
		Queen Elizabeth II Stakes-G1				
5Sep93♦Longchamp(Fr)	gd *1	ⓉRH 1:37³ 3↑ Stk 270000			41½	Eddery Pat
		Prix du Moulin de Longchamp-G1				
3Jly93♦Sandown(GB)	gd *1¼	ⓉRH 2:06¹ 3↑ Stk 376000			54¾	Roberts M
		Eclipse Stakes-G1				
2Jun93♦Epsom(GB)	gd *1½	ⓉLH 2:34³ Stk 1219000			59	Roberts M
		Epsom Derby-G1				
15May93♦Curragh(Ire)	yl 1	Ⓣ Str 1:43 Stk 327000			1hd	Roberts M
		Irish 2000 Guineas-G1				
1May93♦Newmarket(GB)	gd 1	Ⓣ Str 1:35² Stk 293000			23½	Roberts M
		2000 Guineas Stakes-G1				
15Apr93♦Newmarket(GB)	gd 1	Ⓣ Str 1:37⁴ Stk 61000			4½	Roberts M
		Craven Stakes-G3				
17Oct92♦Newmarket(GB)	gd 7f	Ⓣ Str 1:24 Alw 24800			1nk	Dettori L
		Houghton Stakes				
10Oct92♦Newmarket(GB)	gd 7f	Ⓣ Str 1:24³ Maiden 10000			11½	Dettori L
		Westley Maiden Stakes (Div 2)				

Ski Paradise may not qualify as a Group 1 winner, but the 3YO filly four times has been beaten barely at the highest levels. In the richest stakes for 3YO fillies in France (Poule d'Essai des Pouliches), Ski Paradise just missed. She missed narrowly in her last three too, each a Group 1 at Longchamp against older males. Not to be overlooked, when Ski Paradise was entered against Group 2, Group 3, and listed opposition, she did not disappoint. I trust handicappers have been persuaded this is one very classy 3YO filly. She belongs.

Barathea is a Group 1 winner, having won the Irish 2,000 Guineas in May. The 3YO colt has not repeated since, though he did finish second in the half-million-dollar Queen Elizabeth Stakes versus older on September 25. Barathea has confronted Group 1 horses, without exception, since May 1.

Can Barathea win the Breeders' Cup Mile? Of course. The colt fits snugly enough. Yet the full record indicates Barathea may be a cut below the prime, at least now. Barathea belongs more comfortably on the undersides of exactas and trifectas. At a glorious price, the colt may be backed to win.

If a horse has won a lonesome Grade 1 race, or a couple of Grade 1's spaced across months, check to see whether the strenuous efforts tend to knock the horse off form. The next starts may deteriorate into clear-cut losses, as happened following Barathea's Group 1 score in Ireland. The relapses signal a fair warning. The horses can be expected to prevail in Grade 1 company only at a peak, and not following that peak.

Ski Paradise and Barathea can be differentiated reliably on the pattern. The filly has persevered as the sturdier racehorse.

Any horse five years old or older should have won a pair of Grade 1 stakes this year. This will be especially revealing among mature horses that were obviously more accomplished last year. A character in this book is practically prototypical of the species, as the past performances reveal:

Best Pal
Own: Golden Eagle Farm

B. g. 5
Sire: Habitony (Habitat)
Dam: Ubetshedid (King Pellinore)
Br: Mabee Mr-Mrs John C (Cal)
Tr: Jones Gary (25 5 3 4 .20)

126

Lifetime Record :	30				
1993	7	2	1	2	$903,750
1992	5	4	0	0	$1,672,000
SA	10	5	2	1	$1,472,370

16Oct93-8SA	fst	1⅛	:451 1:092 1:344 1:48	3↑ [S]CalCup Clssc 250k	102	1	5	512	55¼	1½	13½	Black C A	LB 126	*.30	90-10	Best Pal1263½ Native Boundary1161¼ Gol
21Aug93-3Dmr	fst	1¼	:46 1:094 1:341 1:592	3↑ Pacifc Clsc-G1	111	7	6	42	2½	21½	33¾	Black C A	LB 124	*.40	98 —	Bertrando1243 Missionary Ridge124¾ Be:
3Jly93-3Hol	fst	1¼	:462 1:101 1:35 2:00	3↑ Hol Gld Cp HG1	117	5	5	54½	21	1½	12½	Black C A	LB 121	*1.10	97-05	Best Pal1212½ Bertrando1185½ Major Im
31May93-8Hol	fm	1¼ Ⓣ	:474 1:112 1:343 1:573	3↑ Hol Turf H-G1	100	6	5	32½	21	32½	23½	Black C A	LB 122	7.40	102 —	Bien Bien1193½ Best Pal122nk Leger Cat'
10Apr93-8OP	fst	1⅛	:464 1:102 1:353 1:483	Oaklawn H-G1	107	2	7	812	710	65	32½	Desormeaux K J	L 123	2.80	90-19	Jovial1171¼ Lil E. Tee1231¼ Best Pal1231¼
6Mar93-5SA	fst	1¼	:471 1:11 1:351 2:002	S Anita H-G1	105	1	8	76½	73¾	74¾	55	Desormeaux K J	LB 124	*1.40	88-13	Sir Beaufort119no Star Recruit117hd Maj
Wide, climbing, lost shoe																
24Jan93-8SA	fst	1$\frac{1}{16}$	:234 :47 1:11 1:414	Sn Psql H-G2	102	3	3	33½	3½	1hd	22¾	Desormeaux K J	LB 124	*1.00	92-15	Jovial1152¾ [D]Best Pal124½ Marquetry11
Came out, impeded foe 5/8; Disqualified and placed 5th																
9May92-10Pim	fst	1$\frac{3}{16}$	:473 1:112 1:354 1:544	Pim Specl H-G1	104	7	3	31½	31	22	44¼	Desormeaux K J	L 126	*.60	84-23	Strike the Gold114¾ Fly So Free1161¼ Tw
11Apr92-8OP	fst	1⅛	:46 1:094 1:351 1:48	Oaklawn H-G1	121	6	5	55	53¼	1½	11½	Desormeaux K J	L 125	*.70	96-20	Best Pal1251½ Sea Cadet120½ Twilight A
7Mar92-5SA	fst	1¼	:46 1:094 1:34 1:59	S Anita H-G1	123	4	5	53¼	1½	13	15½	Desormeaux K J	LB 124	*1.70	99-10	Best Pal1245½ Twilight Agenda1242½ De
9Feb92-8SA	fst	1¼	:463 1:102 1:35 1:594	C H Strub-G1	119	5	3	31	1hd	11½	11¼	Desormeaux K J	LB 124	*1.20	95-11	Best Pal1241¼ Dinard1208 Reign Road11
Four wide backstretch, steadied near 3/8 pole																
18Jan92-8SA	[illegible]	[illegible]	:47 1:111 1:353 1:481	Sn Fernando-G2	121	4	7	73¾	4¾	1½	13½	Desormeaux K J	LB 122	2.80	89-21	Best Pal1223½ Olympio1225½ Dinard120

WORKOUTS: Oct 22 Hol 4f fst :47 H *3/16* Oct 11 SA 6f fst 1:122 H *2/10* Oct 6 Hol 1 fst 1:392 H *1/1* ●Sep 30 Hol 7f fst 1:26 H *1/4* Sep 24 Hol 6f fst 1:132 H *2/6* Sep 19 Hol 5f fst 1:00

Southern California's champion Best Pal survived my first cut, but I immediately lost interest. Only one of his 1993 performances (July 3) could be translated to victory in the Breeders' Cup Classic, and the October 16 prep, against easy Cal-bred competition, was entirely misleading. The Beyer Speed Figure proved as ordinary as the race itself. Leading California owner-breeder John Mabee supplemented an otherwise ineligible Best Pal to the Breeders' Cup Classic for $360,000 (12 percent of the purse), an extravagant gamble. At 9–5, second choice, Best Pal finished tenth of thirteen. In the future, handicappers should not be so fooled.

Procedure aside, handicappers can never afford to disregard their brains. Anomalies exist. An amazingly curious pattern was embedded in the past performances of one of 1993's standouts. Do handicappers recognize a peculiar pattern?

Lure
Own: Claiborne Farm

B. c. 4
Sire: Danzig (Northern Dancer)
Dam: Endear (Alydar)
Br: Claiborne Farm & Gamely Corp (Ky)
Tr: McGaughey Claude III (—)

126

Lifetime Record :	17	10	5	0	$1,442,573					
1993	7	5	2	0	$692,323	Turf	10	7	3	0
1992	7	4	2	0	$729,910	Wet	2	0	1	0
SA Ⓣ	0	0	0	0		Dist Ⓣ	4	3	1	0

16Oct93-6Bel	sf	1 Ⓣ	:224 :454 1:103 1:354	3↑ Kelso H-G3	111	2	6	43	31	11½	13¼	Smith M E	125	*.70	83-29	Lure1253¼ Paradise Creek1205 Daarik112½	
30Jly93-8Sar	fm	1$\frac{1}{16}$ Ⓣ	:24 :471 1:11 1:404	3↑ Daryl's Joy-G3	108	2	4	43½	41½	11	13	Smith M E	122	*.20	90-15	Lure1223 Fourstardave1222 Scott The Great1151¼	Rated, r
27Jun93-5Atl	fm	1$\frac{3}{16}$ Ⓣ	:47 1:104 1:35 1:531	3↑ Csrs Intl H-G2	115	1	1	12	12	12	21	Smith M E	123	*.80	93-08	Star Of Cozzene1201 Lure1239¼ Finder's Choice1142¼	L
6Jun93-8Bel	gd	1¼ [T]	:481 1:12 1:353 1:584	3↑ ET ManhattanG2	114	5	3	2hd	2hd	11	2¾	Smith M E	124	*.60	95-14	Star Of Cozzene118¾ Lure1247 Solar Splendor1122¼	Stumb br
Stumbled at the break, raced gamely																	
14May93-11Pim	fm	1⅛ Ⓣ	:464 1:104 1:351 1:473	3↑ ET Dixie H-G3	109	8	3	2½	1hd	13½	11½	Smith M E	124	*.80	97-03	Lure1241½ Star Of Cozzene1192 Binary Light1151¾	
30Apr93-8CD	fm	1⅛ Ⓣ	:47 1:104 1:342 1:461	3↑ ET Classic HG3	112	4	1	1½	11	11½	1¾	Smith M E	123	*1.10	101 —	Lure123¾ Star Of Cozzene1182 Cleone116no	Goo
4Apr93-7Kee	fm	1 Ⓣ	:23 :454 1:102 1:342	Alw 28800N$Y	107	7	2	1hd	1½	12½	14	Smith M E	123	*.50	98-08	Lure1234 Rocket Fuel118nk Kiri's Clown112½	Ridden
31Oct92-7GP	fm	1 Ⓣ	:222 :454 1:09 1:324	3↑ B C Mile-G1	112	1	1	12½	11	13½	13	Smith M E	122	5.40	109 —	Lure1223 Paradise Creek122nk Brief Truce1221½	Goo
10Oct92-5Bel	sf	1 Ⓣ	:222 :46 1:102 1:361	3↑ Kelso H-G3	102	4	2	32	21	22	22¾	Smith M E	111	2.70	78-19	Roman Envoy1172¾ Lure1112 Val des Bois-Fr118	
14Sep92-7Bel	fm	1$\frac{1}{16}$ [T]	:243 :47 1:104 1:41	3↑ Alw 33000	110	7	2	2½	12	15	110½	Smith M E	113	*1.00e	93-14	Lure11310 Mucho Precious1173¼ Scuffleburg115	
6Jun92-6Bel	my	7f	:213 :441 1:084 1:222	Riva Ridge-G3	79	5	4	44½	45	77¾	611	Smith M E	122	2.00	81-08	Superstrike-GB1151¼ Three Peat1222½ Windundermywings115	
21Apr92-8Kee	my	1$\frac{1}{16}$	:232 :471 1:122 1:44	Lexington-G2	100	1	3	31½	11	1hd	2nk	Smith M E	B 118	0.40	86-16	My Luck Runs North115nk Lure1184 Agincourt115	

WORKOUTS: Oct 14 Bel [T] 4f gd :493 B (d) *3/7* Oct 9 Bel [T] 5f fm :594 H (d) *1/3* ●Oct 2 Bel [T] 5f gd 1:01 B (d) *1/5* Sep 27 Bel 4f sly :51 B *4/7* Sep 20 Bel 4f gd :493 B *18/51* Sep 11 AP 4f fst :492 B *20/67*

In seven 1993 starts, Lure had not won a Grade 1 stakes. The brilliant Danzig colt had won just one Grade 1 title ever. Of course, that was the Breeders' Cup Mile of 1992, when Lure was a 3YO.

Andrew Beyer adored Lure in the 1993 Mile and throughout the prerace discourse that week he reiterated the irrefutable reasoning: "Lure easily bested the top milers in the world in the Breeders' Cup Mile when he was a 3YO. He's a much better horse as a 4YO and there's no discernible reason to expect he won't do it again."

The most avid class handicapper on the globe cannot toss Lure from the Mile, his specialty. A quintessential miler, Lure in 1993 had pursued the Early Times Handicap series, trying to snatch a million-dollar bonus for winning the three. He missed because (a) Star Of Cozzene proved an excellent challenger and (b) middle distances are Lure's limit. Moreover, the country's major tracks do not card Grade 1 miles on the grass. If they did, Lure surely would be a multiple Grade 1 winner at the distance, a happenstance handicappers must appreciate.

In the Sprint, the multiple Grade 1 test does not apply, for a reason analogous to Lure's single Grade 1 title. Not enough Grade 1 sprints are programmed. Instead, divide the field into thirds. Accept the top third on speed figures as the main contenders. Award extra credit to speed figures that were recorded in Grade 1 and Grade 2 competition.

Of the second third, prefer any that will be positioned within striking distance of the leaders at the second call and possesses one of the two most powerful closing punches in the field.

In the championships for the juveniles, favor the fastest colt and filly, with stronger preference for any that already has won a Grade 1 route. Rank the 2YOs on speed figures, top to bottom. Accept as contenders any colt or filly whose latest speed figures look competitive, provided the races in the recent record reveal a pattern of real improvement.

Eliminate any juvenile whose speed figures are clearly slower than the top contenders' or whose stakes races look unremarkable in comparison to overnight races. As its speed figures and stakes performance suggest, the 1993 winner of the Norfolk Stakes was best discarded:

Shepherd's Field										Lifetime Record :	4 2 1 1	$146,100	
Own: Camptown Stable		Ro. c. 2 (Feb) Sire: Spectacular Bid (Bold Bidder)							1993	4 2 1 1	$146,100	Turf	0 0 0 0
		Dam: Ransomed Captive (Mr. Leader)							1992	0 M 0 0		Wet	0 0 0 0
		Br: Roger Gebhard (Ky)						122	SA	1 0 0	$120,000	Dist	1 1 0 0
		Tr: MacDonald Brad (4 1 1 0 .25)											

```
10Oct93-6SA fst 1¹⁄₁₆  :223 :46 1:10 1:43   Norfolk-G2   87 6 5 42½ 43 41 1½  McCarron C J  LB 118 b 8.00 89-11  Shepherd'sField118½ RamblinGuy118½ Ferrara118½          Split
4Sep93-6Dmr fst  6f    :221 :452 :572 1:094  Md Sp Wt    89 10 7 53 .31½ 2hd 1½ McCarron C J  LB 118 b *1.50 90-10  Shepherd'sField118½ ⓓDrouillyRiver118² SmoothRunner118nk   '
14Aug93-4Dmr fst 6f    :221 :45 :571 1:10    Md Sp Wt    78 4 4 41½ 31½ 32 32  McCarron C J  LB 117 b 3.70 87-13  Ferrara117¹½ Devil'sMirage117hd Shepherd'sField117⁴       Edge
28Jly93-6Dmr fst 5f    :22 :454     :583     Md Sp Wt    68 3 8 88½ 88½ 55½ 22½ McCarron C J  LB 117 b 12.50 101-07 Showdown117²½ Shepherd'sField117hd DrouillyRiver117²     Bro
WORKOUTS: Oct 22 SA 4f fst :491 H 15/25  Oct 7 SA 3f fst :353 H 4/28  Oct 1 SA 1 fst 1:411 H 2/5  Sep 25 SA 7f fst 1:263 H 8/14  Sep 20 SA 5f fst 1:023 H 50/56  Sep 14 Dmr 3f fst :372 H 13/17
```

Extended to win the Norfolk, if Shepherd's Field's speed figures had continued to improve, the colt would have become an interesting contender. But the stakes figure, at the route, instead declined. The colt has run too slowly to be taken seriously in the Breeders' Cup Juvenile. Shepherd's Field did not get a call. Many 2YOs fit a similar pattern.

Once the contenders have been identified, a few trusty guidelines help to sort them further.

In the Sprint, when separating contenders, prefer horses that not only qualify as outstanding sprinters, but also have won Grade 1 stakes at middle distances. These are the power sprinters. Pure sprinters cannot contain them, no matter how fast they can run. Previous Sprint champions Precisionist, Very Subtle, and Gulch fit the profile nicely. Precisionist had won Grade 1 titles at classic distances. Among mere sprinters, Precisionist was a monster. It's no fluke that Precisionist took the 1985 Sprint in hand following a lengthy layoff.

One-dimensional sprinters like Eillo, Thirty Slews, and Cardmania can prevail only when the Grade 1 middle distance winners are missing, which was the unfortunate circumstance in 1993.

In the Classic, favor horses whose best efforts have occurred at classic distances, and not at middle distances. The difference can be remarkable, far more serious than most handicappers realize. The 1993 running can be the model for all times.

Bertrando was never an authentic mile and a quarter runner. On unbiased surfaces, Bertrando has waltzed at nine furlongs and labored at ten furlongs. Bertrando may have been the horse to beat in the 1993 Classic, all right, but class analysts understood the 4YO would be extended late. If something challenged Bertrando severely, the challenger was destined to win. No one imagined the challenger would be an obscure French import bearing pari-mutuel odds of 133–1. And no one can deny the challenger was much the best.

In the juvenile races, play the fastest 2YOs at the route. If the speed figures are too close for comfort, favor the juveniles that have set, pressed, or stalked the fastest pace.

In other Breeders' Cup events, prefer the horses that have run the swiftest both early and late against the most advanced opposition. In other words, the horses that have consistently demonstrated the fiercest combinations of speed and class. Those potential champions figure to win. Be skeptical of wide margins of victory, when the competition is strictly lower class.

When dealing with fanciful 3YOs entered against their elders in Breeders' Cup competition, the sophomores should already have won a Grade 1 or Grade 2 stakes open to older horses. That kind of competitive seasoning can be crucial. When New York's Sky Beauty lined up against Hollywood Wildcat and Paseana in the 1993 Distaff, her record looked like this:

Sky Beauty had spent the entirety of 1993 beating up on unexceptional 3YOs in New York. Fair enough. The filly had done all that was required. But following a layoff from August 14 to October 10, trainer Allen Jerkens surprisingly reentered Sky Beauty in an affair called the Rare Perfume Stakes, a Grade 2 limited to 3YOs. Sky Beauty won, without being pushed.

Why trainer Jerkens did not prepare Sky Beauty in the Beldame Stakes or in a similar top-grade stakes open to older fillies and mares eludes me. How would Sky Beauty respond when she confronted Hollywood Wildcat and Paseana, a filly and mare she could not simply accelerate past? During Breeders' Cup week, several New York handicappers issued decidedly negative opinions on Sky Beauty's chances. Her speed figures had remained stubbornly below the top females, and so had the quality of her opposition.

In the running, Sky Beauty unleashed a prominent run while wide on the far turn. When the front runners responded, however, Sky Beauty quickly faded. Even if Sky Beauty had leveled, persevered, and stayed close, she almost surely would have been defeated. The time to gain the experience of an exhaustive stretch battle against the cream of the older division is not on Breeders' Cup day.

As the handicapping process concludes, but handicappers find themselves precariously on the fence about a number of Breeders' Cup candidates, adhere to a simple caveat. If the price will be low, discard them. If the price will be high, embrace them.

THE BETS If the handicapping can be relatively uncomplicated, the wagering is not. Overlays carry the cause, but customarily the program presents plenty of them. Combinations of underbet and overbet contenders in the exotics provides an antidote of sorts, but matters can veer out of control.

What to bet? How much to bet? What to do?

A pragmatic strategy directs handicappers to proceed on multiple fronts simultaneously, not unlike a military maneuver intent on defeating an enemy having superior forces. The advent of simulcasting and cross-track betting has opened a strategic front heretofore unexplored. Favorites, co-favorites, and low-priced contenders now can be covered at advantageous prices, but handicappers must act preemptively.

The future-books have become an outlet for low-priced contenders handicappers strongly prefer. In 1993, Hollywood Wildcat would be 6–5 on race day, but 30–1, 15–1, 10–1, and 5–1 in Las Vegas and Mexico from August to October. At slightly lower opening lines, similarly higher odds were available early on winners Lure and Kotashaan, known quantities in August. The risk the horses may not reach the starting gate is real, but minimal. If handicappers have decided on a leg or two by August, or earlier, playing the future-books makes perfect sense.

A second tactic sends certain win-bets to tracks where the horses might be relatively underbet. Knowing Sardula would be hammered at Santa Anita, I played the Juvenile Fillies at Philadelphia Park. Of course, Sardula lost. Later I learned the tactic had been a waste of time. Sardula went 2–1 at Santa Anita, and 2–1 at Philadelphia Park. No matter. Getting the edge, or attempting to, remains the objective.

With the win-bets covered in the future-books and out of town, on race day I fastened my action on the "rollover" Pick-3s, and occasional exactas. Additional win betting was possible, but for value only, on contenders at ridiculously generous odds, a regular attraction on Breeders' Cup day.

I got a convenient break to open the card. As usual, Oak Tree at Santa Anita had programmed a trio of local stakes to surround the Breeders' Cup championships. The first was a $100,000-added seven-furlong sprint stakes for females, 3UP. Trainer Bob Baffert, a high percentage winner, had entered Arches Of Gold, the sensational sprinter at Santa Anita the previous winter. The trainer at that time had predicted Arches Of Gold would win the Breeders' Cup Sprint.

Baffert's boast now seemed ironically bittersweet. Arches Of Gold figured to triumph on the Breeders' Cup card, all right, but on the undercard. She was definitely best in the seven-furlong Cascapedia Stakes. She did win, smartly, and paid a fair $6.60. I had invested a key bet, and was pleasantly in front by $575, a bankroll now to be re-invested in the Pick-3 rollovers.

On Breeders' Cup eve, I had carefully separated my roster of contenders in each race into two groups, the A-team and B-team. The betting strategy was triple-barreled: link the A horses in Pick-3 parlays with one another on the main ticket ($10); combine the B horses in each leg with the A horses in the other two, or the B horses in two legs with the A horses in the third leg ($3); link the B horses in each parlay with one another on the minor ticket ($1).

I was not prepared to watch a contender in each of the three-race parlays win, and not collect the mutuel.

A broad definition of A and B contenders serves the strategy well. The A horses will be either (a) favorites that should be properly bet or underbet, or (b) contenders that enjoy a decent chance to win while being significantly underbet.

The B horses will be either (a) favorites that should be overbet, or (b) all other contenders.

In Pick-3 wagering, judgments regarding probable odds must be intuited, from morning lines and the handicapper's experience, as the bets are placed before handicappers know the odds in two of three races. As savvy handicappers might agree, the blackout can be tremendously advantageous.

Odds-on favorites are best discarded. Even when they win, odds-on favorites generate underlays. When odds-on choices lose, however, the Pick-3s pay generously, to put it mildly. If odds-on favorites display the slightest crack, or might be patently false, à la Dehere, in the 1993 Juvenile, handicappers should not fail to cover *all* the other contenders. If handicappers believe odds-on favorites will not lose, pass the races.

On Breeders' Cup day, for Races 3 through 8, I arranged the A, B contenders as follows (morning lines in parentheses):

	A-TEAM	B-TEAM
3rd Juvenile Fillies	Sardula (2–1)	Phone Chatter (9–5)
		Heavenly Prize (5–2)
4th Distaff	Hollywood Wildcat (2–1)	Dispute (9–2)
		Paseana (9–5)
5th Mile	Lure (7–5)	Bigstone (8–1)
	Ski Paradise (12–1)	Paradise Creek (15–1)
		Wolfhound (20–1)
6th Juvenile	Brocco (5–2)	Dehere (6–5)
	Flying Sensation (6–1)	
7th Turf	Kotashaan (2–1)	Bien Bien (5–1)
	Inrepidity (6–1)	Hernando (8–1)
	Hatoof (12–1)	Apple Tree (8–1)
8th Classic	Bertrando (2–1)	Diazo (20–1)
	Pleasant Tango (20–1)	Kissin Kris (12–1)

Baffled by the Sprint, where I wanted 8–1 or greater on four contenders, and the bettors offered less on each, I passed. Cardmania, not among my four, in my opinion won as an underlay at 5–1.

Eventually I eliminated Dehere altogether, a decision that

helped when the colt was lowered to 3–5. Dehere bled, and was no factor.

To represent the possibilities, I've reconstructed a portion of my rollover Pick-3s, the three parlays encompassing the Mile. Actual odds have been posted alongside the horses' names. Finish positions appear in parentheses.

RACES 3–4–5

A. Sardula 2–1 (2nd)
   Coup De
      Geni 7–1 (4th)
   to

A. Hollywood
      Wildcat 6–5 (1st)
   to

A. Lure 6–5 (1st)
   Ski Para-
      dise 18–1 (2nd)

COST: $40

PAY: ($40)

RACES 3–4–5

B. Phone
      Chatter 2–1 (1st)
   Heavenly
      Prize 9–5 (3rd)
   to

A. Hollywood
      Wildcat 6–5 (1st)
   to

A. Lure 6–5 (1st)
   Ski Para-
      dise 18–1 (2nd)

COST: $12

PAY: $52.50

RACES 4–5–6

A. Hollywood
      Wildcat 6–5 (1st)
   to

A. Lure 6–5 (1st)
   Ski Para-
      dise 18–1 (2nd)
   to

RACES 4–5–6

B. Dispute 9–2 (4th)
   Paseana 5–2 (2nd)
   to

A. Lure 6–5 (1st)
   Ski Para-
      dise 18–1 (2nd)
   to

A. Brocco 3–1 (1st)
  Flying Sensa-
    tion 6–1 (4th)
COST: $40
PAY: $212
	A. Brocco 3–1 (1st)
	  Flying Sensa-
	    tion 6–1 (4th)
	COST: $12
	PAY: ($12)

RACES 5–6–7

A. Lure 6–5 (1st)
   Ski Para-
     dise 18–1 (2nd)

to

A. Brocco 3–1 (1st)
   Flying Sensa-
     tion 6–1 (4th)

to

A. Kotashaan 3–2 (1st)
   Intrepidity 4–1 (13th)
   Hatoof 15–1 (5th)

COST: $120

PAY: $302

RACES 5–6–7

B. Bigstone 12–1 (6th)
   Paradise
     Creek 8–1 (8th)
   Wolfhound 9–1 (10th)

to

A. Brocco 3–1 (1st)
   Flying Sensa-
     tion 6–1 (4th)

to

A. Kotashaan 3–2 (1st)
   Intrepidity 4–1 (13th)
   Hatoof 15–1 (5th)

COST: $36

PAY: ($36)

TOTAL COST: $260   TOTAL PAY: $566.50   NET: $306.50

Several additional combinations of A, B contenders were bought, but the strategy is sufficiently represented. In the five races (3 through 7), three favorites and two second choices prevailed. Ouch! I cashed three Pick-3s, but the payoffs were kept below $100. When Arcangues astonished everyone in the Classic, paying $269.20, I missed that leg, and therefore the three parlays linked to the Classic (Race 8).

My Pick-3 rollovers amounted to a push. Not a single three-race parlay that I caught approached the $1,000 payoff I had imagined. The critical leg was the Mile. If Ski Paradise, an A-contender, had upset Lure, the three parlays embracing the 18-1 shot would have returned thousands. I would have collected on two of them.

Agreeably, the Lure to Ski Paradise $2 exacta combination did pay $68.40. The combination was one of two exacta combinations I boxed on the card. The other coupled Kotashaan and Hatoof. Both combinations hooked overbet favorites and underbet contenders from the A-teams, an exacta strategy I recommend.

Having lost with Sardula in Philadelphia and Diazo in the future-book, and thwarted in the Pick-3 rollovers, I nonetheless prospered by the day's major objective. The stretch charge of the Distaff became a sight to behold. From the top of the stretch to the finish line, without a breather, defending champion Paseana and 3YO challenger Hollywood Wildcat fought one another ferociously. Headed in mid-stretch, the challenger rebounded by a nose. The Distaff eventually would be rated the best race of 1993.

As the pair battled through the stretch, my thoughts wandered back to the 1992 Distaff, where Paseana trounced my key bet of the day, Versailles Treaty, another 3YO challenger. Now she was doing it to me again. I had been completely confident Paseana could not regain her top form again. My 15–1 in Las Vegas and 10–1 in Mexico were the day's big bargains, but now Paseana had the 6–5 favorite by the jugular and would not let go.

Prepared to lose as the horses battled, I wondered how Paseana could be doing this on this decisive day, threatening again to deny the heir apparent, when earlier she had (a) lost to the ex-claimer Southern Truce, (b) barely withstood the stretching-out sprinter Bold Windy, and (c) been gobbled up easily by the mare Re Ross. Three weeks ago at Keeneland, Paseana had been extended to rebuff Grey Cashmere, who was just a horse.

"Class," yelled my Breeders' Cup companions, "she's got a ton of past class.

"She almost got you looking the other way again. Let it be a lesson learned."

I pass the lesson along. It would have been dearly expensive, the lesson, but through the combined talents and relentless efforts of Neil Drysdale, Eddie Delahoussaye, and Hollywood Wildcat, by the thinnest nose, the future books owed me $3,500.

The post–Breeders' Cup discourse fastened relentlessly on the fantastic upset in the Classic by the unheralded French import Arcangues. He was a 5YO, a Grade 1 winner once, who looked like this on paper:

Arcangues
Own: Wildenstein Daniel

Ch. h. 5
Sire: Sagace (Luthier)
Dam: Albertine (Irish River)
Br: Allez France Stables Ltd (Ky)
Tr: Fabre Andre (—)

126

Lifetime Record:	**15**	**4**	**2**	**2**	**$298,530**					
1993	**4**	**1**	**0**	**0**	**$98,361**	**Turf**	**15**	**4**	**2**	**2**
1992	**5**	**1**	**1**	**0**	**$76,504**	**Wet**	**0**	**0**	**0**	**0**
SA	**0**	**0**	**0**	**0**		**Dist**	**0**	**0**	**0**	**0**

20Oct93♦ Longchamp(Fr)	hy	*1 3/16 ⓣRH	$2{:}07^{3}$	3↑	Stk 90000 Prix Dollar-G2	$4^{9\frac{3}{4}}$	Jarnet T	132	2.00	— —	Knifebox 126^{8} Fanmore $126^{1\frac{1}{2}}$ Marildo 130^{nk} *Chased in 4th, never on terms with run*
3Jly93♦ Sandown(GB)	gd	1¼ ⓣRH	$2{:}06^{1}$	3↑	Stk 376000 Eclipse Stakes-G1	$6^{5\frac{1}{2}}$	Jarnet T	133	5.50	— —	Opera House 133no Misil $133^{1\frac{1}{2}}$ Tenby 122^{3} *Held up in last, effort on uphill 2f out, neve*
30May93♦ Longchamp(Fr)	fm	*1⅛ ⓣRH	$1{:}50^{3}$	4↑	Stk 158000 Prix d'Ispahan-G1	$1^{1\frac{1}{2}}$	Jarnet T	128	6.60	— —	Arcangues $128^{1\frac{1}{2}}$ Misil $128^{\frac{1}{2}}$ Shanghai $128^{1\frac{1}{2}}$ *Reserved in 6th, rallied 1-1/2f out, led 1f out, driving*
2May93♦ Longchamp(Fr)	hy	*1 5/16 ⓣRH	2:21	4↑	Stk 159000 Prix Ganay-G1	7^{14}	Jarnet T	128	6.20	— —	Vert Amande 128^{nk} Opera House 128^{3} Misil 128^{nk} *Unhurried in 5th, weakened thr*
4Oct92♦ Longchamp(Fr)	sf	*1½ ⓣRH	2:39	3↑	Stk 1763000 Prix de l'Arc de Triomphe-G1	$7^{6\frac{1}{2}}$	Mosse G	130	12.00	— —	Subotica 130^{nk} User Friendly 120^{2} Vert Amande $130^{1\frac{1}{2}}$ *Mid-pack throughout, neve*
20Sep92♦ Longchamp(Fr)	gd	*1¼ ⓣRH	$2{:}07^{2}$	3↑	Stk 67000 Prix Prince d'Orange-G3	1^{6}	Jarnet T	126	2.30	— —	Arcangues 126^{6} Prince Polino 121^{hd} Arazi 121^{3} *Held up in last, rallied to lead over 1f ou*
4Jly92♦ Sandown(GB)	sf	*1¼ ⓣRH	$2{:}10^{4}$	3↑	Stk 493000 Eclipse Stakes-G1	8^{5}	Jarnet T	133	5.00	— —	Kooyonga $130^{1\frac{1}{2}}$ Opera House $133^{1\frac{1}{2}}$ Sapience $133^{\frac{1}{2}}$ *Chased leader in 2nd, led 3f to 2f out, weaken*
31May92♦ Longchamp(Fr)	sf	*1⅛ ⓣRH	$1{:}54^{3}$		Stk 157000 Prix d'Ispahan-G1	2^{nk}	Jarnet T	128	17.00	— —	Zoman 128^{nk} Arcangues $128^{1\frac{1}{2}}$ Exit To Nowhere $128^{2\frac{1}{2}}$ *Tracked in 3rd, bid 1-1/2f out,*
5Apr92♦ Longchamp(Fr)	sf	*1¼ ⓣRH	$2{:}10^{2}$		Stk 77200 Prix d'Harcourt-G2	$6^{4\frac{1}{2}}$	Jarnet T	127	*.40e	— —	Fortune's Wheel 123^{1} Pistolet Bleu $127^{1\frac{1}{2}}$ Art Bleu 123^{hd} *Towards rear, mild bid 1-1/2f out, nev*
20Oct91♦ Longchamp(Fr)	sf	*1½ ⓣRH	$2{:}37^{3}$	3↑	Stk 88300 Prix du Conseil de Paris-G2	3^{2}	Jarnet T	128	*.90	— —	Sleeping Car $121^{\frac{1}{2}}$ Deja $121^{1\frac{1}{2}}$ Arcangues 128^{2} *Tracked leader, led over 1f out, soon headed a*
15Sep91♦ Longchamp(Fr)	gd	*1½ ⓣRH	$2{:}28^{2}$		Stk 119000 Prix Niel-G2	$3^{\frac{1}{2}}$	Eddery Pat	128	*.30e	— —	Subotica 128^{nk} Pistolet Bleu $128^{\frac{1}{2}}$ Arcangues 128^{2} *Tracked leaders, led 3f out, clear over 2f out, he*
15Aug91♦ Deauville(Fr)	gd	*1¼ ⓣRH	$2{:}06^{4}$		Stk 85700 Prix Guillaume d'Ornano-G2	2^{nk}	Jarnet T	127	1.50	— —	Glity 121^{nk} Arcangues 127^{hd} Kotashaan 124^{2} *Trailed for a mile, rallied 2f out, erratic t*

As did all stunned handicappers, I revisited Arcangues's record in detail, and came away shaking my head at the price. The horse was no plug. Arcangues usually was respected by the European bettors, and he was just 12–1 in the 1992 Prix de l'Arc de Triomphe, Europe's greatest race. The trainer was André Fabre, by consensus the continent's best.

One of Fabre's post-race zingers startled me: "When this horse runs his race, he's a world beater." Oh, really? Where was the comment in the pre-race discourse? I could not recall reading a positive piece about Arcangues, although associates insisted to me they had. And how did it come to pass that no one, or virtually no one, thought to bet on the horse?

On Sunday, the next afternoon, I was joined for lunch in Santa Anita's turf club by Scott Finley and Steve Klein, two of the shrewdest handicappers of my acquaintance. Finley had visited briefly at our table early on Breeders' Cup morning, and he had alluded to Arcangues in positive ways. Knowing how Scott can spread his opinions in the exotics, after the Classic had been concluded and the mutuels included a Pick-3 worth no less than $16,003.50, my initial reaction was that Finley probably had covered the bonanza. After all, the first two legs, Races 6 and 7, had been won by co-favorites.

Finley had not included Arcangues in Pick 3 combinations.

But when he observed the gigantic odds, he did use Arcangues in the national trifecta. He cashed. A $1 ticket with Bertrando and Kissin Kris in the place-show holes paid 1,900–1.

Steve Klein did even better by Arcangues. Klein had driven to the race book at L. F. Caliente, in Mexico, where handicappers might shop for odds on Breeders' Cup races at any track on the board, including Aqueduct, Laurel, Calder, Hawthorne, Remington Park, Bay Meadows, and Santa Anita. A dedicated seeker of overlays, Klein recognized Arcangues as the amazing overlay he was. Betting at the five-minute mark, Klein put $40 to win on Arcangues's chances.

At what track did Klein choose to bet, get the highest odds?

Would handicappers believe Oak Tree at Santa Anita, where the races were live?

"The horse was a better price here [Santa Anita] than anywhere," reported Klein.

The reason is well worth remembering.

On Breeders' Cup day, as on Kentucky Derby day, as on a few other widely popular cards, the greatest amount of silly money will be dumped in the host track's pools. On the Breeders' Cup Classic, 55,130 bettors at Santa Anita wagered $2,606,477 to win, the lion's share of the money uninformed or misinformed. At other tracks receiving the simulcast, at intertrack sites, at OTB parlors, and at other sites offtrack, racing's regular handicappers gather. These wiseguys do not traffic much in silly money. So longshots like Arcangues typically will pay the most where the crowd sets the odds — at the host track.

Steve Klein's $40 bet to win on Arcangues returned a profit of $5,384. That's a value bet for the ages!

In the aftermath of the Breeders' Cup, other stakes do seem anticlimactic. On the Sunday after in 1993, Santa Anita carded a trio of added-money features, a thick-enough slice of the weekend's stakes festival. After the homework, I relished all three. I blanked.

And during Oak Tree's getaway week, I slumped. On the final days, I cut my play, consoling myself that the upcoming and concluding stakes festival of 1993 was a personal favorite.

Hollywood Park's fall season opens with a deluge of advertisements for the track's international Turf Festival, a schedule of grass stakes encompassing a pair of weekends. The turf festival has been designed not only to entice European stakes stars staying in the States following the Breeders' Cup but also to introduce the appropriately bred juveniles to stakes competition on the grass. As turf racing suits my taste, I anticipated the Hollywood Park races avidly.

But a slump is a slump is a slump is a slump. On the weekend before Thanksgiving, I found not a single foreign import worthy of a wager. The grass stakes went instead to local overbet favorites.

That Tuesday I flew to Philadelphia for Thanksgiving holidays with my brother and his family, which includes my six-year-old goddaughter, an amazing competitor in driveway "hoops." Katie shoots with money up (quarters), and wins, but it's the competition she loves.

Excursions to Philadelphia invariably involve a visit to the OTB parlor in the West Philly suburb of Upper Darby, where I grew and learned and played, located a few city blocks from the family home. It's a splendid parlor, modern, clean, decorous, comfortable, with lavish burnished-wood furnishings, expensive English racing art adorning the walls, large leather chairs in the bar area, big-screen televisions, and pleasant dining service, with small TV monitors on every table.

I went there on Saturday with a gaggle of local handicappers for the late-afternoon simulcast from Hollywood Park, the stakes festival program that featured two quarter-million dollar grass stakes for 2YOs, one for colts, a second for fillies. I was assigned the role of West Coast expert on demand. The objective was to spot a juicy overlay having an outstanding turf sire. I assured my companions it remains one of the most generous and most overlooked betting opportunities in the game.

Naturally, I found none. An even-money favorite and low-priced contender won the juvenile stakes. Worse, I could not collect on a race during the Hollywood simulcast, mounting evidence of a continuing slump.

We stayed for dinner. That night the Upper Darby OTB was receiving the simulcast signal from Penn National Race Course, the small oval in central Pennsylvania (Grantville) presenting some of the finest minor-league horse racing in the nation, including a turf program that impresses. No grass racing this night. Central Pennsylvania was being buffeted by a swirling, driving rain storm. The dirt races went on, of course.

Over dessert I discovered a Starter Handicap open to horses that had started for a $5,000 claiming price in 1992 or 1993. All the horses had competed at Penn National in $5,000 claiming races, or thereabouts, or in the continuing $5,000 starter series there — with one exception.

The exception was a shipper to Penn National from The Meadowlands, where the shipper himself recently had finished second in another $5,000 Starter Handicap. The shipper's recent record was filled with wins and close calls near the $5,000 claiming level at The Meadowlands.

The shipper was not the favorite at Penn National. He veered from 5–2 to 3–1 and back. The Meadowlands may be a small ways up the turnpike from Penn National, but a $5,000 Starter Handicap at The Meadowlands does not remotely resemble a similar race at Penn National, which is jammed with local stock. The shipper was a class stick out.

The shipper's dope did not show conclusive evidence of off-track ability, but I realized I would not enjoy my dessert unless I had supported the horse. Just then, as if on cue, a friendly waitress wanted to know whether I desired dessert.

Wait right here, I implored her, and strolled purposefully to the nearest Autotote machine, bet to win quickly, a key amount, returned, and ordered a Chocolate Devastation. Just before the

Devastation arrived, the shipper from The Meadowlands frol-
icked in the Penn National goo and won by the length of the
stretch. I devoured the dessert, delighted by the sweet taste, and
amused by the thought that this may be just the kind of class
mismatch that can snap a racetrack slump.

The next afternoon the Hollywood Turf Festival climaxed with
the half-million Grade 1 Matriarch Stakes, a big-ticket item for
older fillies and mares. The co-favorites would be Flawlessly and
Toussad, the latter a member of my post-Breeders' Cup Horses
To Watch list. The list was select:

Ski Paradise	Tabasco Cat
Meafara	Luazur
Toussad	Supah Gem
Pleasant Tango	Coup De Genie
Diazo	

Toussad had finished fourth in the Mile, despite a load of
trouble. In the same race, Flawlessly had been thrashed, although the ladies' 1992 champion had encountered trouble too.
I had not expected Flawlessly would start again in 1993 for
Charles Whittingham, but there she was. I preferred Toussad,
but against Flawlessly I wanted a sensible price.

It was much ado about nothing. I could not get to the Upper
Darby OTB parlor for the simulcast. In a thrilling race and finish, Flawlessly barely defeated Toussad. Having saved the bet,
inadvertently, I accepted the outcome as additional evidence the
slump might be ebbing.

Heavily publicized data regarding Horses To Watch exiting
the Breeders' Cup championships suffer the same inadequacies
attaching to the prerace historical data. Nine repetitions amount
to too meager a sample. Handicappers best compile personal

lists, and watch for overlays wherever they should reappear. The data indicate rather strongly that Breeders' Cup Turf graduates have been nailing a disproportionate share of their next starts, as many as 60 percent.

More interesting than the Horses To Watch following the Breeders' Cup are the Horses To Beat. The list from year to year is easily compiled. I present mine in 1993:

Cardmania	Brocco
Phone Chatter	Kotashaan
Hollywood Wildcat	Arcangues
Lure	

Handicappers will recognize the seven horses as the winners of the 1993 championship events. I am being neither facetious nor foolish. Every Breeders' Cup winner should be expected to lose its next start, and without exception. I especially looked forward to wagering against the 1993 Classic icon Arcangues. Instead of 133–1, Arcangues might be 8–5 in his 1994 debut. Another underlay is always welcome.

The reasoning should ring familiar, and ring true. The ranking Grade 1 stars rarely are prepared to fire their fiercest shots following a layoff. It wouldn't make sense, and an all-out assault on a stakes purse below the season's major objective will not be happily indulged. So the horses are permitted to lose. Handicappers should expect that. Nonetheless, the crowd will overbet the horses. A greater chance for alerted handicappers to tab a few talented overlays at irresistible prices.

Even Breeders' Cup winners that do not earn a rest following the glorious day can be expected to disappoint next out, for the same reason that Dancing Brave and a trail of European champions have tended to disappoint following a win or close call in the Prix de Arc de Triomphe. The horses have been primed to a best-ever peak for the championship bout. Afterward, they will have passed that peak.

As if to testify eloquently on the matter, three of the 1993 Breeders' Cup winners ran again before the year elapsed. Two of them lost, most memorably Brocco at 2–5, after having looked so sensational five weeks before. The third prevailed as an odds-on choice. Who needs it?

DECEMBER

In preparation for the ninety-day Santa Anita season, re-winding the cycle, my custom is to stay away in December. I kept to custom in 1993, with a subtle concession to this book project. I would scout the entries for a big-ticket, maximum-bet, getaway stakes horse on which to draw the final curtain. One gorgeous spot play!—that's what I wanted for my 1993 Christmas.

December's days slipped by without a take. Soon I fastened on the weekend of December 18–19, when the leading southern California juveniles Sardula and Brocco would be battling for rich purses at Hollywood Park. In step with my Horses To Beat rationale, I was willing to wager enthusiastically against either of the 2YOs, or both.

I could not detect a worthy opponent for Sardula in the Starlet Stakes, which she won by a length in a labored stretch drive that had remained undecided inside the sixteenth pole.

But the Horse To Beat most engagingly was Brocco, who I imagined would enter the gate at 2–5, which he did. Brocco had been quite lightly raced (three races), unusual for a Breeders' Cup prospect, but even so the colt presumably had peaked on Breeders' Cup day, and therefore could be vulnerable now.

The date was the Hollywood Futurity, at a half-million dollars definitely a significant pot for the West's top twos. Despite extra effort, I could not find a solid bet against Brocco. I just let go. Not in attendance, after the race I watched the replay as Brocco struggled in the final sixteenth against a 16–1 winner. The past performances looked like this:

Valiant Nature not only switched from turf to dirt, but also he went wire to wire. Not an easy transition, and not an easy overlay to spot. Nothing about Valiant Nature's grass win indicated he might outrun Brocco on the main track, not even the odds lowered from the inaugural race. The lower odds surely related to the colt's stout turf pedigree. Indeed, few horses run equally well on dirt and grass.

When the speed and pace figures for the Hollywood Futurity came to life, they proved no less than stunning:

Valiant Nature	112	112
Brocco	110	110

The speed figures qualify as the highest among the juveniles in years. If the numbers were accurate, the two colts could be accepted as classic prospects for 1994 absolutely. In defeat, Brocco had run fully five lengths swifter than he had in the Breeders' Cup Juvenile. Brocco may have flattened in the Futurity's final sixteenth, but he suffered no loss of reputation.

Brocco was a good one. But so was the new kid on the block: Valiant Nature.

My personal stakes festival of 1993 would not come to a close without one final sudden delightful surprise. I got my last big bet, after all. The opening-day (December 26) feature at Santa Anita winter is the Malibu Stakes. It's a Grade 2, seven-furlong sprint limited to 3YOs, purse of $100,000-added. On examining the entries, I could scarcely believe my eyes:

Cimply A Winner	Diazo
Gilded Time	Glowing Crown
River Special	Concept Win
Mister Jolie	Pharaoh's Heart
Bat Eclat	

Without consulting the past performances, I simply knew my inspiration and benefactor Diazo should win. Furthermore, at the sprint distance, Diazo might be an attractive third choice, behind stakes winners Gilded Time and River Special. The others were outgunned.

My intuition had been heightened by equally convincing feelings that neither Gilded Time nor River Special should win.

Review the past performances of the three Malibu Stakes contenders. Why should Gilded Time and River Special lose? Why should Diazo win?

Gilded Time was favored because he had run a superb six furlongs in the Breeders' Cup Sprint, finishing an admirable third following a year's hiatus. He also had won the Breeders' Cup Juvenile as a 2YO of 1992 at Gulfstream Park, the second line in the record. The performance documents Gilded Time's high class.

Why should Gilded Time lose?

Figure analysts recognize the "bounce" pattern, notwithstanding the seven weeks since the comeback effort. A year's absence and a strenuous comeback against the cream of the division foreshadows a big bounce next time; almost a certainty. Moreover, Gilded Time's speed and pace figures for the Sprint remain two lengths below par for today's Malibu.

To shine today, Gilded Time must set or press a blistering contested pace for seven furlongs, which is no walkover.

Away too from March 14 to November 27, River Special may also be destined to "bounce" in the Malibu. Not only that, his speed and pace figures on the comeback attempt (102–101) fell several lengths below today's par (110). River Special needed another warm-up.

Diazo was beautifully spotted in the Malibu. As he had in the Arkansas Derby and impressively in the Kentucky Derby, Diazo had loomed up menacingly toward the leaders in the Breeders' Cup Classic. At the prestretch call, he looked to have a decent chance. Instead he faded, outrun late.

Diazo was never an authentic classic contender, but I had rated the colt the top sprinter and middle-distance sophomore of 1993. During Santa Anita in winter, Diazo had delivered the fastest 3YO speed and pace figures of the meeting; 105–110. Later, in the Pegasus, Diazo had recorded the fastest 3YO Beyer Speed Figure of the year, a 109 at nine furlongs.

As for seven furlongs, Diazo already had handled the distance in eye-catching style at today's track. Still-developing 3YOs can change distances far more readily than their older counterparts. The Malibu pace figured to be swift and competitive early, favoring Diazo's off-pace rally.

As the wagering began, Diazo was bet heavily, but as post time neared, his odds drifted up. My salvo was $500 to win, and I wrestled with doubling that, but did not. As the gates were loaded, Diazo settled at 7–2, a terrific price.

With Gilded Time, River Special, and a third horse battling neck and neck on the front, down the backside Diazo ran a distant last. At the three-eighths pole, Diazo still seven-and-a-half lengths in arrears, I admit to pangs of doubt. Then Diazo commenced a sustained rally on the far turn along the rail.

My confidence restored, I nudged a neighbor to insist I should have doubled down. As the result chart testifies, the outcome would not be as predictable from that point as I had imagined:

EIGHTH RACE

Santa Anita

DECEMBER 26, 1993

7 FURLONGS. (1.20) 41st Running of THE MALIBU STAKES. Purse $100,000 Added (Grade II). 3–year–olds. By subscription of $100 each to accompany the nomination, $250 to pass the entry box and $750 additional to start, with $100,000 added, of which $20,000 to 2nd, $15,000 to 3rd, $7,500 to 4th and $2,500 to 5th. Early Bird nominations to the '94 Santa Anita Handicap are automatically nominated to the Malibu Stakes subject only to entry and starting fees. Weight, 124 lbs. Non–winners of $200,000 twice in 1993, allowed 2 lbs; Of such a race in 1993, 4 lbs; Of $100,000 in 1993 or $460,000 since October 5, 6 lbs; Of $60,000 in 1993 or $30,000 since October 5, 8 lbs. (Claiming races not considered). Starters to be named through the entry box by the closing time of entries. A trophy will be presented to the owner of the winner. Closed Wednesday, December 15, with 12 nominations.

Value of Race: $109,700 Winner $64,700; second $20,000; third $15,000; fourth $7,500; fifth $2,500. Mutuel Pool $744,378.00 Exacta Pool $695,352.00 Quinella Pool $84,998.00

Last Raced	Horse	M/Eqt. A.Wt PP St	¼	½	Str Fin	Jockey	Odds $1
6Nov93 8SA6	Diazo	LB 3 120 4 8	7hd	72½ 4½	1½	Pincay L Jr	3.50
27Oct93 8SA1	Concept Win	B 3 116 6 4	42½	42½ 2½	22	Stevens G L	9.20
16Dec93 8Hol3	Mister Jolie	LBb 3 116 3 5	51	51 51	3no	Delahoussaye E	23.80
21Nov93 7Hol1	Bat Eclat	LB 3 118 8 6	8	8 71	41¾	Solis A	20.60
25Nov93 8Hol6	Glowing Crown	LBb 3 116 5 7	62	62 6½	57½	Atkinson P	74.50
6Nov93 2SA3	Gilded Time	LB 3 116 1 3	1hd	1hd 1hd	6¾	McCarron C J	0.80
8Dec93 8Hol1	Pharaoh's Heart	LBb 3 116 7 2	2hd	2hd 3hd	7¾	Nakatani C S	7.00
27Nov93 3Hol3	River Special	LB 3 117 2 1	31½	31½ 8	8	Valenzuela P A	10.60

OFF AT 4:07 Start Good. Won driving. Time, :22, :44, 1:08⁴, 1:21 Track fast.

$2 Mutuel Prices:

6–DIAZO	9.00	5.20	4.60
8–CONCEPT WIN		7.00	5.60
5–MISTER JOLIE			8.20

$2 EXACTA 6–8 PAID $64.20 $2 QUINELLA 6–8 PAID $38.60

Ch. c, (Mar), by Jade Hunter–Cruella, by Tyrant. Trainer Shoemaker Bill. Bred by Paulson Allen E (Ky).

DIAZO angled to the rail leaving the chute, moved up inside leaving the turn and into the stretch to gain the lead inside the furlong marker and gamely bested CONCEPT WIN under urging. CONCEPT WIN, close up between rivals in the initial stages, tracked the dueling leaders slightly off the rail down the backstretch, angled out to come four wide into the stretch and battled gamely outside the winner the final sixteenth to just miss. MISTER JOLIE, settled well off the rail down the backstretch, came five wide into the stretch to loom a threat in midstretch but could not match the top pair. BAT ECLAT raced wide throughout and finished well. GLOWING CROWN, well placed a bit off the rail to the stretch, lacked the needed late rally. GILDED TIME was sent up inside to gain the lead before going a quarter mile, dueled inside to the stretch, drifted out a bit and gave way readily in the final furlong. PHARAOH'S HEART, four wide early, dueled three deep to the stretch and also had nothing left the final furlong. RIVER SPECIAL, vied for command between rivals to the stretch, steadied briefly between rivals into the stretch and gave way. CIMPLY A WINNER (1) WAS WITHDRAWN. ALL REGULAR, EXACTA, QUINELLA AND DOUBLE WAGERS ON HIM WERE ORDERED REFUNDED AND ALL HIS PLACE PICK NINE, PICK SIX AND TRIPLES WERE SWITCHED TO THE FAVORITE, GILDED TIME (3).

Owners— 1, Paulson Allen E; 2, Glen Hill Farm; 3, Appleton Arthur I; 4, Walter Mr & Mrs Robert H; 5, Franks John; 6, Milch & Silverman & Silverman; 7, Burroughs & Horton; 8, Golden Eagle Farm

Trainers—1, Shoemaker Bill; 2, Proctor Willard L; 3, Drysdale Neil; 4, Stute Melvin F; 5, Van Berg Jack C; 6, Vienna Darrell; 7, Mitchell Mike; 8, Hess R B Jr

Overweight: River Special (1).

Scratched— Cimply A Winner (15Dec93 8HOL3), Sir Hutch (20Nov93 7HOL1)

POSTSCRIPT Now in front, at the sixteenth pole Diazo was challenged severely by the excellent stakes sprinter Concept Win, a 9–1 outsider. Diazo would be fully extended to prevail. Had the colt not dug down for more, and summoned more, he would have been beaten.

An instinctive reaction chided me to think that without the benefit of an inside trip around the far turn, Diazo likely would have lost. Later, the speed and pace figures reinforced the instinctive reaction. Diazo's numbers: 101–108. Pace figures are unimportant for closers, but the speed figure, two lengths below par, is a classified allowance figure, not a graded stakes figure.

I felt fortunate. Following the Kentucky Derby, the Pegasus Stakes, the Jockey Club Gold Cup, the Breeders' Cup Classic, and now the seven-furlong Malibu Stakes, the gallant 3YO Diazo probably required a rest.

The post-Malibu discourse in the media followed a different tack. The pundits lauded Diazo's performance and in the conventional manner proudly pronounced the colt an outstanding deserving favorite for the two stakes remaining in Santa Anita's unique Strub series for new 4YOs.

As often, my dissent. As loudly as I had hailed Diazo throughout the second half of his 3YO campaign, I now retreated just as confidently. A tired Diazo would be an underlay next time. I predicted he would finish out of the money. My alternative would qualify for my first major wager of 1994.

It was Pleasant Tango.

Wanting to conclude this adventure on a high note, I resolved that Diazo's glorious triumph in the opening-day Malibu Stakes would be my final stakes hurrah of 1993. Diazo became a fitting ending.

I did not bother to determine how much Diazo had paid at the simulcast sites that were not commingling with Santa Anita's pools. Something important I learned in 1993 that I had not expected to learn applied to cross-track betting. Cross-track betting consists of funny angles.

At Santa Anita, Gilded Time was a pitiful 4–5 odds-on choice in the Malibu Stakes. He would not be overbet in that aggressive manner anywhere else. Diazo, that is, paid as much or more at Santa Anita than he would at numerous simulcast sites, perhaps all simulcast sites.

The lesson should be clear. If unfamiliar horses can be underbet by unfamiliar bettors, familiar horses can be overbet by familiar bettors. So strikingly familiar horses that have been stakes stars in the local community likely will be even more overbet at the host track, à la Gilded Time.

And that's why Diazo might be expected to pay more at home than elsewhere. And that's why the unfamiliar unheralded Arcangues paid the most money at the overcrowded host track on Breeders' Cup day.

It's a brand-new world of stakes racing out there. For well-versed handicappers, the payoffs can be magnificent, as the next section indisputably tells. The lesson has not been lost on your protagonist. I intend to repeat the stakes adventures next season, and the next, and the next.

I urge contemporary handicappers to resolve to do the same.

THE
CONVENIENT
POST-RACE
ANALYSIS

Simulcast handicappers who resolve to attack the nation's stakes schedules in the calculated manner promoted by this book will be positioning themselves for a number of seasonal rewards.

For openers, it's profitable. The experience has confirmed the suspicion at the outset that contemporary handicappers should become as expert as they can on class evaluation in the stakes. In the era of simulcasting and cross-track betting, it pays.

Table 1 displays the results during Santa Anita winter for $20 and $200 bettors, respectively. Table 2 shows what transpired at other tracks from March to December. Table 3 presents the bottom line for all tracks after the entire season.

Review the results:

Although the level of financial success at Santa Anita exceeds

TABLE 1
STAKES AT SANTA ANITA, WINTER 1993
Plays, Wins, Net Profit, and ROI for $20 and $200 Win Bettors

	$20 WIN	$200 WIN
Plays	36	36
Wins	12	12
% Win	.33	.33
Bet	$720	$7,200
Gross	$2,276	$22,760
Net	$1,556	$15,560
ROI*	2.16	2.16

*ROI means Return On Investment and is based upon the dollar return ($1); i.e., for each dollar wagered at "all tracks" from Jan.–Dec. 1993, bettors can expect to receive $1.68, or 68 percent profit (see Table 3)

twice the level of investment, the profits can be discounted by two extenuating circumstances.

First, the subjective bias. The bettor (me) is highly experienced and completely familiar with Santa Anita winter racing; the horses, the eligibility conditions, the horsemen, and the track conditions. Simulcast handicappers cannot expect similar results, at least not at first.

Data newly reported in Maryland has indicated out-of-state simulcast bettors as a group might be expected to lose half again as much as the track take on the west coast simulcast. As a rule, in the beginning, untutored unversed out-of-state simulcast bettors will be prone to lose more than they should.

Second, two of the one dozen stakes winners at Santa An-

TABLE 2

STAKES AT OTHER TRACKS, APR.–DEC. 1993

Plays, Wins, Net Profit, and ROI
for $20 and $200 Win Bettors

	$20 WIN	$200 WIN
Plays	72	72
Wins	27	27
% Win	.37	.37
Bet	$1,580	$15,800
Gross	$3,883	$38,830
Net	$2,303	$23,030
ROI	1.46	1.46

ita 1993 were outrageous overlays, El Atroz at $88 and Visible Gold at $48. Handicappers cannot expect to duplicate either. At the same time, neither winner was an angle that struck like lightning. Both qualified as contenders on handicapping fundamentals whose odds in contentious fields careened crazily off-center. Both horses, in fact, became multiple stakes winners in 1993. On January 8, 1994, one of them, Visible Gold, scampered wire to wire again at a mile on the turf and paid all of even money.

Outrageous overlays do triumph in the natural scheme of events, and alert handicappers do spot them, and sometimes they do bet them smartly.

Although the profits during Santa Anita winter can be discounted, they should not be denied. A decent correction cuts the profits by half. The ROI on the dollar becomes 1.58, closer to

TABLE 3
STAKES AT ALL TRACKS,
Jan.–Dec. 1993
**Plays, Wins, Net Profit, and ROI
for $20 and $200 Win Bettors**

	$20 WIN	$200 WIN
Plays	108	108
Wins	39	39
% Win	.36	.36
Bet	$2300	$23,000
Gross	$6159	$61,590
Net	$3,859	$38,590
ROI	1.68	1.68

reality, and still invigorating. The $20 bettor nets $778 and the $200 bettor nets $7,780, which is not peanuts.

The most interesting results are displayed in Table 2. Now the subjective bias and outrageous overlays have been mini-mized, if not altogether eradicated. The shape of events looks reassuringly normal, from the number of bets (72), to the win percentage (.37), to the money won and the dollar return (1.46). The $20 bettor nets $2,303 and the $200 bettor nets $23,030, sums that mimic reality for talented handicappers.

Indeed, inadvertently I missed a seriously underbet winner (Latin American, New Orleans Handicap, Fair Grounds) that would have padded the $200 bettor's pocket by another $5,000.

Simulcast handicappers might resolve to duplicate the results presented in Table 2. Although not easily, the win percentage is attainable by anyone who cares, and so is the money-won. Flat bets are recommended. Keeping records is imperative. Results can be charted routinely. In a positive situation, among winners, advantages that attach to fixed-percentage or Kelly wagering long haul cannot be manifested across a season of limited bets.

If handicappers sense themselves impressed only by the profits accumulating for bigger bettors, they need not be unimpressed by the profits awaiting smaller bettors. Most dedicated handicappers fall in between the extremes. No one who normally bets $20 should determine arbitrarily to hype the bet size tenfold in anticipation of the impressive profits. Successful racetrack speculation does not occur in an accelerated linear progression. Bet size increases realistically when predicated upon prior experience and enlarged incrementally.

Simulcast bettors unaware of or uncertain of success levels might begin with flat bets of $20. At the end of a season documenting positive results, or when boredom has cast its spell, inflate the bet size, not to $200 but to $40 perhaps, or $50, or $60, two to three times the original amount. As seasons elapse and success persists, escalate the bet size to $200, or $300 perhaps, or $400, as comfort zones tolerate and capital funds permit.

Bet size, to recall, should be 5 percent (or less) of the capital at risk; no more.

Depending upon well-established pyramids of success (a full season, twice replicated) handicappers can estimate seasonal profits reasonably well by relying upon Table 2 and typical bet sizes. The $50 bettor can expect to collect two and a half times the profits of a $20 bettor, or $5,800. The $100 bettor can expect to win $11,500 if he persists in wagering for eight months and wins 37 percent of the bets, attainable results.

Table 3 suggests that handicappers who concentrate on the stakes divisions effectively throughout the year can do splendidly. Apply the same betting ratios to estimate personal bottom lines. Surely the point to be stressed is that handicappers, regardless of bet size, have ample incentive to transform themselves into successful simulcast bettors.

Simulcasting trends will only accelerate and intensify. It's convenient to stay ahead of the times and the crowd as much as technological developments allow, and to grab a long head start on the opposition, other handicappers not up to snuff on the simulcast menus and the stakes horses best qualified to win. My experience has provided a number of timely tips in anticipation of handicappers' inevitable questions:

In pursuing the national stakes calendar, how best to proceed?

How best to exploit the cross-track betting opportunities?

What are the relevant information resources?

HOW TO PROCEED? It's crucial to follow winter racing at a flagship track closely; if possible, daily.

This book urges handicappers to begin at Santa Anita, but Gulfstream Park can be comparably significant. The edge accorded to southern California is linked to (a) the rapid expansion of the area's simulcasting network, and (b) the depth and quality of the circuit's stakes divisions.

Santa Anita, Hollywood Park, and Del Mar are fast becoming a national circuit. Stakes winners and close runners-up there will be prominent contenders in the several stakes divisions throughout the core season and the shipping from southern California to other stakes races has become virtually nonstop.

The same competitiveness is true of New York stakes horses, of course, yet the shipping out of state has been less prevalent, Gulfstream Park and Oaklawn Park excepted. The interchange between the flagship tracks on each coast is characterized by shipments west to east. Southern California stakes prospects make appearances in New York exceedingly more often than Big Apple stakes stars venture west.

Handicappers in the South, Midwest, and Southwest can follow Gulfstream Park or Santa Anita or both during winter as they please, but by all means choose one of the two tracks and pay attention. Simulcasting schedules may impose themselves on handicappers' choices, but inexorably the two main sources of the finest winter racing will be widely accessible.

Keep abreast of the nonclaiming 3YOs, the allowances as well as the stakes. As surely as the trek to the Kentucky Derby is well publicized, the probable winners of other assorted derbies will not be well comprehended. And few handicappers bother to identify the post-Derby 3YOs that might pay sizable windfalls later, à la Diazo in 1993.

As summer beckons, shift the handicapping emphasis to the older stakes divisions. Look longingly for shippers that might stick out at outposts where they likely will be underbet.

In fall, focus on the stables' preparations for the Breeders' Cup, especially the less-remarked ramifications, such as accepting low-priced overlays in the major preliminaries, isolating ineligible Cup prospects shipping instead to other stakes races, and attacking the future-books. Future-book betting on the Kentucky Derby usually amounts to fool's play (Winning Colors excepted), but as the Breeders' Cup nears, the future books are crying out to be exploited by perceptive handicappers.

If handicappers can get 15–1 on a Hollywood Wildcat, or Lure, or Kotashaan, or a Bertrando within sixty to ninety days of the championships, that's a fabulous bet at relatively low risk. Will the horses make it to the gates? Probably. Take the chance. In addition, take extreme future-book odds on any other stakes stars having a decent chance on Cup day.

If schedules allow, try to travel. Go to Florida, or New York, or Los Angeles, or Hot Springs, or Maryland, or Chicago, or all of the above. Get around. Show up anywhere an intriguing stakes festival has been planned. Sample a couple of the festivals every year. Visit Las Vegas once, twice, or three times, and do not be bashful about confronting the stakes at each simulcast site on the local board.

Watch the simulcasts of stakes races carefully. Inspect the entries of stakes races at the several tracks included in the regional edition of *Daily Racing Form,* sniffing out opportunities for cross-track wagers that might pay boxcars.

The simulcast handicapper's cause would be abetted greatly if the industry formulated a policy of simulcasting all Grade 1 and Grade 2 stakes to all operating tracks. Simulcast bettors might lobby for the policy effectively.

Most important of all, as stated insistently, become a blooming expert on the class factor. In the stakes, ultimately class reigns. As ever, the several fundamentals will be significant, and other factors can be decisive, but the best races will be won most frequently by the best horses. Handicappers able to relate speed and pace figures to the quality of the opposition will enjoy an enviable edge.

The Grade 1 horses defeat the Grade 2 types, the Grade 2 types beat the Grade 3 and listed kind, and Grade 3 and listed horses handle the open and restricted stakes routinely. Comprehend the stakes hierarchy, and honor it. It's critical to understand what's what and who's who in the various stakes divisions.

WHAT ABOUT CROSS-TRACK BETTING? As simulcasting expands, pari-mutuel pools are increasingly commingled and cross-track betting opportunities have been dwindling. Furthermore, cross-track betting can be annoyingly complicated and impractical. So far, relatively few handicappers have prospered in any enduring sense by cross-track wagering.

Nonetheless, cross-track betting still affords alert, aware handicappers several juicy propositions in any season. On my largest bet of 1993, Bertrando was 2–1 in southern California, 4–1 in New York, and 7–1 in Philadelphia. No one can be apathetic about exploiting that edge.

Having said that much, probably the keenest disappointment of 1993 was the spare array of cross-track bets I encountered. To be sure, I chose an unlikely season. The 3YOs will be remembered as among the slowest stakes winners in years and the older handicap divisions proved thin. I look forward to the future with greater optimism.

Regardless, the practical constraints to cross-track betting will be plentiful. Once the attractive possibilities have been identified—no minor consideration—access depends upon a network of agents to place the bets. In the main, the network consists of friends and associates who happen to be available and willing.

In this rarefied context, I do not recommend elaborate schemes. The fantastic vision of a well-knit network of handicappers on site at local tracks and equipped with cellular phones whereby they advise associates located hundreds or thousands of miles away of the odds near post time, perhaps placing heavy bets on overlays as instructed, does not square with a handicapper's day at the races. It's despairingly messy.

An informal survey of semi-professional handicappers has suggested few bettors bother with the pursuit of cross-track wagering. A repetitive theme of the responses alludes to the alternative emphasis on exotic wagering. That is, bigger bettors apparently have become so preoccupied with the exactas, trifectas, serial triples, and Pick-6s at the local tracks, few of them attend to cross-track bets to win on stakes prospects running partway across the country.

Fair enough, but the general discourse on cross-track payoffs continues and nobody denies they would delight in collecting the minor windfalls that regularly startle.

A middle ground erects a select network of friends who can alternate as trusted handicappers and trusted agents. Agreements can be reciprocal. A three-ply network of agents might be stationed at (1) common shipping and receiving tracks within the home track's region, (2) Las Vegas, and (3) an out-of-state simulcast site that produces consistent overlays. The first station should be obvious, as between southern California and northern California, or between New York and New Jersey.

Las Vegas qualifies as the catchall outpost for betting on horses shipping to stakes at other tracks. The race books of Vegas honor the several tracks on the boards, which embraces virtually all major and medium-class tracks. A dependable out-of-state simulcast site can cover the majority of opportunities that arise from separate pools. In 1993, I chose Philadelphia Park.

When the interstate wrinkles have been ironed out, exotic wagers encompassing stakes races carded concurrently at multiple tracks will be promoted, featuring national pari-mutuel pools. Unfamiliar stakes horses will be prominent in every leg. This is exactly the style of cross-track betting this book has been intended to inform. With bonanza payoffs commonplace, the serial triple in particular can be stunningly rewarding. The wager has the potential, nothing less, to replace the Pick-6 as the handicapper's preferred fountain of riches. To a large degree, that has occurred already in southern California.

Handicappers in the know will merit a tremendous edge in the national Pick-3s. For those handicappers, the national exotica cannot arrive soon enough.

INFORMATION RESOURCES Computer technology cannot substitute for comprehensive handicapping, but it certainly can support the cause. If handicappers do not construct personal speed and pace figures, for example, they might (a) rely on the Beyer Speed Figures, or (b) download alternative professional figures from assorted data bases. The "other" figures may supply a precious edge, not because they will be more accurate or more reliable necessarily than Beyer Speed Figures, but because far fewer handicappers will be applying them.

The best I have seen to date come out of the Colts Neck online data base, of Colts Neck, New Jersey. Professional Online handicapper Andy Cylke, of San Diego, downloads Colts Neck's speed figures daily, and touts them persuasively. Subscribers receive a graph of recent figures which reveals concrete patterns of performances above and below today's par. The cost is relatively low. I have observed Cylke as he applied the Colts Neck data at Del Mar and at the race books of Mexico (various tracks), and they work admirably. Playing in southern California and other tracks far from north New Jersey, Cylke has cornered the precious edge; not many other local handicappers will be sharing the Colts Neck data. As full-card simulcasting spreads, services such as Colts Neck's will practically be mandatory.

In evaluating horses' abilities, any computer logic that has been demonstrably effective in getting winners and a positive return on investment qualifies as extending the same potential advantage: fewer bettors will be sharing that logic. Thus the chance for more rewarding results.

Other information resources include trainer performance and trainer pattern data, absolutely for New York and southern California, where the bulk of the shipping of blueblooded stakes horses originates. The reference extends to every major track. How do trainers fare with shippers? Simulcast handicappers want to know. The Bloodstock Research (BRIS) data base, of Lexington, Kentucky, is a powerful source of trainer statistics.

A comprehensive, high-quality source of a vast array of handicapping data for southern California races is *Today's Racing Digest*, a daily publication which in 1994 began to extend its distribution channels to several out-of-state simulcast sites. Publishing adjusted times, speed and pace prodections, track profiles, trainer statistics, workouts, and race-by-race analyses, the *Digest* contains something for everybody. A consultant to the publication, I do not hesitate to salute *Today's Racing Digest* to simulcast handicappers everywhere.

And another helpful resource for handicappers who have not yet come to terms with the intricacies inherent in class evaluation of non-claiming races, the stakes especially, is a bellwether text on the topic. I recommend *The Handicapper's Condition Book*, not entirely because I wrote it, but also because the book's been heralded unanimously by other leading authorities and has stood the test of time remarkably well.

Enough. Handicappers do not require an oversupply of information resources to cope effectively with stakes races. More than information resources, most handicappers need instead the knowledge and skill to recognize the best horses when they see them.

* * *

A few close colleagues aware of this special project have asked me, after paying attention to so many stakes races, which horse did I judge to be best of show in 1993?

I do not hesitate. It was Lure. The splendid son of Danzig distinguished himself unmistakably as the most brilliant turf miler of recent times, maybe of modern times. Just as speed is the hallmark of thoroughbred class, brilliance on the track becomes the trademark of champions.

The best racehorses of all are denoted by the capacity to take the top horses in the land on a fruitless chase in rapid time, by brilliance over distance, à la Secretariat, Seattle Slew, Affirmed, Spectacular Bid, and few others. At a mile on the grass, Lure did that. His Breeders' Cup Mile of 1993 was the year's signature performance: brilliant, decisive, towering.

Fanned wide on a swiftly contested pace into the clubhouse turn, while gunned, Lure gained the lead and advantage into the backstretch at what looked at the moment to be too heavy a cost. Lure stayed in front of a talented international cast into the upper stretch, and then surged to the wire unthreatened. The speed and pace figures would be sensational: 118–115, the very best in 1993 on grass.

Only a true-blue champion could have overcome the gridlock rush to the clubhouse turn while wide at full throttle, and Lure accomplished the task in total command. On that memorable afternoon, Lure was the single winner to go from start to finish on the front. It was a virtuoso performance, by the season's deserving Horse of the Year.

In closing, handicappers should understand too that playing the national stakes calendar is fun. I thoroughly enjoyed it. I suspect a majority of handicappers would. After all, fun and profit, the twin towers of the great game of handicapping . . .

What else do handicappers need to know?